CRUISING GUIDE

to

San Francisco Bay

by

Carolyn and Bob Mehaffy

CRUISING GUIDE
to
San Francisco Bay

by

Carolyn and Bob Mehaffy

Paradise Cay Publications
Post Office Box 29
Arcata, California 95518-0029

The text of this book is composed in Palatino font.

Library of Congress number 96-068869

ISBN 0939837315

Published by Paradise Cay Publications

Cover design by Anthony Sebastian

Charts by Allan Cartography

Title page: Getting under way in Sausalito anchorage

Back cover: Authors' photo by Richard Guches

PREFACE

In this revised edition of *Cruising Guide to San Francisco Bay,* we have added four coastal destinations that are important to San Francisco Bay sailors: Drakes Bay, Tomales Bay, Bodega Harbor, and Pillar Point Harbor. Another significant change is that many of the charts and sketches of destinations in this revision are now computer-generated images based on the latest NOAA charts. The quality of all the pictures from the first edition has also been greatly improved in this revision. In addition, we've updated the entries for anchorages and marinas.

The *Cruising Guide to San Francisco Bay* will continue to fill a much-needed niche for both local and visiting sailors. It is still the only complete guide to the many destinations for cruising sailors in San Francisco Bay. In this guide are general tips for safe, comfortable, and pleasurable Bay cruising and a description of each destination that includes directions for the approach, anchoring and berthing possibilities, facilities available at each site, and some highlighted attractions of the area.

San Francisco Bay is not, strictly speaking, a bay at all but part of an immense estuary. From Alviso at the southern end to Suisun City at the northern end, this estuary extends more than 75 miles, and from the Golden Gate to Stockton and Sacramento at the eastern end, almost 100 miles.

The specific destinations are grouped according to location. Local sailors generally designate as the Central, or Main, Bay that portion bounded by the Golden Gate, the Richmond-San Rafael Bridge, and Central Basin (immediately south of the Oakland-San Francisco Bay Bridge). The South Bay, according to sailors who live there, begins below the Dumbarton Bridge; however, other sailors on the Bay frequently use the term "South Bay" for the anchorages and marinas below Central Basin on the west shore of the Bay and below the Bay Bridge on the east shore. For the purposes of this book, we have adopted the latter use. The North Bay commonly refers to San Rafael Bay, San Pablo Bay, and Suisun Bay, lying north and east of the Richmond-San Rafael Bridge and extending to the Benicia-Martinez Bridge. The river destinations of Petaluma and Napa are reached from San Pablo Bay, and Suisun City is accessible from the western side of Suisun Bay. (The Sacramento-San Joaquin Delta destinations also begin in the North Bay, but we have not included the Delta in this book because Hal Schell has already covered that area extensively in his *Guide to Cruising California's Delta.*) The coastal and offshore destinations suitable for day or weekend cruises from San Francisco Bay have been included in this revised edition; they are, in addition to the Farallon Islands, Drakes Bay, Tomales Bay, Bodega Harbor, and Pillar Point Harbor.

Cruising Guide to San Francisco Bay includes all public and private marinas in San Francisco Bay, as well as yacht clubs, that accommodate cruising boaters. It includes all safe and legal anchorages we have been able to discover. (We eliminated some anchorages that local boaters told us about because we judged, after researching them, that these anchorages were either unsafe without local knowledge and experience or illegal. If you discover anchorages that you believe we should have included, please write to us in care of the publisher.)

We took *Carricklee*, our Hardin 45 ketch, into virtually every marina and anchorage to determine the safety and comfort of the destination. In addition, we explored marinas and anchorages by sportboat and by car to find out more about facilities and attractions in and around each destination. We talked with harbormasters, yacht club members, chandlery managers, shopkeepers, park rangers, and anyone else with a few minutes to spare for us.

In giving sailing directions for the approach to each marina and anchorage, we have given the bearing in **degrees magnetic** because we believe most small craft are fitted with magnetic compasses. We've given distances in **nautical miles** and depths in **feet**. Points of the compass are abbreviated, for example, **N** for north and **SE** for southeast.

Acknowledgments

We are deeply indebted to the scores of people who took the time to talk with us as we visited the many destinations covered in this book. We are grateful, too, to our good friends and buddy boaters Jim and June Ball, who accompanied us on many of our research cruises, and to our sailing friends Dick Honey and Jo Anne Kipp, who shared their local knowledge of the South Bay with us Northerners. Bob Smith's *Complete Guide to Harbors, Anchorages, & Marinas*, Northern California Edition, and Roger L. and Robert R. Dinelli's *The Northern & Southern California Boater's Guide to Harbors & Marinas* were both immensely helpful as references. *San Francisco Bay Shoreline Guide*, a California State Coastal Conservancy Book, edited by Rasa Gustaitis, was invaluable in locating outdoor activities along the shores of the Bay. Our immense gratitude also goes to photographers and friends Brian Bates, Merlin Bradshaw, and David Dawson for letting us use some of their photographs. Mike Landis was both generous and patient as he assisted us with the layout. Finally, we appreciate the editorial advice and encouragement of Brian Fagan, author of the venerable *Cruising Guide to Southern California's Offshore Islands*, and of Matt Morehouse, editor and publisher, Paradise Cay Publications.

Some portions of this book have appeared in *Cruising World* and *Northwest Yachting* magazines.

CONTENTS

ABOUT THE BAY AND BOATING

ANCHORAGES AND MARINAS

SAILING SAN FRANCISCO BAY

San Francisco Bay. For sailors throughout the United States and around the world this wondrous estuary, including two smaller "bays"— San Pablo and Suisun, fed by the San Joaquin and Sacramento rivers and numerous small streams—has long been a destination to dream about. From the earliest written account of San Francisco Bay, set down in his log by Manuel de Ayala in August and September of 1775, this nearly perfect harbor for commercial and military ships has been lauded. While the number of these ships in San Francisco Bay has diminished greatly in the second half of the 20th century, their absence has been more than compensated for by the numbers of pleasure boats—both sail and motor—afloat on these still voluminous and sparkling waters.

Richard Henry Dana, having sailed into this bay on a trade ship in 1835, alerted the world to the multitudinous beauties to which sailors might attend here:

We sailed down this magnificent bay with a light wind, the tide, which was running out, carrying us at the rate of four or five knots. It was a fine day; the first of entire sunshine we had had for more than a month. We passed directly under the high cliff on which the Presidio is built, and stood into the middle of the bay, from whence we could see small bays making up into the interior, large and beautifully wooded islands, and the mouths of several small rivers. If California ever becomes a prosperous country, this bay will be the centre of its prosperity. The abundance of wood and water; the extreme fertility of its shores; the excellence of its climate, which is as near to being perfect as any in the world; and

The *Balclutha* moored at Aquatic Park

9

its facilities for navigation affording the best anchoring-grounds in the whole western coast of America—all fit it for a place of great importance.
—Two Years Before the Mast.

The *great importance* San Francisco Bay has for pleasure boaters results largely from the harmonious conjunction of water, weather, landscape, and "the City." The water, a deep, pure blue under the California sunshine, can be placid in one part of the Bay, accommodating the sailor seeking a relaxing sail, and roiled up in another part with current and wind, guaranteeing a rollicking ride for the thrill-seekers. A day without winds somewhere on the Bay is a rare day, especially during the spring, summer, and fall months. These winds are often in the 10-to-12-knot range early in the day, climbing in the afternoon, particularly in certain areas of the Bay, to 20, 25, or 30 knots. Those looking for the pleasures of some boisterous sailing need only to look around: somewhere in this bay they'll most often find the right conditions. On the other hand, a motorboater can usually find somewhere on the Bay a place to escape unwelcome winds.

An extraordinary thing about cruising in the San Francisco Bay is the plethora of destinations. If you have but a week to spend here, your first emotion will almost surely be frustration at your inability to do any more than dabble in the possibilities. Do you want a cool day with little sunshine in a secluded anchorage? It's here. Do you want, the very next day, a slip in a sunny, warm marina near a large selection of facilities? It, too, is here, as are just about any other combinations you can desire. You can choose anchorages near nature preserves, mountain trails,

The Golden Gate Bridge

10

sandy beaches, marshlands, and historic sites or marinas near biking and walking paths, museums, and libraries.

The one option you don't have in the Bay itself is tropical weather among palm trees. However, San Francisco Bay proper contains only a portion, though surely the major portion, of the destinations available to boaters. To the north, this Bay joins San Pablo Bay, which in turn connects through the Carquinez Strait to Suisun Bay to the east. The Petaluma and Napa rivers flow from the north, into San Pablo Bay. The Sacramento River flows into Suisun Bay. You can readily find the palm trees and hot, if not tropical, summers in the valleys accessible along these rivers. From San Francisco Bay, boaters can easily navigate these other bays and the rivers to add to the enormous natural variety of this splendid destination.

The City of San Francisco is not the least of the many attractions this destination offers to boaters. Dylan Thomas, the Welsh poet, said of the *city* of San Francisco, "It is and has everything." Had he been a sailor, he could have said the same for the Bay. But he got it just right for the City as well as for the Bay he failed to include. And part of the *everything* of cruising by sailboat or motorboat in San Francisco Bay *is* the City, even if the only piece of the City the sailor takes in is its beauty seen from the water.

Thomas, writing to his wife, Caitlin, went on to describe San Francisco:

The wonderful sunlight there, the hills, the great bridges, the Pacific at your shoes. . . . And the city is built on hills; it dances in the sun for nine months of the year; & the Pacific Ocean never runs dry.

John Steinbeck, a native Californian, was no less enthralled:

When I was a child growing up in Salinas we called San Francisco "the City." . . . A strange and exclusive word is "city." Besides San Francisco, only small sections of London and Rome stay in the mind as the City. . . . San Francisco put on a show for me. I saw her across the bay, from the great road that bypasses Sausalito and enters the Golden Gate Bridge. The afternoon sun painted her white and gold—rising on her hills like a noble city in a happy dream. A city on hills has it over flat-land places. Over the green higher hills to the south, the evening fog rolled like herds of sheep coming to cote in the golden city. I've never seen her more lovely.
—Travels with Charley.

Because the City rises, sometimes precipitously, from the Bay to Nob Hill, to Telegraph Hill, to Russian Hill, her beauty is displayed as tableaux of many levels—white houses stepping up the steep streets, deeply tinted green trees interspersed; Presidio Park showing little but a swatch of dark green, its eucalyptus and cedar trees concealing the many buildings squatting beneath them; Golden Gate Park extending an invitation into its emerald gardens; and, at dusk, the lights of Coit Tower and the Transamerica pyramid illuminating two eras in the City's history. If you never go ashore to discover all that makes this *the City*, you will nonetheless have savored much of its beauty from gliding along the waterfront.

Fog rolling in over the Marin Headlands and under the Golden Gate Bridge

Both Thomas and Steinbeck remark on San Francisco's glorious sunshine. A part of this city equally tantalizing, though not as much to those wanting to sail as to those sitting in marinas or anchorages enjoying the view, is the thick marine layer that frequently lies offshore, a backdrop for San Francisco, the Golden Gate Bridge, the Marin Headlands, and Sausalito during mid-day, waiting to come in like sheep to cote, as Steinbeck says. When it does move in, in effusive white, woolly clouds, the fog horns of Point Bonita, Mile Rocks, Point Diablo, the Golden Gate Bridge, and Lime Point sound their deliciously mournful tunes, a sound most resonant of the sea.

The City, however, is not the only site of civilization drawing you to this Bay. Among the sites we invite you to explore in this book are the many anchorages that are relatively secluded, given the population around the Bay, and the many marinas and yacht clubs where you can moor your boat while you get acquainted with cities from the size and complexity of Oakland to the modesty and simplicity of Petaluma. Spend some time in the Berkeley Marina, from which you can get acquainted with one of the country's most prestigious universities. Or explore a former shrimp-processing operation from the anchorage at China Camp in San Pablo Bay.

San Francisco Bay has everything for your cruising pleasure: an extraordinary and intricate system of estuaries and rivers; varied winds and weather patterns; hills, mountains, and flat valleys; and cities and towns of every size.

About the Bay
and
Boating

This is the land the sunset washes
   —Emily Dickinson

1 A BRIEF HISTORY OF SAN FRANCISCO BAY

If history is, as the historian Carl Becker claims, the record of the events of the past, then the history of San Francisco Bay is scant indeed before the Gaspar de Portolá expedition of 1769. Mistakenly believing the body of water he saw from the Montara Mountain on November 4, 1769, to be a portion of Drakes Bay (which Sebastian Cermeño had named Bahía de San Francisco in 1595), Portolá had no notion of the importance of his discovery. Only after Juan Manuel de Ayala, the first European to sail into the Bay, mapped it extensively in 1775 was this recognized as a separate and immensely significant bay.

THE PEOPLE

When the water went down and the land was dry O'-ye planted the buckeye and elderberry and oak trees, and all the other kinds of trees, and also bushes and grasses, all at the same time. But there were no people and he and Wek'-wek wanted people. Then O'-ye took a quantity of feathers of different kinds and packed them up to the top of Oon'-nah-pi's and threw them up into the air and the wind carried them off and scattered them over all the country and they turned into people, and the next day there were people all over the land. —Coast Miwok tale

Native Americans

Despite its lack of *history* in Becker's definition, the San Francisco Bay has nonetheless been the site of continuous human occupation for many centuries, probably for at least the past 5,000 years. Among the attractions for boaters are exhibits around the Bay that explain and illustrate how life along these shores must have been before the arrival of the first Europeans in the late eighteenth century. The indigenous peoples who were hunting and fishing on the shores of San Francisco Bay when the first Europeans arrived in the late 18th century formed four tribes, each based on a common language: the Coast Miwoks, the Ohlones, the Wintuns, and the Yokuts. These tribes seemingly lived a simple, relatively stress-free life, with abundant supplies of fish, game, and vegetation to provide food, clothing, shelter, and rudimentary tools.

That life has now disappeared entirely, with but a few descendants remaining from these four Bay Area tribes. The tribal people were replaced, successively, by Spanish and then Mexican missionaries and ranchers, American merchant sailors and traders, gold miners and soldiers, and, today, urban dwellers of every occupation.

Spanish and Mexican Explorers

Throughout the Bay Area are fascinating relics of the Spanish era that began in San Francisco some 200 years after it had begun along the Pacific Coast to the south. The pervasive fog that lies off the coast of San Francisco for many days of the year shrouded the Bay from the view of Spanish mariners who had, under the command of Sir Francis Drake, discovered Drakes Bay in 1579. Once Ayala mapped San Francisco Bay in 1775, the Spanish began to change the civilization that had existed relatively unchanged for 5,000 years or more. In 1776 the Spaniards set up, first, a fort—the Presidio—and a church, dedicated to San Francisco de Asís but today called Mission Dolores. In the 19th century the surrounding land on the north, east, and south sides of the Bay was divided among a few huge Spanish and, after 1821, Mexican land grants, the Vallejo and Peralta ranches among the largest with Vallejo's ranch estimated to have covered as much as 170,000 acres. The Hispanic era effectively ended with the Gold Rush.

U. S. Settlers

Even before the Gold Rush, Americans had begun to arrive by both ship and the Oregon trail. William Richardson's house, built in 1835 near Mission Dolores, was the first establishment of an American enclave here called Yerba Buena ("good herb"). After U. S. soldiers captured the Presidio on July 9, 1846, they erected the Union flag over Yerba Buena, and the city was renamed San Francisco on January 30, 1847. The Treaty of Guadalupe Hidalgo made California a U. S. territory in 1848.

Coit Tower, one of boaters' favorite landmarks

The discovery of gold in the American River at Coloma, northeast of Sutter's Fort (Sacramento), hastened the granting of statehood to California in 1850, when it became the thirty-first state.

GROWTH OF THE CITY

The Gold Rush brought to San Francisco—and consequently to the Bay itself—dramatic changes, beginning with a jump in population from 300 to 25,000 in but a few months. Many men who did not make their fortunes in the gold fields returned to the Bay Area and stayed as squatters. Despite the provisions of the Treaty of Hidalgo of 1848 guaranteeing that the property rights of the Californios (as the residents from Mexico and Spain were called) would be respected, the Californios could not defend their ranches against these squatters because of the sheer sizes of the ranches and the enormous expense of guarding their boundaries. The financial drain of protracted legal battles led, in

Mission San Rafael Arcangel

most cases, to the Californios' having to sell their holdings. Missions, forts, adobe houses, and their usual accoutrements from this Hispanic period survive around the Bay Area to give one a sense of life here before the Gold Rush changed it all.

Of particular interest to sailors are the many modifications to the Bay itself that began with the gold miners and gold mining and have, to some degree, continued to this day. Approximately one-third of what was the San Francisco Bay before 1850 has been either filled in or diked off, beginning with the unusual filling in of the cove of Yerba Buena by the many ships that sailors with gold fever abandoned. Some of these ships became hotels or other commercial establishments. As the ships deteriorated from neglect and sank, they served as the foundation for new buildings along the waterfront. The gold mining itself also facilitated the filling of the bay: hydraulic mining sent millions of tons of sediment down the Sacramento and San Joaquin rivers and into the Bay, altering not only its shoreline but its depth and composition as well. The damming of the rivers, and the diminished run-off, continues to affect the composition.

If the Gold Rush brought long-lasting and sometimes undesirable changes to the geography of San Francisco Bay, its effects on the City were no less enduring and, in some ways, no less unwelcome. Prosperity for the Bay Area was certainly not among those unwelcome changes. With the phenomenal growth of population in the 1850s and 1860s, the economy responded vigorously. Demands for beef, food crops, and lumber and the ever increasing need for freight, steamship, and stagecoach lines to transport both these products and the population resulted in many new jobs. In 1852 Wells Fargo began as an express and banking agency. The elite of the City built expansive and expensive homes on Rincon Hill and in South Park in the 1850s and on Nob Hill in the 1870s.

The hills of San Francisco gave these homeowners magnificent panoramic views of the Bay, but these same hills presented quite a challenge to transportation. The first cable car, demonstrated in 1873, promised a solution. For the next twenty years, the cable cars on as many as eight different lines not only climbed the hills in the center of the city but linked outlying areas to San Francisco. Electric street cars and trolleys replaced most of the cable cars in the 1890s; buses with gasoline engines completed the job in the 20th century. Visible today from Aquatic Park, one of the few remaining cable cars continues to clank up Hyde Street to Nob Hill several times daily.

Another section of the City experiencing dramatic growth was the Barbary Coast, between lower Broadway and Pacific Avenue, inland now from the fishing pier, Pier 7. Named after the notorious coast of North Africa where pirates congregated, the San Francisco version of the Barbary well deserved its name. Some writers and filmmakers have romanticized this "colorful" era, but, in fact, some of the unsavory activities that took place here were anything but colorful. Nothing remains of the Barbary Coast today but the stories, both the romantic and the real.

Contemporary sailors exploring the Bay can relive another important change brought about in part by the Gold Rush and in part by the building of the transcontinental railroad. Chinese immigrants arrived in relatively small numbers to seek their fortunes in the gold fields; many more came to join those failed gold miners to work on the railroad.

China Camp State Park

Upon completion of the railroad in 1869, the majority of the Chinese laborers returned to San Francisco. Chinatown is the best known result of the migration of these laborers, but for the sailor the Angel Island Immigration Station and China Camp in San Pablo Bay give further insight into the history of this group of San Franciscans.

A second economic boom lasting 20 years came to the Bay Area with the discovery of the Comstock silver lode in 1859. San Francisco financiers provided the capital for the mining of this lode, and nearly all the supplies for both the mines and the miners passed through Bay waters before being transported overland or up the Sacramento River.

During this time, city leaders had the foresight to set aside land for a public park. Unfortunately, all the available land was sand dunes, and critics of the proposals to create a wooded haven in these barren dunes seemed justifiably skeptical. But Golden Gate Park, built on these dunes, stands today as one of the country's most accommodating and beautiful city parks, the park a long rectangle of green running for more than 3 miles (4, if the narrow Panhandle between Fell and Oak is included) through the heart of metropolitan San Francisco down to the Pacific Ocean.

A few blocks north of the Pacific end of Golden Gate Park, Adolph Sutro (mayor of San Francisco from 1895 to 1897) opened a public bath house in 1896, the largest bath house in the United States at the time. Continuing in popularity well into the 20th century, the Sutro Baths finally closed in 1954, and then in 1966 fire destroyed the building, characterized by its 2-acre glass roof. Just south of the site of Sutro Baths, the Cliff House that today overlooks Seal Rocks is a greatly scaled down version of the Cliff House that Sutro erected there in 1896. The most significant legacy of Sutro for contemporary San Franciscans and visitors is Sutro Heights Park, the ocean property Sutro's daughter, Emma, left to the city in 1938.

The earthquake of 1906 brought a pause, though certainly not a halt, to the growth of San Francisco. The quake, or the fires that followed for three days after, destroyed many of the buildings, including virtually all those downtown. The filling in of Mission Bay with the debris left after the earthquake and fires is one of the other permanent changes to the coastline of San Francisco Bay.

The rebuilding of the City began immediately, and by 1909 San Franciscans were ready to share with the world their city's rejuvenation. City leaders bid for the international fair that had been discussed to celebrate the opening of the Panama Canal in 1904. To transform Harbor View (now called the Marina District, directly east of the Presidio), workers built a seawall and filled in behind it with sand dredged from the Bay. The Panama Pacific International Exposition opened on the site in 1915 with great aesthetic and economic success. The Palace of Fine Arts, rising majestically above West Harbor, is the only building remaining, though the Exposition did result in Marina Green and the Marina Small Craft Harbor, both of which continue to be recreational assets for the City.

Palace of Fine Arts, easily visible from the Bay

The next exposition for San Francisco—and one that also changed the configuration of the Bay—was the Golden Gate International Exposition of 1939-1940 to commemorate the opening of the Golden Gate and the Bay bridges. Engineers created a site for this exposition by adding mud and sand dredged from the Bay to the north shore of Yerba Buena Island and using stone quarried from the tunnel through the island connecting the two sections of the Bay Bridge. The Treasure Island

Museum on Treasure Island

Museum is housed in one of the three buildings remaining from this exposition. Sailors are perhaps even more impressed with the other addition to the Bay: the excellent anchorage in the lee of Treasure Island, Clipper Cove.

Two miles directly west of Treasure Island is another island of historic interest, though, unlike Treasure Island and Angel Island, it has no dock or anchorage for pleasure boats. This island, Alcatraz, is today a part of the Golden Gate National Recreation Area; visitors must come by ferry from the City Front. However, sailors can get a good view of

Alcatraz Island, an excellent landmark

the exterior of the buildings and "the Rock" on which they perch by navigating around the island, being careful not to interfere with the ferry traffic. One can readily understand why this rock was first a military fort, standing sentinel with an unimpeded view of the Golden Gate. One can also well imagine why someone thought its location would make it ideal for a prison. From 1859 to 1907 it was, in fact, both a military fort and a military prison, the latter being only a minor function at that time. Beginning in 1907, Alcatraz became solely a military prison; and between 1934 and 1963, in its most widely known role, Alcatraz was the site of a maximum security federal penitentiary. The Rock had one final spate of national attention in 1969, when Native Americans "captured" Alcatraz and occupied some of the former penitentiary buildings until 1971.

The Bay Area has, since the Gold Rush, attracted a diverse population, with people coming from not only around the United States but from around the world to seek their fortunes. With the onset of World War II, this trend gained impetus. Because of its strategic location, the Bay Area became the center of the West Coast war effort, with several army and navy bases spread around the Bay and two major shipbuilding facilities, Bechtel Corporation's Marinship in Sausalito and the Henry Kaiser Shipyard in Richmond. Men and women of many diverse backgrounds poured into the area to fill the thousands of positions newly created. After the war, both civilians and military personnel who had come to the Bay Area stayed on to call one of the surrounding communities home.

THE MILITARY

Once the Treaty of Hidalgo, signed in 1848, assured California status as a United States territory, the U. S. military began its continuing and often extensive tenure in the Bay Area. Fort Point, on the south side of the narrowest part of the only entrance into San Francisco Bay from

Fort Point, under south end of Golden Gate Bridge

the Pacific Ocean, was the obvious site for the first U. S. fortification. In the late 18th century, Spanish explorers had recognized the strategic importance of this point they called *Punta del Cantil Blanco* (White Cliff Point) and erected a gun battery there. In 1849 the U. S. Army mounted artillery in the remains of the old Spanish fort. Planning and construction of a major fort for the site began almost immediately, later to be officially designated as Fort Winfield Scott, though "Fort Point" has prevailed in popular usage. The masonry fort, from which a shot was never fired at an enemy, has been restored as the Fort Point National Historic Site.

From that modest beginning the U. S. military went on to build various kinds of military installations on the San Francisco Bay shores, some, like Fort Point, for securing the Bay from enemy intrusion, some for debarkation of troops and materiel, some for wartime construction, and others for the training of military personnel. The islands of the Central Bay—Alcatraz, Angel, and Yerba Buena (and the manmade addition to it, Treasure Island)— have all been military outposts. Other military installations (mostly historic now) along the waters of the Bay are Fort Baker, the San Francisco Presidio, Fort Mason, Point Molate U. S. Naval Fuel Depot, Kaiser Shipyards, Oakland Army Base, Alameda Naval Air Station, Moffett Field, Hunters Point, Mare Island Naval Shipyard, Hamilton Field, and Marinship Shipyards.

BOATS, SHIPS, AND FERRIES

The earliest boats we have any record of in San Francisco Bay were the canoes Native Americans made from tule reeds. Early Spanish explorers made drawings of some of these canoes used by the various tribes around the Bay to catch fish, to gather shellfish, and to hunt otters and seals.

Coast Miwok tule boat

The buoyancy of the reeds assured good flotation, but apparently the reeds were not always woven tightly enough to render the canoes watertight. These early inhabitants of the area were excellent basket makers, however, and did weave the tule reeds into waterproof containers to hold everything from acorns to water to steaming mush. These baskets presumably could also be used as bailers in the leaky canoes.

Ayala's mapping of San Francisco Bay in 1775 alerted the world to the enormous potential this well-protected bay promised for shipping. Still, its remoteness kept the numbers of shipping vessels coming in here low during the Spanish and Mexican eras. But the U. S. conquest of California in 1846 began an accelerating period of commercial shipping in and out of the Bay, much of that shipping involving, too, the plying of the rivers and estuaries around the Bay. Cargo and passengers came in, from the East Coast primarily, and agricultural and livestock products and seafood went out. The Gold Rush caused a decided spurt in that acceleration, with close to 1,000 ships in Yerba Buena Cove at times during the 1850s.

Besides the port of San Francisco, several other cities have figured prominently in commercial traffic on the Bay. Benicia, Martinez, Port Costa, and Vallejo thrived in the early 20th century as busy links between the Bay and the agricultural towns to the north. The numbers of merchant ships coming into the ports of Oakland, Alameda, and Richmond rose steadily during the 20th century, with Oakland today continuing to be a prosperous port. Among the other less busy, and thus less well known, ports are Pinole, Hercules, Crockett, Port Chicago, and Antioch.

Between 1882 and 1908, San Francisco Bay was the whaling capital of the world. (The last whaling station in the United States, at Point Richmond, closed in 1971.) The fishing industry in the Bay had taken off during the Gold Rush, when many immigrants drawn here for gold realized they could find much more profit in the rich waters in and outside the Bay. Italian and Dalmatian fishermen in their feluccas— lateen-rigged fishing boats common in the Mediterranean— found bountiful harvest along the coast, while the Chinese were the primary shrimpers inside the Bay, building Chinese junks and sampans for the purpose.

Before the construction of the seven major bridges that connect the opposite shores of the Bay Area, ferry services around the Bay were big business, with at times more than two dozen routes crisscrossing the Bay. First to open in the late 19th century were services from San Francisco to Richmond, Oakland, and Alameda and from Benicia to Martinez. Soon to follow were routes from San Francisco to Marin County and Vallejo, with many additional routes established in the first four decades of the 20th century. Today, few ferry services remain in operation on the Bay.

Recreational boating on San Francisco Bay has no less illustrious history than have the commercial marine enterprises. During the second half of the 19th century pleasure yachts began to populate the Bay. In 1869 the San Francisco Yacht Club was incorporated, with the Pacific and the Corinthian following over the next fifteen years. Yacht racing became popular, but so did the racing of working craft, such as barkentines and schooners. Competitive rowing in the 20th century attracted crowds of spectators who lined the banks from the starting docks to the finish line. The coming of gasoline-powered boats facilitated the even wider use of boats for sport hunting and fishing; the Bay Area continues to be a rich source of game and fish.

Sailors today can view remnants of San Francisco's maritime past at the Hyde Street Pier. The highlights of the pier are the three-masted square rigger the *Balclutha*, built in Scotland in 1886; the *C. A. Thayer*, a three-masted lumber schooner built in Eureka, California, in 1895; the *Alma*, perhaps the only surviving scow schooner in the world; and the ferryboat *Eureka*. Replicas of feluccas and a houseboat complete the panorama. At the docks of the Bay Model in Sausalito are other examples: the *Wampana*, a lumber schooner built in St. Helens, Oregon, in 1915, and the last of her kind; and the *Hercules*, one of the last remaining steam tugs, built in New Jersey in 1907.

The *Alma*, a scow schooner

The *Wampana* and the *Hercules* in Sausalito

DAVID DAWSON

BRIDGES

The three major islands of the Central Bay—Angel, Alcatraz, and Yerba Buena—form a pleasing natural pattern for those of us who look for patterns. The works of men and women—the Golden Gate, the Oakland-San Francisco Bay, and the Richmond-San Rafael bridges—form a no less pleasing triangle. Of course, these bridges are enormously important in the economic and recreational life of San Francisco and all the surrounding communities. One immediate change upon the completion of the bridges was the dramatic drop in the number of ferry boats working the Bay. Sailors here must still be on the lookout, however, for ferries making several daily runs from San Francisco to Alcatraz, Angel Island, Sausalito, Tiburon, Corte Madera, and Vallejo and from Tiburon to Angel Island.

For Bay sailors the bridges have another importance: they make ideal "fixed stars" for navigation, and, like those more time-honored fixed stars, the bridges lend unique beauty to the sky above the sailors. Unlike the fixed stars, however, these "stars" fascinate sailors by both day and night. At night the lights on the three bridges, like necklaces of diamonds, appear to be on chains looped above the dark water, all three bridges visible simultaneously from many positions on the water's surface. By day their intricate structures leave Bay Area boaters who take time to contemplate these bridges in awe.

The Bay Bridge, completed in 1936, is a marvel of construction with its eastern cantilevered-trussed section and western suspension span joined by a tunnel through Yerba Buena Island. This tunnel through the rock has the largest diameter of any vehicular tunnel in the world. The Golden Gate Bridge, one of the world's two longest suspension bridges, became the symbol of San Francisco upon its completion in 1937. The construction of this bridge on rocky shores along a tumult of water being pushed through the narrow opening between San Francisco Bay and the Pacific Ocean makes for a compelling story. The newcomer among the Central Bay bridges, having been completed in 1956, the Richmond-San Rafael Bridge curves gracefully in a long, low arc to link the two cities giving the bridge its name. These three bridges circumscribe what most sailors know today as the Central Bay.

To the northeast of the Richmond-San Rafael lie two more bridges, the Carquinez and the Benicia-Martinez. Sailors venturing south of the Bay Bridge can view two other bridges that play major roles in the lives of Bay Area residents, the San Mateo and the Dumbarton. As do the bridges in the Central Bay, these four provide navigational landmarks and engineering interest to Bay sailors.

The Bay Bridge from a sailor's perspective

2 GEOGRAPHY AND GEOLOGY

. . . and the next day before the dawn we were lying to upon the Oakland side of San Francisco Bay. The day was breaking as we crossed the ferry; the fog was rising over the citied hills of San Francisco; the bay was perfect—not a ripple, scarce a stain, upon its blue expanse; everything was waiting, breathless, for the sun. A spot of cloudy gold lit first upon the head of Tamalpais, and then widened downward on its shapely shoulder; the air seemed to awaken, and began to sparkle; and suddenly "The tall hills Titan discovered," and the city of San Francisco, and the bay of gold and corn were lit from end to end with summer daylight.

         —Robert Louis Stevenson, 1879

The topography of San Francisco Bay is what makes this bay a premier cruising destination. Much of its some 400-460 square miles of surface is navigable by pleasure boats, both sail and motor, and its 276 miles of shoreline makes many turns and starts, including three embayments— Richardson, San Pablo, and Suisun. As a consequence, the Bay has dozens of suitable and varied spots for anchorages and marinas. Its ten islands and groups of islands—Angel, Belvedere, Alcatraz, Yerba Buena (and its extension, Treasure), Alameda, Brooks, Red Rock, the Marin Islands, the Brothers, and the Sisters—furnish additional destinations, though only Angel, Belvedere, Yerba Buena/ Treasure, and Alameda have reliable anchorages and/or marinas

Nine California counties border the Bay shoreline—San Francisco, San Mateo, Santa Clara, Alameda, Contra Costa, Solano, Napa, Sonoma, and Marin; each of these counties has unique features a boater can savor, in some cases only while sailing by, in other cases by anchoring or tying up and going ashore. Cityscapes and landscapes lend a constantly changing view. Coast redwoods, coast live oaks, Douglas fir, eucalyptus, pines, madrone, and buckeyes grace the hillsides that are geometrically scored by lines of streets. Beaches and marshes are replete with snowy egrets, blue herons, willets, curlews, stilts, sandpipers, and avocets pecking in the mud and sand at low tide.

The marine influence determines, for the most part, the climate of the Bay itself and its shoreline, resulting in cool, wet winters and cool summers with frequent fog or wind. However, many boating destinations of the San Francisco Bay are quite near "banana belts," where the cold air drains away from the slopes. These bayshore sites get more heat year around.

Adding to this expanse of the Bay are the navigable rivers and sloughs that extend the potential destinations for boaters by many miles

Willets on the wing at Newark Slough

Pastoral scene on the Napa River

and in many directions. A cruise up one of these rivers or sloughs will take you past wetlands and grainfields, pastures and salt evaporation ponds. These rivers and sloughs generally have warmer, less windy summer weather and cooler, wetter winter weather than the Bay.

As rich as all this variety available in the Bay is today, we nevertheless like to imagine the appearance of the Bay in years, centuries, even millennia past. In 1775, when Juan Manuel de Ayala mapped the Bay, he observed a body of water quite different from the one we observe today. The bay he saw, however, almost surely closely resembled the bay the first indigenous people discovered when they migrated to these shores between 5,000 and 10,000 years ago. An almost identical bay also greeted the participants in the Bear Flag Rebellion who raised the United States flag above the Presidio in 1846. But major changes to this bay began to occur only four years later, with the coming of the Gold Rush. Hydraulic mining sent millions of tons of sediment down the Sacramento River, silting the Bay. At the same time, with the rapid growth in population in the Bay Area, the filling of the Bay proceeded unbridled in response to the demand from both commercial and private interests for waterfront property. Today, primarily as a result of these two factors, the water of the Bay has only about 400-460 square miles of surface, rather than the over 700 square miles it had in 1846. Some coves, islands, beaches, creeks, sloughs, and wetlands mapped by Ayala in 1775 have disappeared altogether. Others have been altered drastically.

But change has ever been the nature of Nature, too. The San Francisco Bay we know today is in large part the product, though surely not the final product, of cataclysmic changes over millions of years. Some 200 million years ago, the Pacific Ocean Plate, one of several huge pieces making up the earth's fractured and dynamic crust, began to push eastward under the western edge of the Continental Plate. The vertical warping that resulted formed the land mass we now call the Bay Area. About 30 million years ago, the Pacific Ocean Plate began to move in a northwest direction, sliding past the Continental Plate toward Alaska. This slide continues today along the San Andreas Fault, at the rate of one to two inches a year. The San Andreas Fault System, which includes the Calaveras and Hayward faults, extends from Point Arena in Mendocino County to the Mexican border, where it has formed the Gulf of California. And we all know that this fault system continues to alter the topography of the Bay Area.

Volcanic activity beginning about 25 million years also contributed to the forming of what is today the Bay Area. These volcanos combined with the folds, faults, and uplifts caused by the movement of the plates to form the Bay Area's mountains plus the Sierra Nevadas about 3 million years ago. With the rising of the Sierra Nevadas and the Coastal Range came increased rainfall and increased water flow into the Central Valley, creating the great river system of what is today called the Delta, so named because the three major cities of the Delta in the second half of the 19th century— Sacramento, Stockton, and Antioch— form a triangle, the symbol for the Greek letter "delta."

The two major rivers, now called the Sacramento and the San Joaquin, carrying water down from the Sierras to the ocean then, as today, converged at Suisun Bay and passed through the Carquinez Strait. Exactly where the water then flowed into the Pacific Ocean geologists are unsure, but they believe the present outlet, the Golden Gate, dates from about one million years ago.

Rocks protecting Fisherman Bay on Southeast Farallon.

At about the same time the downward warping of the earth's crust between the San Andreas and Hayward faults formed the basin where the Bay is now. The river funnelling through Carquinez Strait began to carve out a valley in what we call the Central Bay, digging out a 350-foot canyon at the narrow gap in the Coastal Range, now the Golden Gate. In the South Bay less boisterous rivers formed the Santa Clara Valley.

The present filling of this basin between these two faults began about 10,000 years ago. At that time the Pacific Coast shoreline lay about where the Farallon Islands are, 27 miles offshore. Then, as the glacial melt raised the sea level, perhaps as much as 400 feet, the waters of the Pacific poured through the Golden Gate, filling the basin and the river valleys. The result is an extensive shallow body of water, with two-thirds of its water less than 18 feet deep and only one-fifth more than 30 feet deep, the deepest places being the ancient river bed between Angel Island and Tiburon and the Golden Gate. This body of water, which geologists say is really an estuary, "a closed embayment where fresh and saltwater mix," drains about 40 percent of California's water.

The Golden Gate. Think of all that has come about because of that rupture in the Coastal Range. The ocean has flowed in, giving us an exceptionally well-protected and extensive bay where we might have had a marshy lake after the last ice age. The fog and the sea breezes reach the Bay Area through this same entrance, tempering the heat that prevails to the east and making possible, some claim, the best sourdough bread in the world. Not to be neglected is the nautical result of the slenderness of the Golden Gate. Where the girdled water comes out of the Bay into the ocean, a lively meeting of opposing forces occurs. Called the Potato Patch, as the legend goes because potato scows lost their loads here with some regularity but just as likely because the water looks like nothing so much as potatoes dug up and lying about in clumps and lumps, this interface has given many a sailor pause. A sailor can neither enter nor exit San Francisco Bay without being reminded of the enduring legacy of the Golden Gate.

3 WIND, WEATHER, AND SEASONS

WIND

Gray-eyed Athena sent them a favorable breeze, a fresh west wind, singing over the wine-dark sea.
—The Iliad

Of all its attributes that lure men and women from around the world to sail on San Francisco Bay, the singing wind has the most persuasive voice. Those fortunate enough to get out on the Bay aboard a sailboat go home with glowing stories about these fabled Bay winds.

Carricklee **on a beam reach in Central Bay**

Of course, not every boater on the Bay desires the winds. On summer weekends, sails dot the Bay; powerboats add only an occasional accent. Those singing summer winds that sailboaters find so alluring elicit no enthusiastic responses from powerboaters.

The Causes of the Wind in San Francisco Bay

San Francisco Bay is perhaps the only place in the world where boaters can, with relative assurance, expect to sail almost any afternoon from March through October, confident the winds will blow at 20 knots or more. These consistent and dependable winds result from two primary causes. California's great Central Valley, the envy of farmers the world over, produces bountiful crops because of the deep top soil and the 100-degree temperatures common during the summer months. That valley heat siphons the cool marine air in through the Golden Gate, across the Bay, and toward the Valley. The hotter the Valley, the stronger the winds on the Bay.

The Pacific High Pressure Zone also plays a part in keeping the Valley hot and the Bay winds blowing. During the winter, the high moves south, allowing storms to push into Central California. Along about March, however, the high moves north again and parks itself approximately 1,000 miles offshore of San Francisco, blocking most storms at sea. If the high were not positioned off the coast, the storms could come through and cool the Central Valley. This cooling would result in comparable temperatures in the Valley and in the Bay, as is the case during the winter months; the winds on the Bay would then be gentle breezes. As it is, the high pushes the storms to the north, giving Oregon and Washington summer rain, green grass, and light winds. The Central Valley remains hot, and Bay sailors gleefully listen to the "beat of the offshore wind" (Kipling, "The Long Trail"). These summer winds on the Central Bay are dependable, blowing with authority almost every afternoon between March 15 and November 15.

Winds on the Bay generally run in cycles. If the Central Valley is enduring one of its exceptionally hot spells, when the temperatures exceed 100 degrees for several days, the winds will blow at 25 knots on the Central Bay. After a few days, however, the temperature in the Valley will gradually decrease, and the winds on the Bay will subside. When the temperature in the Valley drops to about 90 degrees, winds of 15 to 20 knots and warmer temperatures will prevail on the Bay. After a few days of this more gentle weather in both areas, the cycle of the hot Valley and the windy Bay will begin again. Some weather people and boaters claim a new cycle begins every six days.

Early spring and late fall bring milder temperatures for the Central Valley, so the winds in the Bay decrease somewhat. March, October, and November have a number of light air days on the Central Bay in some years. In other years, boaters find boisterous winds throughout November and even into December.

Avoiding San Francisco's Winds

But those boaters who don't care for heavy winds shouldn't despair. Those famous, or, for some, infamous, Bay winds don't typically blow 24 hours a day. In fact, the winds generally begin just before noon.

Those who prefer to avoid the heavy winds of the afternoons can do so by being at their destinations before noon and getting settled in. For this reason, on a typical summer day many anchorages around the Bay begin filling up before noon.

Although many boaters choose to anchor or dock their boats before the heavy winds begin blowing across the Central Bay, others who want to avoid a rollicking ride find sheltered areas to explore. These heavy winds that can make the Central Bay uncomfortable for smaller

Spinnakers in gentle morning breezes east of Angel Island

sailboats and powerboats don't extend to all areas of the Bay. When most parts of the Central Bay have winds of 25 knots, the area close to the San Francisco shoreline south of the Bay Bridge will typically have 15-knot winds and calm water. Similarly, boaters can find light winds on the east side of Angel Island and the Tiburon Peninsula. And many other areas exist, of course, where boaters go when they don't feel like bashing into waves, for example, "up the river" to Napa, Petaluma, or the Delta.

Though the winds do occasionally blow strongly all night in some anchorages and marinas, the winds commonly die out to almost nothing at night. As in the day, any winds that do blow at night are generally westerly or northwesterly, with but an occasional east wind during the fall and winter months.

The Winds Outside San Francisco Bay

Boaters who venture outside the Golden Gate past Point Bonita expecting to find the same wind conditions in the ocean as in the Bay often get a surprise. The heat of the Central Valley has little effect on the strength of the wind at sea. Rather, the winds at sea are an extension of those in the North Pacific Ocean on that particular day. We have seen days where the winds were blowing 25 knots on the Bay but were flat after we passed Point Bonita. Conversely, we have seen days when the ocean was being blasted by gale-force winds and the Bay was experiencing nothing more than gentle breezes.

Typical ocean winds west of San Francisco blow from the northwest, but like all ocean winds, they vary. In the winter they might come from any direction and will generally be light unless a weather front is moving through the area. In the spring and summer, the northwesterly winds generally blow strongly during the late morning, afternoon, and early evening hours. Then during the late evening, night, and early morning hours, the winds decrease, and sometimes cease altogether.

Because of these wind patterns in the Pacific Ocean off San Francisco, most who make an ocean passage watch the weather carefully before departure. If the winds are blowing strongly outside the Gate, boaters leave well before noon, using the motor until they clear Point Bonita. When they are a few miles offshore, they can adjust the sails and get serious about sailing.

Because the prevailing winds off the Northern California coast roughly parallel the coastline, northwest to southeast, the wind strength increases markedly near any point on the coastline that juts out into the ocean noticeably. Rounding such a point while heading into the wind can be treacherous, especially for small boats. Boaters heading north to Bodega Bay or Tomales Bay, for example, will find rounding Point Reyes in the afternoon difficult. To make this passage more comfortable, most boaters spend the night at Drakes Bay and round Point Reyes early the next morning.

SAN FRANCISCO BAY FOG

O the mutter overside, when the port-fog holds us tied,
And the sirens hoot their dread!
 —Rudyard Kipling , "The Long Trail"

Literature abounds with stories of the San Francisco Bay fog. Jack London began his novel *Sea Wolf* with a mid-bay collision caused by this heavy fog. In fact, however, fog inside the Bay is rarely the kind that results in zero visibility. What passes for a typically foggy day on the Bay is more commonly high fog, or a marine layer, that obscures the sun completely but leaves good horizontal vision.

San Francisco's fog results when the Pacific Ocean winds encounter the coastal water that is cooler than the water mid-ocean. As the ocean meets the Pacific coast, the cold water that has been deep is forced to the surface. The warm winds that have travelled the Pacific Ocean, carrying great amounts of water vapor, cross this area of cooler water and create coastal fog. Air travelers looking out the windows of the airplane see this thick, cottony fog as they approach San Francisco. The bottom of this fog may be no more than 200 feet off the water's surface, and it rarely extends more than 1,000 feet above the water. This relatively thin layer usually burns off inside the Bay by midday or shortly after. Above the Pacific Ocean outside the Bay, however, the fog may obscure the sun for a solid week at a time.

Fog over Angel Island

The typical San Francisco Bay fog dominates the weather picture between March and November at least part of each day. Often developing just before dark, this fog is more persistent in some areas than others. The fog rolls in through the Golden Gate and then moves down the City Front, enveloping Emery-ville and Berkeley and sometimes Richmond. Later in the evening, it often covers the entire coastal Bay Area.

Every month the pattern of fog is different. March, which many local boaters consider the beginning of the boating season, typically has few foggy days. April has more foggy days. And May, June, July, and August have many foggy days, August having the most. September, October, and November, like the spring months, have fewer foggy days than the summer months. In the winter months—December, January, and February—the occasional zero-visibility day may surprise boaters. We have been caught out sailing when the thick winter fog moved in and left us unable to see the bow of our boat from the cockpit.

This thick fog common in the winter rarely rolls into the Bay in the spring, summer, or fall, but you will occasionally find it around the Golden Gate in the summer. In early August 1982, Bob was making a voyage to Hawaii and departed the dock in Richmond at 0700 in bright sunshine. By the time he and his crew got within one mile of the Golden Gate Bridge, they sailed into a fog bank so thick they could not see the bridge, Fort Point, Mile Rocks, Point Bonita, Seal Rocks, or the buoys marking the ship channel. In fact, they could barely see the bow of the boat for the first 24 hours of the trip to Hawaii. While this anecdote illustrates that low, thick fog can form in the summer, happily such fog is rare.

STORMS

And I have asked to be
  Where no storms come,
Where the green swell is in the havens dumb,
  And out of the swing of the sea.
    —Gerard Manley Hopkins, "Heaven-Haven"

Storms on San Francisco Bay occur almost exclusively during the winter months because of the Pacific High sitting offshore from April to November. San Francisco seldom receives more than 15 inches of precipitation annually, and most of that falls during December, January, February, and March, with rain being unusual between May 1 and November 1. Fortunately, the Bay does not have real storms like those in most other areas of the world. A typical heavy-weight San Francisco storm might bring 40-knot winds and one inch of rain; considering the hurricanes and typhoons that strike other areas, that's not a storm.

SEASONS

The Bay really has only two seasons, winter and summer. Between come transition periods distinct enough to be called spring or autumn.
    — Kimball Livingston, *Sailing the Bay*

The beginning of spring, March 21, roughly coincides with the beginning of the sailing season for most Bay sailors. Of course, a few boaters take to the water every weekend of the year, but the number is scant before the second or third weekend of March. Between the middle of March and the last weekend of April, the date

Sailors waiting for wind along the City Front

of the official Opening Day celebration, more and more boats appear on the Bay every weekend. Spring sailing is characterized by inconsistent winds, occasional days with light rain, and cool days and nights. Nevertheless, boaters who have refrained from taking their boats out during the winter suddenly appear on the Bay.

Summer sailing begins in early May, when winds are predictable. Every afternoon between Alcatraz and Angel Island the winds blow in excess of 20 knots. And the fog is predictable, too, covering the entire Bay from late evening one day until noon the following day. The temperatures become warm enough so boaters can sleep overnight on their boats while at anchor. All in all, this time of the year is blissful for boaters.

Fall sailing unofficially begins the first weekend after Labor Day. The weather commonly becomes more agreeable at this time of the year: winds become less boisterous, fog—if it forms at all—burns off early in the day, and temperatures rise, encouraging shirt-sleeve boating. In most years this gentle fall weather continues into November, ending only when the Pacific High retreats to the south and leaves the storm door open. When the rains begin to fall sometime in November and the temperatures drop enough to make being out of doors less than enjoyable, boating on the Bay decreases. After that, only the die-hard boaters take their boats out of their marinas regularly.

Most boaters use the winter months to work on their boats, making repairs and improvements for the next season. When a particularly warm weekend occurs in December, January, or February, some Bay boaters are once again out, but not in force. Winds typically are light and temperatures too cool for enjoying nights aboard in the deserted anchorages unless you have a heater on your boat.

PREDICTING THE WEATHER

There is really no such thing as bad weather, only different kinds of good weather.
—John Ruskin

Boaters around the world pride themselves on being able to predict weather and thus stay out of trouble. This ability is necessary in most areas. San Francisco Bay boaters, however, have not gone out of their way to develop this ability, since Bay Area weather offers few surprises during the most common sailing season—March through October. Even in November, the most noteworthy surprise the weather holds is an occasional rain shower. December, January, and February bring increased chances of heavy winds and rain, and they also bring a threat of the dense fog that hugs the ground and reduces visibility to zero.

4 TIDES AND CURRENTS

There is a tide in the affairs of men,
Which, taken at the flood, leads on to fortune.
—Shakespeare, *Julius Caesar*

San Francisco Bay boaters must understand tides or suffer the consequences. One friend had a frightening experience resulting from his inattention to the tide. He was sailing a Rhodes 19 inside the Bay near the Golden Gate Bridge, when the wind died about an hour before sunset just as a large ebb tide started to flow. Since his boat had no engine, he could do nothing more than watch as he and the boat were swept under the bridge and past Point Bonita into the Pacific Ocean. When the tide changed, long after sundown, he was sitting in a dark ocean without food or drink on a boat without lights. Luckily, a light breeze came up, the tide turned, and he was able to ride the flood tide back to Sausalito. He arrived back at the dock after midnight, a hungrier and wiser man. The lesson to be learned from his experience is simple: take heed of the powerful current that results from the tide in the Bay.

The more common nautical mishap that results when boaters in the Bay don't watch the tides is a grounding. San Francisco Bay is but a shallow basin that the waters of the Pacific Ocean filled after the last ice age. Additionally, the rivers and streams continue to deposit sediment in the Bay. Many boaters have anchored their boats in protected coves or in the lee of the land, enjoyed dinner and one of the Bay's spectacular sunsets, and tucked into their bunks to get a good night's sleep, only to awaken during the night to find the boat aground. Particularly hard on the props on powerboats, going aground can also be frightening for those sleeping aboard a sailboat because the boat may fall over on its side.

CAUSES OF THE TIDES

The moon and the sun have more to do with tides than anything else. Both have a gravitational pull on our oceans. As a result, the water in our oceans and bays bulges toward these bodies. The moon, because it is much closer than the sun, has the most to do with tides. When the moon orbits the earth, the water is pulled toward it. As the earth rotates on its axis and orbits the sun, the same occurs but to a lesser degree. These gravitational pulls result in ebb and flood tides.

Every day the water ebbs (falls) and floods (rises) twice. The two highs and two lows each day differ significantly. Typically in the

San Francisco Bay Area, one high tide will be as much as 3 feet higher than the other one every day, and the same is true of the two low tides on any given day. Thus, prudent boaters on the Bay keep a tide book nearby at all times.

Because of the moon's pull, we need to consider the moon's orbit of 27.3 days around the earth. Looking at the tide book, you will note that the high and low tides coincide with the phases of the moon. On the left margin of your tide guide are the symbols for the various phases of the moon. You will also see the letter **P**, representing *perigee*, meaning that on that particular day the moon is closest to the earth on its monthly orbit. On that day the pull of the moon on the water is at its strongest, and the difference

Low tide at Alviso

between the highest high tide and the lowest low tide is greater than on any other day of the month. This tidal difference can be as much as 12 feet in San Francisco Bay.

When the sun and moon get lined up with the earth and exert their pulls on the same side of the earth simultaneously, *spring tides* occur. These tides are, of course, not the tides of spring; they occur every 13.6 days year around. Rather, they are the extreme high and low tides resulting from this conjunction of the moon and the sun.

When the moon and sun are the farthest from being lined up, *neap tides* result. On those days with neap tides, the range between high and low tides is small, sometimes no more than 2 or 3 feet. The average difference between high and low tides is 4.5 feet during neap tides. Both the neap and spring tides are, of course, influenced even more significantly by the moon when it is at perigee. We all depend on our tide books to calculate for us the effects of these many and varied influences on the tide.

CURRENTS IN THE BAY

As the tides rise and fall, the water moves in and out of the Bay, producing currents. The speed of these currents depends on the size of the tide. When the moon is at its perigee, the maximum ebb current at the Golden Gate Bridge will occasionally reach 6 knots. Aboard a sailboat with a top speed of 5 knots, which is fairly typical, you can end up seeming to be sailing toward the Central Bay at a great rate under the Golden Gate Bridge but in fact be slipping steadily out to sea. On those days when a large ebb is flowing, you will see boaters sailing backwards! Be familiar with currents in the Bay to keep yourself from being carried away by them.

The second reason to consider currents is to minimize the time required to get to your destination. Going against a current, you will clearly decrease your speed made good over the bottom. For instance, if you're going through the water at 6 knots against a 4-knot ebb current, your boat will actually be making good only 2 knots over the bottom. Consider making the 20-mile trip from Sausalito to Vallejo as a typical cruise, and you can easily see how important a knowledge of the currents can be. Assuming your boat averages 5 knots, this trip will take about four hours with no current. If you depart Sausalito during slack water before a large ebb current, however, you can easily add three or four hours to your trip. By contrast, leaving Sausalito on slack water before a large flood, you can cut your travel time by an hour. Using the current to help you can result in making a passage in half the time you'd take if you went against the current.

Currents should also concern cruising boaters in the Bay because of the effects they have on anchored boats. A 5-knot current will put a tremendous strain on your anchor. If your ground tackle is not heavy enough or not properly set, your anchor will drag. To make sure you don't drag, begin with an anchor that is adequate for securing your

Bay current keeps anchor lines taut.

boat. Don't make the mistake of cruising in the Bay with an anchor smaller than the size recommended. Go one size too large rather than one size too small.

Consider, too, that currents change direction. If you anchor facing north on the east side of Angel Island when the current is going out, you will be facing south when the current is coming back in. If you don't take into account this change in current, you can end up dangerously close to the shore, a pier, or a rock.

Current and wind work together to produce some curious results. We all know that a 10-knot wind can make an anchored boat hang back on the end of its anchor line—but not if a strong current is running counter to the wind. When you anchor at China Camp and a 10-knot wind is blowing over the hill, for example, the wind will often strike your boat abeam instead of on the bow because the 2-knot current has more effect on the direction your boat points than a 10-knot wind. This seeming anomaly can be disconcerting the first time you observe it.

If current and wind work together to produce disconcerting results, adding tide to the equation can produce even more dramatic problems. Many a boater has dropped anchor at low tide, let out a little scope, and settled in for dinner or a cozy night's sleep. A little later a flood tide lifts the boat enough to reduce the amount of scope on the anchor line, and the current and wind cause the anchor to drag. Bay sailors soon learn to take tide, current, and wind into consideration when they anchor.

The fact that 40 percent of all the water that runs off California's mountains—obviously a tremendous volume of water—drains out through San Francisco Bay suggests that river flow is another large variable affecting currents. In fact, though, 80 percent of all currents in San Francisco Bay result from tides and are thus remarkably predictable.

USING TIDE BOOKS

Most boaters use as their boating bible the small complimentary booklet titled *Tides and Currents: San Francisco Bay & Tributaries*. If you decide to anchor, you can use this little book to determine whether the tide is low or high so you can accurately estimate how much scope to let out.

Boaters in San Pablo Bay or the San Francisco Bay south of the Bay Bridge *must* rely on tide books if they wish to avoid sitting in the mud. At low tide many areas are simply unnavigable for a boat that draws 5 feet or more. Below the San Mateo Bridge and in the north part of San Pablo Bay, water depths outside the channel are less than 10 feet almost everywhere at low water. Before leaving the marina in that part of the Bay, study the tide book so you know the time

Boats in the mud at low tide in Alviso

of the high and low water as well as the state of the current.

Many boaters suggest that you should enter exceptionally shallow water areas only at low tide or on a flood tide so you can get off quickly if you do go aground. Aground at high tide, you can be in serious trouble when the tide ebbs. A 6-foot tide can leave your boat lying on its side. Even going aground during an ebb can create a serious problem because you may wait a long while for the incoming tide to float your boat off the ground.

Not all boaters consider the same parts of their tide books important. Many who do their boating in the Central Bay look only at the pages that show currents at the Golden Gate. They frequently care primarily about any current that will slow their progress but worry little about going aground. If the current is your concern, study the current page to determine the exact time the current will reach maximum velocity and what the speed will be at the Golden Gate. If you're boating in another part of the Bay, you must add a correction factor to calculate the time of that maximum tide. The tables giving the correction factors for both tide and current are found in the beginning portion of the tide book. Once you find the correction factor, you simply need to add it to the figures from the tide tables to determine what time you can safely go into an area with shallow water. If your boat is in Redwood City, for example, you must add one hour and six minutes to the time of the high tide at the Golden Gate.

Using the tide book can make all your Bay sailing safer and more efficient. If you are going from the Central Bay to Napa, for instance, you want to know the time of the maximum flood current so you can use it to speed you on your journey. To lessen the risk of going aground, you also want to know the times of the high and low water since you'll be going through some shallow water. Your best option, then, as you make your way up the Napa River, is to leave Vallejo on a flood tide. Indeed, very few Bay Area boaters leave the dock for anything more than a casual day sail without first checking the tide book.

5 EQUIPMENT FOR SAFETY AND COMFORT

A ship of the best form will not show its good qualities, except when it is at the same time well rigged, well stowed, and well worked by those who command it.
– Chapman Piloting

For Bay cruising, you need little more than a sturdy boat to enjoy these waters. Many people we have known began visiting anchorages and marinas aboard a small boat with no frills. Over the years, they have bought larger, more comfortable boats and added equipment that has enhanced the enjoyment of their hobby. Although we all seem to add more and more equipment to our boats, little of it is required. The following presentation describes some of the essential equipment—anchors, lines, safety gear—as well as the non-essential equipment commonly found on boats cruising San Francisco Bay.

ANCHORING AND MOORING EQUIPMENT

First, equip your boat with four dock lines so you can tie up at the marinas you visit. If you normally keep your boat at a Bay Area marina, these dock lines should be in addition to the ones you use to tie up in your marina so you won't have to remove your lines from your dock every time you go out to enjoy the Bay. Be sure to have at least one extra long dock line to use for a spring. Guest berthing facilities in the marinas we visit are often end ties requiring one or more spring lines to keep our boat in place. To be prepared, we carry two 50-foot dock lines as well as a number of shorter ones.

A long line will also be handy when you visit Ayala Cove on Angel Island and want to tie up to the mooring buoys. We customarily use one 200-foot anchor line when we tie up to

Boat on an end tie using spring lines

those buoys, tying off one end of the anchor line to a stern cleat, slipping the bitter end through the ring on the top of the buoy, and then tying off that end to our other stern cleat, forming a 100-foot-long vee between the stern of our boat and the buoy. We then motor ahead to the buoy we plan to tie our bow to and slip another line through the ring on the top of that buoy, just as we did with the stern line. Since the buoys are often at least 100 feet apart, you'll need one medium-length line for the bow, at least 50 feet long, to tie up in this manner.

Assuming you'll also want to anchor out to enjoy some of the beautiful anchorages the Bay has to offer, you'll need good ground tackle. Begin with a serious anchor. Most cruising boaters equip their boats with a primary anchor that is at least one size heavier than the recommended size. For recommended sizes for your boat, consult your local chandlery or look in the West Marine catalog.

Boaters have favorites when it comes to anchors, so you can expect to find that people have widely divergent opinions when you ask them what type of anchor you should buy. If you were to check the anchors on cruising boats in the Bay area, you would almost certainly find that a majority of them have a CQR for a primary. The second most common anchor is likely to be a Danforth style (including the West Marine Performance and the Fortress). The third is the Bruce, and the fourth is probably the Delta. The apparent popularity of each of the types above should not dictate the type you put on your boat. Rather, you should consider what type of cruising you plan to do. If you plan to cruise only the San Francisco area, you would be well advised to put a Danforth-type anchor aboard. It will hold particularly well in the mud bottoms found most often in the Bay and Delta.

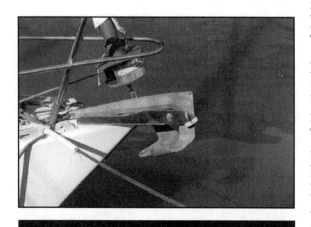

Bruce anchor as a primary

You will most likely choose a secondary anchor that is quite different from your primary. Looking for an anchor that will hang over the bow comfortably, many boaters choose the CQR or Bruce for a primary. However, because neither stows well in a locker or on the stern rail, these same sailors choose something else for a secondary anchor. The most common secondary anchor aboard Bay Area cruising boats is probably a Danforth-type anchor because it stows easily under all the normal equipment in lockers. An apparent contradiction exists: most boats have a CQR or Bruce for a primary anchor because they stow most easily on a bow roller, even though a Danforth-type anchor would probably hold better in most Bay Area situations. Few boaters wish to dig their anchor out of a locker every time they want to anchor.

Once you've chosen an anchor, you'll need to select a rode. You can use either an all-chain rode or a nylon and chain rode. An all-chain rode is best if you plan to do any long distance cruising in the future. Many anchorages in Mexico and the South Pacific have coral patches on the bottom that will make short work of a nylon rode, so Bay cruisers who have plans to visit these areas in the near future generally equip their boats with all-chain.

If your plans focus on only California cruising for the next few years, you can outfit your boat with a rode made up of 35 feet of chain and 200 feet of nylon. The advantages of the nylon/chain rode over the all-chain are many. First, the nylon/chain rode is lighter. Too often a cruiser puts 400 feet—and thus 400 to 600 pounds— of chain in the bow of the boat, causing the boat to hobby horse in rough water. The second advantage to a nylon/chain rode becomes apparent when you weigh anchor. With a nylon/chain rode, you can use your muscles to get your anchor aboard, but if you have an all-chain rode and a 66-pound anchor, as we do, you'll have no choice except to use a windlass. And putting a windlass on your boat is expensive—*very* expensive if your boat is large. Another economic advantage is that chain costs three times as much as nylon. A final advantage is that you'll enjoy more quiet with nylon. Chain can always find a way to rub against our boat's bobstay when we are anchored.

Despite the advantages to a nylon/chain anchor rode, we have an all-chain rode because we plan to visit Mexico and the South Pacific in the near future. Since we have the chain in the bow locker, we just go ahead and use it. We also have nylon/chain aboard, but it is not as convenient as using the all-chain that is at the ready.

Many cruising boats have windlasses on the bow. A windlass is virtually mandatory if you have a large boat with an all-chain anchor rode. We know some cruisers with boats under 30 feet with one-quarter inch chain who pull their anchors up without a windlass, but they are

Manual anchor windlass

Electric anchor windlass

the exception. And they have strong backs.

If you decide you need a windlass for your boat, you can choose between an electric or a hand-powered model. As you might guess, the hand-powered models are less expensive. Not only is the initial purchase price about one-half that of the electric, but the installation costs of the manual are much less. The electric windlass requires, at a minimum, two heavy battery cables, often as much as 35 feet long, a solenoid, and a foot-operated switch. And installing an electric windlass is much more involved than installing the manual. But bringing in 150 feet of chain with an electric windlass takes less time and requires far less effort than with a manual windlass.

Stowing your anchor as you sail around the Bay also deserves some forethought. If you leave your anchor on a bow roller, as most Bay cruisers do, be sure it is securely locked in place. You can secure it by putting a pin through the anchor mount and the anchor, if your anchor mount has such a hole. Many cruisers have cruised for years without such a pin, however; they simply tie the anchor securely to the anchor mount before they make a passage where they might be banging into waves. We have a friend who can testify to the need to secure the anchor. He was sailing through the Carquinez Strait one night on his way back to the Bay when he realized his anchor was being dragged along behind him. He got it back aboard without getting it fouled in his prop, but he recognizes how lucky he was.

Remember to protect your boat by seizing the pin in the anchor shackle. Because the pin in that anchor shackle is so hard to remove when you want to take it out, you may be tempted to say that you don't need to get out the seizing wire and take care of it, but ask someone who lost a boat when that pin backed out in the middle of the night; you will immediately get an emphatic recommendation to seize the pin. We have never had a pin back out, but we know cruisers who have, so our anchor shackle has a pin held in place by seizing wire.

CLOTHING

You can easily pick days that are not rainy to cruise the Bay since rain in the area between May 1 and November 1 is rare. But the lack of rain shouldn't suggest that you'll need to bring along only a pair of shorts and a tee shirt to be comfortable cruising the Bay in the summer. As legendary as the San Francisco fog are the cool summers on the Bay.

The secret to being comfortable while sailing in the San Francisco Area is layering. A few days a year are warm enough to wear shorts and a tee shirt, but generally you'll want to wear long pants and a long sleeved shirt, at the very least. When you're under way, plan to wear a layer over that long-sleeved shirt whenever the winds are blowing. And if the water is flying, particularly on a sailboat, you'll be comfortable in foul weather gear. Those who don't put that foul weather gear on often end up with wet clothes, a "zero at the bone" experience when a 20-

knot wind is blowing on San Francisco Bay.

If you're planning to do some coastal cruising or extensive Bay cruising in the winter months, you should buy clothes designed especially for this weather. The layer next to your skin should be

Bay sailors in layers

made of polypropelene or some similar man-made material. Do not use cotton because it will get damp and only add to the chill. Most cruisers buy Patagonia or REI long underwear for this purpose. REI offers three weights of long underwear. The heaviest is even available with a zipper turtleneck that many find much warmer than underwear with a tee shirt neck.

The second layer for cold weather should be made of some sort of polar fleece. You can wear a bunting jacket with or without a windbreaker outer layer. If you wear foul weather gear over the bunting jacket, you probably won't need the windbreaker, and you'll feel less bound up when you try to move quickly. Many cruisers on the Bay prefer wool sweaters or sweatshirts under their foul weather gear. The "best" choice depends on you, but be prepared for the chilly weather on the Bay.

The top layer should be a good quality foul weather suit. You can buy quality equipment at any of the larger chandleries or from mail order catalogs. Traditionally, outerwear made by Henri-Lloyd, Musto, Helly Hansen, and Douglas Gill have been the number one choice, but the West Marine Explorer has been receiving great reviews in recent years. Expect to pay $300 and more for a good set of foul weather gear. You can buy cheaper foul weather gear, but it may not keep the water out. Some say the one-piece suits keep them drier, but those we tried were uncomfortable. We can also tell you from personal experience that the

Foul weather gear

two-piece suits with the bib overall tops are more comfortable in serious weather than the one-piece models, even though they are inconvenient when you are trying to use the head in a rush. Try a variety of foul weather suits on before you buy.

You can also buy foul weather gear that has a built-in safety harness and built-in flotation. We find these not only expensive but bulky. When we want a safety harness or a PFD, we simply put those items over whatever outerwear we have on. Still, if you don't have a PFD and a safety harness, you might be able to save money by buying a jacket equipped with harness and flotation.

We know people who go boating on San Francisco Bay in bare feet in the summer, but we aren't among them. Many boaters have found that bare feet and boating result in broken toes. We recommend wearing heavy duty deck shoes or boots.

Good deck shoes with non-skid soles will keep you from sliding around, especially when the decks are wet (which will be most of the time on the Bay). On a sailboat, you'll have a particularly hard time remaining on your feet if you don't have good deck shoes. Leather deck shoes look good and hold up longer than any of the others we have tried. We have leather shoes made by Timberland and Sperry that we have worn for over ten years while boating, and, although they show the wear, they are still comfortable and effective. By contrast, the cheaper canvas shoes bought on sale for $30 have lasted for a season or two at the most.

Some boaters like the deck sandals that have non-skid soles. Most Bay area boaters find that bare feet, or almost so, are cold feet, however, so sandals have only a minimum number of adherents among boaters around San Francisco.

In wet weather, sea boots can make an otherwise uncomfortable day a pleasant day. Sea boots are also a great idea when you are sailing on a boat that takes a significant amount of water over the bow. Sea boots also make cold weather sailing more enjoyable because you can put on layers of socks. Many boaters buy their boots a little extra large so they can wear two pair of socks, a thin pair made of a man-made fabric next to their skin and a heavier pair of either man-made or wool fabric over those.

DODGER

A dodger for your boat does exactly the same thing as foul weather gear does for your body: it shields the cockpit from the flying water and cold winds. Dodgers come in all shapes and sizes. Some small ones do little more than provide protection for the crew coming on deck through the companionway hatch. The advantages of these smaller dodgers are that they don't destroy the aesthetic lines of the boat and they tend to be relatively inexpensive.

Other dodgers, like the one on our center cockpit boat, completely

48   ABOUT THE BAY AND BOATING

enclose the cockpit area, enabling us to sail in rainy weather without getting wet. These larger dodgers make the cockpit into an all-weather room. The primary disadvantages of these larger dodgers, as you might guess, is that they do not do much for the looks of the boat and they are much more expensive than the smaller ones.

Hard dodger

A new concept in dodgers is catching on quickly: the hard dodger that looks like a soft dodger. The most significant advantages of the hard dodger are that you can stand on top the dodger to reef or furl the sail, they don't deteriorate in the sun as the fabric ones do, and they offer a more secure place to hold onto in rough weather on the Bay.

ELECTRONICS

You can put an endless amount of money into electronics, but for cruising the Bay you need but a few of the electronic marvels on the market.

•**A depth sounder** will give you confidence as you are entering anchorages. With a depth sounder, you can easily determine how much scope you need on your anchor rode. But the depth sounder also helps to avoid shallow areas when you sail up the Napa River or the Petaluma River or into the South Bay. Even as you enter a marina with shallow spots, such as Martinez Marina or Glen Cove Marina, a depth sounder can help you avoid going aground if you enter at a dead slow speed.

Many cruising boats on the Bay have installed the new generation of forward-viewing depth sounders because they like the idea of being able to see the depths ahead of their boats. Some of these new depth sounders can scan the bottom 120 feet ahead of the boat. Such a feature would be extremely useful for a boater transiting a narrow channel such as San Rafael Creek or Westpoint Slough in Redwood City. Some of us are almost hoping our old depth sounders will die so we can install one of these newer units.

•**A VHF radio** is the second critical piece of electronic equipment every cruising boat in the Bay area should have. Because it allows you to talk with harbormasters at marinas, you will appreciate the VHF on almost every cruise. The VHF also allows you to keep in contact with those other boaters you might want to meet up with at an anchorage or a marina later in the day. When we're out on the Bay, we often get calls from friends who know we'll be out on the water on a particular day but don't know our location at a given time.

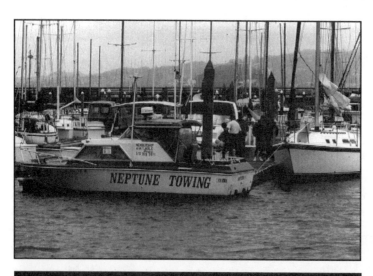

Boater receiving help from vessel assist boat

As well as a convenience item, the VHF radio is also a safety item. In case of an emergency, your VHF radio is your best resource. The Coast Guard monitors Channel 16 and responds immediately to life-threatening situations. If you call asking for help when the situation does not involve a life-threatening emergency, the Coast Guard will refer you to a private vessel assist company, but again your VHF radio will enable you to communicate with those who can help you.

Some boaters bring their cellular telephones aboard instead of installing VHF radios. Boaters make this choice because they can use the same phone in their cars, they can make personal calls without everyone on the Bay listening in, and they won't have to pay the outrageous license fee to the FCC.

We agree that the present fee charged by the FCC is high, but we think putting a cell phone aboard in place of a VHF radio creates more problems than it solves. For example, you can't use a cell phone to talk with other boaters unless they have cell phones. In case another boater near you needs your help, that boater would have no way of communicating with you. The same thing is true, of course, if you experience an emergency and need help from another boater. And with no shore power for recharging batteries while you are sitting in that beautiful anchorage for the week-long vacation, low battery power can also cause a problem. VHF radios are typically wired directly to the boat's batteries, which are rarely so weak as to make communication impossible.

Beyond the depth sounder and the VHF radio, most other electronic aids are non-essential items. You, like many other Bay boaters, may find the following optional electronic aids useful.

•**Radar** can help you find your way into an anchorage or a marina in foggy conditions or after dark. While we know many boaters who have radar units, we know few who use radar regularly inside the Bay. If you plan to cruise southward or northward along the coast, radar becomes much more desirable; for cruising limited to inside the Bay, you can probably spend elsewhere the $3,000 or more a radar installation costs.

•**Knotmeter and log** combinations are on most boats, but they aren't essential for cruising the Bay. Many boaters have enjoyed cruising for years without knowing how fast or how far they have gone. Even though non-essential, the knotlog will help you as you make your way to a new destination. For example, when we make trips up the river to Petaluma or Napa, we regularly watch our log and check the distance we've traveled against the chart so we can more readily identify the next landmark or buoy. If you carefully measure the distance beforehand on your chart, the log also helps you determine the location of a harbor at night or a not readily identifiable anchorage.

•**Autopilots** are, of course, not essential for cruising anywhere but especially not for inside the Bay. Considering that you'll rarely be making a passage to a destination more than a few hours away, the expense of an autopilot is difficult to justify. Again, though, if you plan to visit anchorages and marinas outside the Bay, you might consider installing an autopilot. When making the trip back up the coastline from Monterey, Moss Landing, or Santa Cruz, you'll appreciate an autopilot, particularly if you're shorthanded. If you cruise as a couple, as we do, an autopilot allows one of you to relax or sleep more easily.

•**GPS** units have fallen in price so quickly that many cruisers on the Bay have bought them, telling themselves they are necessary. Nevertheless, you'll not find much use for them inside the Bay. Conceivably, you could use a GPS when making a passage under reduced visibility conditions, especially if you're unfamiliar with the approach to your destination. When your destination is outside the Bay, the usefulness of a GPS unit is another matter. We regularly use our GPS when we make a trip to the Farallon Islands. Because of the marine layer that is common offshore, we can rarely see the Farallons until we're within 4 or 5 miles. By looking at the GPS from time to time, we can tell when we are being pushed off course by current or wind and arrive confidently at the island every time.

SAFETY EQUIPMENT

When the winds blow strongly and the waves are bouncing the boat around, boaters are only one moment of carelessness or one equipment failure removed from the water at any instant. You want to be especially careful not to fall overboard when boating in and around San Francisco Bay because of the cold water. The temperature of the water in the Bay, usually about 55°, makes it unlikely that you will survive for long swimming fully clothed.

Whatever other provisions you make for boating on the Bay, set up your boat to minimize the risk of anyone's accidentally falling overboard. Check lifelines and grab rails regularly, replacing everything that looks even slightly suspect. You'll fall against the lifelines and hang on to the grab rails many times when making sail changes, and you must be confident they will hold. Don't overlook your stanchions. Stanchions held to the deck with screws won't keep you on the boat. To be reliable, stanchions must be through bolted with backing plates on the underside of the deck. In addition, seriously consider the following safety items, some of which are required by Coast Guard regulations:

•**PFD's** (personal flotation devices) are required by the Coast Guard, and common sense also demands them. Regulations require that you have a Type I, II, III, or V personal flotation device for every person aboard if your boat is between 16 and 65 feet. These categories of PFD's, established by the Coast Guard, cover characteristics such as the amount of buoyancy and the construction. The Type I PFD gives the wearer the most support in the water; the others give adequate support. In addition to these wearable PFD's, you must have a device such as a horseshoe ring or a cushion to throw to a person in the water,

The PFD's on the market present the cruiser with almost too many options. The old kapok vest offers tradition and low price, but little more. Bulky and uncomfortable, it gives only the minimum flotation, but it is legal. It has been supplanted in popularity by a jacket that looks similar but has polyethylene foam flotation. This latter jacket is definitely superior in construction, durability, and buoyancy, but it too is uncomfortable. Nevertheless, you'll certainly be glad to be wearing one if you fall overboard.

PFD's with a variety of features, including more buoyancy, have appeared over the last few years. The most promising of the new ones may be those that have inflatable bladders. One even has a built-in safety harness. Inflatable

Inflatable PFD with built-in harness

PFD's have recently received Coast Guard approval, so you will soon be able to legally count them as part of your required equipment if you get boarded. We suspect they'll appear on boats quickly because they are far more comfortable and give twice as much flotation as most other vests. The only drawback is that these vests must be periodically checked and serviced and the expensive cartridges must be replaced each time the vest is inflated.

•**Safety harnesses** should be aboard every cruising boat. Although you'll not need to wear a harness every time you take your boat away from the dock, you should wear one whenever you're in heavy weather or working on deck at night. Too many cruisers go overboard from simple gear failures or mistakes. Since boaters who venture to distant locations—even those within the Bay—can get caught by heavy weather or darkness, safety harnesses, tethers, and jacklines are important safety items. These items should be mandatory for boats venturing outside the Bay.

•**Tethers** are just as important as safety harnesses. In fact, tethers and harnesses should be kept together in a location readily accessible from the cockpit. The most effective tether has a snap shackle on the end that attaches to the two D rings of the harness and a carabiner to attach to the jackline or a padeye.

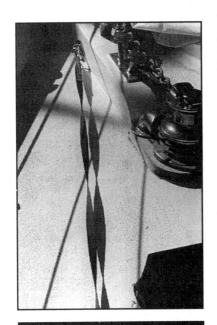

Jacklines of nylon webbing

•**Jacklines** should run from the bow to the stern along each side of the boat. Attach one end of the jacklines to a solid padeye at the bow and the other end to a padeye or cleat near the cockpit or on the stern of your boat. Ideally, you should be able to snap your tether onto the jackline as you get out of the cockpit and then be able to go from the cockpit to the bow without ever disconnecting your tether until you get back to the cockpit. Good jacklines are made of either nylon or dacron webbing or of the same covered wire that lifelines are made of. Jacklines made of webbing won't cause you to slip and fall if you step on them while working on deck as will the ones made of covered wire. The covered wire has a distinct advantage, however; it doesn't stretch as the webbing does.

Set up your jacklines before you depart if you have any notion you'll need them. For instance, in making a non-stop passage from Monterey to Marina Bay in Richmond, you will almost certainly arrive after dark; set up the jacklines before you depart from Monterey rather than waiting until you need them—after dark with the wind blowing 30 knots.

•**Overboard rescue systems** have become increasingly popular on boats in the San Francisco area. The Lifesling is the most common rescue system, perhaps because West Marine markets it so effectively. The Lifesling allows you to drag a line with an attached life-saving device to the person in the water and then to keep that person tethered to the boat until you can haul him or her aboard. All boaters who put these units on their boats would be well advised to practice using them before actual emergencies arise.

Overboard rescue system

•**EPIRB** (Emergency Position Indicating Radio Beacon) could be a good addition if you plan to do a considerable amount of cruising outside the Bay. For destinations inside the Bay, we doubt that you can justify the expense.

•**Life rafts** cause countless debates. Some boaters will not cruise the Bay without rafts aboard while other boaters sail around the world without them. We made numerous trips to Hawaii, Mexico, and the Channel Islands without a life raft, but we brought one aboard when we began ocean cruising full-time a few years ago. Frankly, we can see no reason to purchase one if you plan to cruise only the Bay. If you expect to cruise offshore, however, we can see the justification.

•**Flares** are required on all boats. These may seem superfluous on boats that cruise only inside the Bay, but Coast Guard boarding parties will check for flares as routinely as they check for PFD's. You are required to have three red meteor flares and three red handheld flares. If you choose destinations outside the Bay, carry more flares than this minimum specified by the Coast Guard: double the minimum number of meteor and handheld flares, and add three parachute flares and at least one smoke cannister to your flares kit.

•**Radar reflectors** enhance your chances of being seen by ships and boats in the Bay, especially important if you are still underway after dark or if you get caught in the fog. However, don't count on radar reflectors because many radar operators on large ships can't see small boats even if they have reflectors.

• **Fire extinguishers** are required by the Coast Guard on all boats with enclosed spaces. Boats up to 26 feet with enclosed spaces must have at least one B-1 extinguisher. Boats between 26 and 40 feet must have two B-I extinguishers or one B-II. Boats between 40 and 65 feet must three B-I or one B-I and one B-II extinguisher. Several fire extinguishers strategically spaced throughout the boat are especially important for cruising sailors who will be cooking and using electrical devices out in remote anchorages. Make sure you can get to the extinguishers from every part of the boat. Don't just have one by the galley or in the engine room.

TENDERS

If you cruise only to marinas and tie up to a dock every time out, you obviously won't need a tender. But few cruisers can resist the temptation to anchor out at Clipper Cove, Paradise Cove, China Camp, or any number of other anchorages around the Bay. When they do, they need tenders to explore the area, to get ashore, or to go over to see friends on another boat. If you decide to get a tender, you will have three basic types from which to choose.

• **The hard dinghy** is the tender used by boaters for centuries. The hard dinghy has one outstanding characteristic: it rows well. Many

Rowing a hard dinghy

boaters have gone to the hard dinghy after trying to row an inflatable in windy conditions. People who like tradition also choose hard dinghies because they can quietly explore an anchorage or a coastline without disturbing wildlife or other boaters. Hard dinghies have a couple of disadvantages that keep them from being widely used: they are difficult to get aboard and stow, and they are tippy when being loaded or unloaded.

•**Inflatable dinghies** are chosen for convenience and safety reasons. These dinghies, such as the Avon Redcrest or Redseal, generally come with soft floors. Wood floors are available for soft dinghies, but they are rare because they make the dinghy expensive and heavy. The primary advantage of the soft dinghy is its weight; without wood floors it typically weighs well under 100 pounds. Although most inflatable manufacturing companies made these inflatable dinghies at one time, many have discontinued them recently.

Exploring Gallinas Creek, San Rafael, by sport boat

The disadvantages of these inflatable dinghies are several. They are difficult to row in winds over 15 knots and almost uncontrollable when the winds reach 20 knots. Although many boaters buy small outboards for their soft dinghies to make them more usable when winds blow, the cruisers we've spoken with who use them almost universally complain that the inflatable dinghies are still too slow. Even when powered by an outboard, they will not make more than 6 or 8 knots.

In addition, these inflatable dinghies have serious loading

limitations because of the soft floors. Anything heavy aboard one of these tenders, such as scuba tanks, threatens to fall through the bottom. Furthermore, the soft bottom precludes your standing in it as you load or unload the dinghy, a serious disadvantage.

•**Sport boats** with their removable floorboards have taken over the market. Although their most noteworthy feature may be their load-carrying capacity, sport boats also get high marks for their speed. With a 10-hp outboard on the transom, a 10-foot sport boat can easily plane and travel at almost 20 knots with two or three people aboard.

The speed of a sport boat makes long distance travel quite comfortable. We regularly range up to 5 miles from our anchored sailboat in our sport boat. For instance, when we were up the Napa River recently, we used our sport boat to explore the sloughs south of town and the river through the city of Napa. The shallow depths and bridges would have prevented us from exploring these areas in our sailboat.

If you put a tender of any kind aboard your cruising boat, you should always take the motor off the sport boat when you move from one anchorage or marina to the next. In many instances cruisers have lost their outboards when the sport boats flipped over in the heavy waves on the Bay. Although many of us tow out sport boats after we take the motors off, we all know we should not do that either. We know many cruisers who have lost their tenders both on the Bay and in the ocean when the winds have picked up unexpectedly.

6 NAVIGATION AND SEAMANSHIP

NAVIGATION is the art and science of safely and efficiently directing the movements of a vessel from one point to another.
– Chapman Piloting

CHARTING A COURSE

Charting a course in the Bay is relatively straightforward. Often boaters can see a landmark near their destination when they set out. Bay boaters use landmarks such as the bridges, the islands, a particularly noteworthy building in San Francisco, or the Sutro Tower to help them get to their destinations when they are going only a short distance.

DAVID DAWSON

Transamerica building, a noteworthy landmark

Sutro Tower, another clear landmark

The farther you plan to travel, however, the more carefully you must navigate. Before you depart on a trip, lay out a course and consider how far the destination is and what hazards you will encounter. To lay out your course, you need only a pencil, parallel rules, and dividers. Then, at this stage of the planning, predict how long the trip will take. If you plan a trip to Suisun City, for example, you may decide to spend the first night en route at Benicia. Begin by plotting a course on your chart and measuring distances from one point to the next. Each leg of your proposed course should have the distance and the course written next to it.

During the trip, maintain an up-to-date DR position. That is, write on the chart the exact time you pass major landmarks. You might write on the chart that you passed under the Richmond-San Rafael Bridge at 1015, that you passed Point Pinole at 1225, and that you passed under the Carquinez Bridge at 1630. Keeping a DR will make you more comfortable if the darkness reduces your visibility just after you pass Glen Cove Marina. Your inability to see familiar landmarks on the shore or the rocks just south of Benicia Marina could be a serious problem if you had not just marked your position on the chart as you cleared the Carquinez Bridge. With a good DR position marked, you need do no more than measure the distance to go and follow your predetermined compass course to arrive safely at Benicia for a good night's rest.

Do not rely completely on a GPS, SatNav, or Loran. As helpful as these devices are, they can fail. Besides, they won't warn you of obstructions such as the rocks off Benicia. Only by drawing a course on your chart will you discover the hazards along the route to your destination.

As you travel toward your destination, you will simply follow the courses you wrote on your chart as you did your trip planning. Clearly, you must have an accurate compass in order to follow those predetermined courses. If you don't know whether or not your compass is accurate, have a professional compass adjuster come to your boat to check it.

The price of electronic navigation devices has come down quickly in the last few years. Everyone can now afford them. Furthermore, they are now so easy to use that virtually anyone can operate one within a few hours of purchasing it. As a result, boaters everywhere are becoming careless navigators. Many navigators now put in the coordinates of their destination before they depart from their marina and follow the directions on their screens slavishly. If the coordinates they insert at the outset are slightly off or if their electronic instrument fails for some reason, they could be in serious trouble.

Experienced boaters employ their GPS whenever they go to a destination outside the Bay, but they also maintain an accurate DR at all times. They recognize that if their electronic wonders fail and they don't have their positions marked on a chart as they travel, they will be lost when the fog moves in.

HANDLING A BOAT UNDERWAY

Good seamanship begins with handling the boat correctly while underway. If you are going across the Bay from a harbor to Angel Island, for instance, you must steer the boat smoothly. A boat wandering from side to side confuses other boaters and could cause an accident. Steer the boat with a steady hand, carefully following a compass course or aiming the boat toward a fixed point such as a buoy or a building on shore.

People who take the helm on our boat and have trouble maintaining a steady course are generally those who don't focus on the chore at hand. Many people are unable to keep the boat on course while they're talking. On most race boats and many cruising boats, no one is allowed to speak to the person at the helm except about a boat-related matter. You might consider this rule if you can't both talk and steer the boat.

At the helm on San Francisco Bay

To keep the boat under control, the person at the helm must also understand the effects of the wind and current. Boats have collided with a buoy or a bridge tower because the boaters were not paying attention to current and wind. One sailboater we know was sailing near the south tower of the Golden Gate Bridge, enjoying being heeled over, when the current swept his boat up against the bridge, breaking his boat's mast. When out on the Bay, watch the current flowing by buoys, channel markers, and bridges to determine the speed and the direction of the current.

If you don't yet know how to read current when you look at a buoy or marker, practice by going out on the Bay at different tide/current states. First, look at your tide book under "Current." Pick out the day's date on the left margin and follow across horizontally. The first column will be headed "Slack" and will give you the time of the first slack water of the day. The second column will give you the time and speed of the maximum current during the first tide of the day; the speed will be followed by the letter E or F, indicating ebb or flood tide. Following the time of the flood will be the time of the second slack water. The remainder of the columns present the times of the alternating slack, flood, and ebb currents for that particular day. Then go out on the Bay when the tide book predicts slack water and look at a buoy, preferably one out in the middle of the Bay that is clearly affected by current. Observe that the water around it is quiet. Come back three hours later when a strong ebb or flood tide is flowing and observe the buoy or marker once again. When a particularly fast ebb or flood is flowing, the buoy will be leaning over noticeably, indicating the direction of the flow. The water around the buoy or marker will be bubbling and forming little eddies and whirlpools. Observe the buoy repeatedly to understand what effects current can have.

When boating near a bridge tower, use caution. If your boat is moving slowly as you pass the tower, you can be sucked into the tower by the current. The same is true of buoys and channel markers. Many boaters who thought they had cleared a buoy have been swept into it by a strong current. Those boaters have too often discovered that buoys make holes in boats.

HANDLING A BOAT IN A HARBOR

Although handling a boat while underway can be mastered quite quickly, handling a boat in the close confines of a harbor or marina in San Francisco Bay is more challenging. As your forward motion slows, the effects of both wind and current become more noticeable. Observe both as you enter an anchorage or marina. For example, when you plan to pick up a mooring or a slip at Ayala Cove on Angel Island, prepare for wind gusts of 15 knots and currents of 1.5 or even 2.0 knots. By observing other boats already moored in the Cove, you can determine if a cross current is flowing. If the boats are directly in line between

Read buoys to gauge the current.

Beware of current close to towers of Bay Bridge.

the two buoys they are tied to, you shouldn't have to worry about being swept to one side or the other as you attempt to pick up your mooring. If the boats nearby are to one side or the other of a line between the two buoys and the mooring lines are tight, a heavy cross current is flowing. In this case, picking up moorings is going to be challenging. When such conditions prevail, many boaters pick up the bow buoy first and then put a dinghy or sport boat in the water to pick up the stern buoy.

Wind is the most common negative influence you will encounter when anchoring or entering a slip in the Bay Area. Experienced boaters would always design marinas so boats could enter and leave slips going directly upwind or downwind. Unfortunately, in many marinas the prevailing winds blow at right angles to the slips. In these marinas, including the one where we keep our boat, boaters are challenged to keep their boats under control as they enter slips. The strong winds that blow through some marinas in the afternoons during the summer require

Handling a boat in Berkeley can be challenging.

extra caution. Marina Bay, Berkeley, and Emeryville marinas experience especially strong winds.

To enter a slip in windy marinas, anticipate the effect the wind will have on your craft. As the speed of your craft slows, the wind will blow the bow of your boat off downwind first. The more freeboard on your boat, the more rapidly the wind will blow the bow off course. Large powerboats and sailboats alike are difficult to handle if a crosswind of 15 knots or more is blowing. When entering a slip, favor the upwind side of the slip, and enter the slip faster than you would like, depending on a strong engine and reverse gear to slow the boat before it hits the front end of the slip.

As you practice maneuvering in a marina, you will find that the prop, in most cases, pulls your boat either to starboard or port when you use reverse gear. A left-hand prop will move your boat to starboard when you are backing up, no matter what you do with the rudder. A boat with a right-hand prop will try to move to port in reverse. Once you get your boat moving fast enough in reverse, the rudder will exert some control over the direction you go, but most boats will have to be moving in excess of 2 knots for the rudder to counteract the pull of the prop. In the close confines of a marina, that speed is often not practicable. The alternative is to compensate for the pull of the prop, one area of seamanship that only practice will make perfect.

When he was 84 years old, Ralph Flowers, one of Sausalito's favorite characters, showed us how to handle a boat in a marina. A group of us were aboard a small ketch that was widely known as being impossible to keep under control when backing up. Ralph took the helm and flawlessly backed it out of the slip and down the long, tight channel behind Sausalito Yacht Sales, astounding us all. When asked how he got the boat to do what he wanted it to, he answered that it was simply a matter of getting the boat moving at a good speed and of practicing, in his case for 60 years.

Since you have more room to maneuver, anchoring is easier than entering a slip in a marina when the wind is blowing strongly. Before you stop the boat, make certain you have the bow headed directly into the wind. Even so, get the anchor down quickly because the bow will be trying to pass the stern as soon as the boat stops. As the bow slips off to one side or the other, let out anchor rode until you have an adequate scope and then run the engine in reverse at approximately one-half throttle for one minute to set the anchor. Adequate scope is 7-1 if you use a nylon anchor rode and 4-1 if you use an all-chain rode. (The extra weight of the all-chain rode will prevent the boat from pulling out the anchor.)

Because most anchorages in the San Francisco Bay Area are in shallow water, you will almost never let out more than 200 feet of rode, even if you are using nylon. At China Camp, for example, most boats anchor in 10 feet of water, so letting out 70 feet of nylon line will assure good holding. Since we have an all-chain rode, we let out only 50 or 60 feet of chain at China Camp.

Whenever you anchor near other anchored boats, carefully observe how those other boats are anchored. If they are on single hooks and you anchor bow-and-stern, you run the risk of causing a collision. The other boats will swing freely in the wind and current. Your boat anchored bow and stern of course will not.

Observe how other boats are anchored.

Although boats rarely anchor bow-and-stern in Northern California waters due to the heavy current, you must be prepared to do so if you anchor near others who have bow and stern anchors down.

HANDLING A BOAT IN HEAVY WEATHER

Handling a boat in calm water may not be a great challenge, but handling it in high winds and heavy seas will challenge you. Good seamanship in heavy weather calls for keeping the boat under control at all times. Whether in heavy weather on the Bay or in the Pacific Ocean, you must throttle back if you're operating a powerboat or shorten sail if you're operating a sailboat. Pounding into the waves will make everyone aboard uncomfortable and put unnecessary stress and strain on your vessel. We occasionally see a powerboat traveling at 15 knots across the Bay with water flying everywhere, pounding so badly that we can hear the banging at a distance of a mile or more. When we get closer, we can see passengers inside holding on to whatever they can. Only the person at the throttle has fun in such a case. The same excess can be found aboard sailboats when the captain refuses to shorten sail and everyone ends up cold, wet, and terrified. A sailboat that is pushed so hard that the rail is under water not only would afford the crew more comfort with a reefed main but would also go faster. In the worst case, carrying too much sail can result in a torn sail or a broken mast.

When you're cruising in the ocean, don't challenge the sea. Banging into waves in the Bay makes little sense, but driving into huge waves in the ocean is crazy. If you attempt to drive directly into the steep waves enroute to the Farallon Islands, for instance, green water coming over the bow will sweep the entire length of your boat. To avoid both the discomfort and the danger inherent in this situation, fall off and quarter the seas.

Handling a boat in heavy weather also requires special attention to avoid collisions. We all quite naturally want to get under cover when rain or salt spray begin to fly. Then the risk of collision increases. When we go inside on a powerboat or get behind the dodger on a sailboat, our visibility becomes seriously impaired. Sailboats present a special risk under such conditions because the headsail completely blocks a large area of forward vision. You must deliberately check for traffic in that blind area on a regular basis. On some boats you can see under the genoa by getting down on the low side of the boat, but on other

BRIAN BATES

Even a small staysail can block the view.

boats you must go out on deck to be sure you're safe from collision.

On those days when you get caught out by fog, be especially careful. A radar reflector hoisted in the rigging may help other boats and ships see you, but posting a lookout in heavy fog will also be necessary. A lookout on the bow can hear approaching traffic long before anyone in the cockpit can.

GOING AGROUND AND GETTING OFF

San Francisco Bay has many areas of shallow water, and most boaters who have enjoyed cruising the area for a number of years have gone aground at one time or another. We have been aground, in either our sport boat, our sailing dinghy, our sloop, or our ketch, in several cruising areas in the Bay. If you go exploring to get to know your cruising area, you, too, may find yourself aground, whether in a Swan 65 or an Avon sportboat.

Experienced cruising sailors consider going aground in San Francisco Bay, in most circumstances, merely an inconvenience. Most simply assume it comes with the territory in a bay with an average depth of only 18 feet. Surely no one deliberately goes about looking for a good place to go aground, but it happens when boaters are adventurous.

When exploring areas such as the South Bay near Alviso or Redwood City, where you know you might go aground, use extra caution. Keep that chart nearby in the cockpit, and watch the depth sounder continuously as you move slowly into the suspect area. But even before you enter the area, know the tide state. If the tide is ebbing, don't go into an area where you know you might go aground. Boaters who go aground on an ebb risk having to sit and watch as their boats are left high and dry, often for many hours. We re-

Seriously aground in Westpoint Slough

cently went exploring Westpoint Slough in the Redwood City area. We were warned ahead of time that going aground was a definite possibility, so we timed our entrance into the Slough to coincide with the beginning of the flood tide. Sure enough, we did go aground, and we couldn't get our 35,000-pound boat off the mud bar by using an anchor as a kedge. We didn't worry, however, because we knew the incoming tide would float us off—as it did in a little over two hours. The ideal situation for those boaters who go aground is to have the tide on a flood.

Good seamanship requires not only that you plan ahead so that you risk going aground only on a flood tide but also that you have a strategy worked out ahead of time to get your boat off immediately if you go aground when the tide is ebbing. If a boat goes aground when it is barely moving, you can sometimes use reverse gear to get off. Be aware, however, of the danger to your engine if you do. When your boat is aground in mud and you use reverse gear, the prop will almost certainly kick up mud that may be sucked into your engine, destroying the impeller in your sea water pump. As soon as you lose your pump, of course, you can forget using your engine, even when you do float off, until you replace the impeller.

One alternative is to get a kedge anchor out immediately. If your boat is not too deeply embedded in the mud, you can often kedge off. We have done so many times. Keep a long anchor line, at least 200 feet, and an anchor at the ready whenever you know you might go aground.

Although some people try to kedge the boat out stern first, this endangers rudders and props, so we don't do it. The grounded boat should come out bow first the way it went in. Typically, the water ahead of the boat is shallower than the water behind it. For this reason, we generally deploy the kedge from the bow and lead it aft off the quarter. We can pivot the boat, breaking the suction of the keel in the mud and then pull the boat almost 180° from the direction it was traveling when forward motion stopped.

Another practice we have successfully used is to move everyone aboard to the bow to lift the weight off the stern. If you have enough people aboard, the weight transfer can help lift the transom off the bottom and allow you to back off using the engine. Use this technique with caution if you are in the mud, of course, since you can easily suck the flying mud into your engine's impeller. Another option for sailboaters is to put up the mainsail and jib to create an angle of heel that may free the keel. Be cautious, however, that you don't drive your boat farther into the shallow area using this technique.

AVOIDING COLLISIONS

Perhaps no other aspect of seamanship deserves as much attention as avoiding collisions with other vessels. When two sailboats collide, of course, the risk to people on the boats is slight because the boats are generally traveling at less than 5 miles per hour. If two fast-moving powerboats collide, however, people can be seriously injured. And if either a sailboat or a powerboat collides with a ship, the results can be disastrous. The ship will usually not sustain any damage; in fact, the crew members of a huge ship that collides with a pleasure boat are often unaware that the ship has been involved in a collision.

Parts of the Bay have heavy ship traffic. The Central Bay between the Golden Gate and the Bay Bridge, for example, has a surprising number of ships transiting every day. The Bay waters near Oakland frequently have container ships moving around. And tankers arrive or depart often from the Richmond pier just south of the eastern end of the Richmond-San Rafael Bridge. VTS (Vessel Traffic System) has established shipping lanes inside and outside the Bay.

Container ships are a major challenge for navigators.

These lanes are marked clearly on your charts. Know where these lanes are. You can cross or travel up or down them, but recognize that ships have right of way in them.

Inside the Bay, you can be confident that a professional pilot is aboard any ship moving into or out of the Bay. These professionals have years of experience and know the shipping lanes inside the Bay and along the San Francisco coast. They know well where they cannot take the ship because of shallow water or Coast Guard regulations. In fact, their options are few. Remember that those large ships can't stop for you. A 700-foot ship cannot even begin to slow down or turn in less than a mile. If you get in front of a ship traveling at 15 knots, all the pilot can do is sound the ship's horn to warn you.

Few pleasure boats collide with ships inside the Bay because visibility is generally good and because a professional pilot keeps watch at all times. A different situation exists outside the Bay. All of us who have sailed the ocean for years know of countless instances when we have encountered ships that apparently have no one on watch. For the safety of your boat and those aboard, assume no one aboard the ship sees you. You must stay alert to avoid ships.

The weather variable should also concern you. When the marine layer settles down, keep an especially vigilant watch. Don't assume that someone on the ship will be watching you on radar. We learned a frightening and valuable lesson once in a heavy fog along the coast. We could hear two ships' fog horns nearby and could hear the prop of one of them thumping as it cut into the water. Soon we heard crewmembers of the two ships talking by VHF radio, discussing their positions. They said they could easily see one another on radar. We made radio contact, asking if either of them could see our sailboat on radar. Neither could, in spite of the fact that we had a radar reflector in the rigging. We were probably within a mile or two of one of the ships, a Standard Oil tanker, but we were invisible. In such a case, only keeping a good watch will keep you safe.

Not only does fog make it difficult for radar aboard ships to detect you, but bridges also prevent radar from identifying your boat. Captain J. L. Shanower, a San Francisco Bar Pilot, told us that he worries particularly about pleasure boats near the Golden Gate Bridge when he takes a ship in or out of the Bay in reduced visibility. He has had many near misses in the area because boaters assume their boats will show up on radar. Not so. The bridge makes a large image on the screen that blocks out all boats under it.

MAKING THE BOAT AND CREW SAFE

Coast Guard requirements and common sense require you to have PFD's, flares, a horn, and fire extinguishers aboard any boat you would take out for a Bay cruise. Having this safety equipment aboard

Assume no one on ships can see you.

is not of much use unless it is readily at hand. PFD's, for example, are typically stowed in the bottom of some locker to keep them out of the way, rendering them useless in an emergency.

Falling overboard is perhaps the most serious threat to boaters on the Bay. Often the person who falls overboard has been boating for years. In fact, experienced boaters may be at greater risk than novices because experience on the water sometimes leads to overconfidence and carelessness.

Regardless of what you might have deduced from movies and news items, people who fall overboard are not in danger of being eaten by sharks. Rather, people who fall overboard drown. Because they are usually fully clothed, they do not last long in the water. Just for the sake of knowledge, jump into a swimming pool sometime dressed in the three or four layers of clothes typical for a Bay area boater. As soon as all that clothing becomes water logged, probably in less than a minute, swimming or even keeping yourself afloat becomes nearly impossible. If you were to fall overboard in San Francisco Bay or the Pacific Ocean, the waves would wash over your face as the soaked clothes pulled you ever lower into the water. Add to that the 55° water temperature, and you have a fatal scenario.

More and more boaters on the Bay are wearing PFD's at all times. That makes sense. But staying aboard in the first place also makes sense. If the weather is rough, don't hesitate to rig your jacklines and put on your safety harness.

Fire at sea is a frightening danger for boaters. A chance always exists of a galley fire, so an extinguisher should be kept near the galley. But the danger from a fuel fire is even greater if your boat is powered by a gasoline engine. Many boats have fuel leaks at one time or another. A diesel fuel leak may create offensive odors and a terrible mess in the bilge, but if the fuel aboard is gasoline, a leak creates the potential for an explosion. When fueling the gasoline-powered craft, you are also at risk because of the build-up of static electricity. Be sure to keep the metal nozzle of the filler hose grounded on the fill pipe on your boat.

And while you are thinking about fuel and your boat, remember that you must avoid spilling fuel into Bay waters. When fueling your boat, block your scuppers so that the little fuel that does spill on deck as you fill your tanks can't run overboard. The fine you will be charged for spillage is high.

Maxi-racer along the City Front.

Anchorages
and
Marinas

One of the greatest fascinations that cruising holds for me is the landfalls.
—William Washburn Nutting

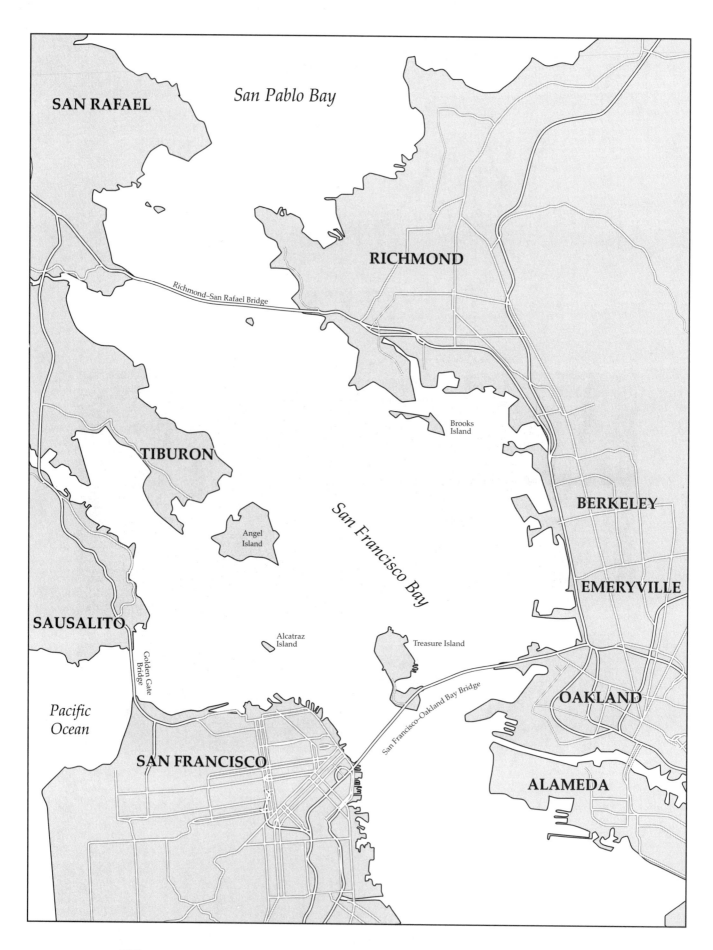

SAN RAFAEL

San Pablo Bay

RICHMOND

Richmond–San Rafael Bridge

TIBURON

Brooks
Island

BERKELEY

Angel
Island

San Francisco Bay

EMERYVILLE

SAUSALITO

Alcatraz
Island

Treasure Island

*Golden Gate
Bridge*

OAKLAND

*Pacific
Ocean*

San Francisco–Oakland Bay Bridge

SAN FRANCISCO

ALAMEDA

7 THE CENTRAL BAY

It's North you may run to the rime-ring'd sun,
Or South to the blind Horn's hate;
Or East all the way into Mississippi Bay,
Or West to the Golden Gate.
—Rudyard Kipling, " The Long Trail"

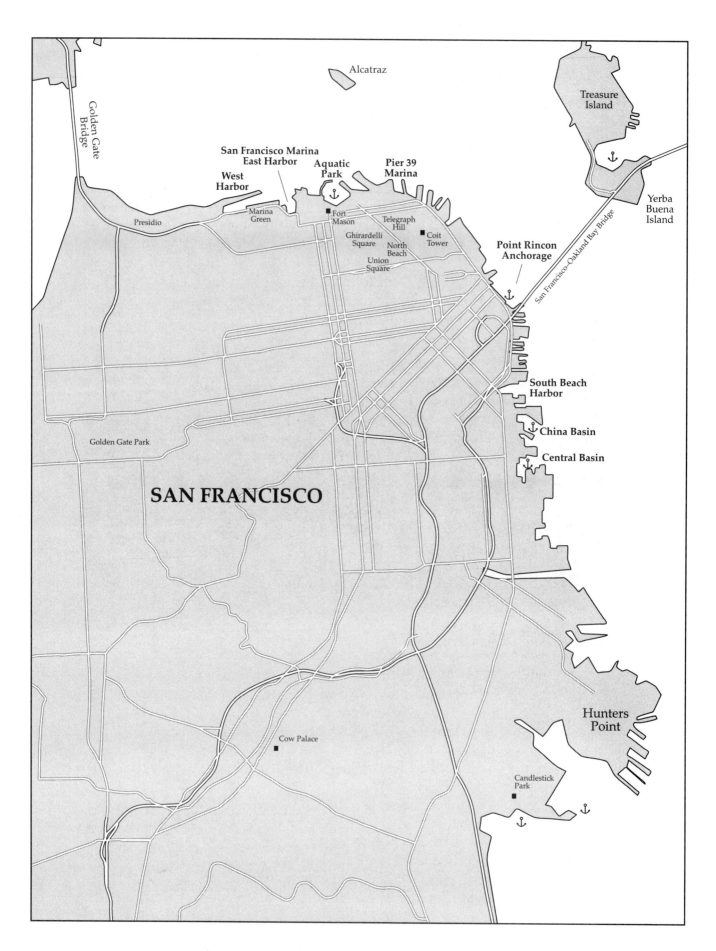

Golden Gate Bridge

Alcatraz

Treasure Island

San Francisco Marina East Harbor

Aquatic Park

Pier 39 Marina

West Harbor

Yerba Buena Island

Presidio

Marina Green

Fort Mason

Telegraph Hill

Ghirardelli Square

Coit Tower

Point Rincon Anchorage

North Beach

Union Square

San Francisco–Oakland Bay Bridge

South Beach Harbor

China Basin

Central Basin

Golden Gate Park

SAN FRANCISCO

Hunters Point

Cow Palace

Candlestick Park

SAN FRANCISCO CITY FRONT
Chart #18649, #18650, or #18652

The San Francisco City Front, the waterfront from the south tower of the Golden Gate Bridge to just south of the west span of the Oakland-San Francisco Bay Bridge, is an ideal place to begin a cruise of the San Francisco Bay.

Along this stretch, much of San Francisco's colorful history has been played out. At the west end of the City Front is the Presidio, one of the first two European settlements. (The other settlement was Misión San Francisco de Asís at Laguna de los Dolores, or, today, Mission Dolores.) In 1775 Spanish captain Juan Bautista de Anza planted a cross at what is today Fort Point to mark the site for a fortified camp. The more than 1,000-acre Presidio is now in transition from a luxuriantly forested U. S. Army base, dating from 1847, to a part of the Golden Gate National Recreation Area.

Mission Dolores

Presidio building on Montgomery Street

From the point where the Bay Bridge today connects to the land northwest to Broadway was the pueblo of Yerba Buena, the commercial center from 1835 on for the Mexican land grant rancheros spread throughout the Bay Area. In 1847, the name of the village became San Francisco. During the latter half of the 19th century Yerba Buena Cove was filled in, and most of the forty-two wharves forming the hub of the city's prosperous waterfront were built.

Along the City Front are two yacht clubs, three public marinas, and four anchorages. Practically speaking, though, only the marinas and anchorages are realistic options for overnight visitors. The yacht clubs, St. Francis and Golden Gate, have guest docks, but they are rarely available for cruising sailors. South Beach Harbor, Pier 39 Marina, and San Francisco Marina, on the other hand, typically have some guest space.

The anchorages and marinas between the Golden Gate Bridge and the Bay Bridge will give you unparalleled views of the three bridges (the third, the Richmond-San Rafael) linking the shores along the Central Bay. Alcatraz and Angel Island lie to the north of the City Front, and beyond the two islands are the hills of Sausalito, Tiburon, and Belvedere Island. To the east Yerba Buena Island, where the two spans of the Bay Bridge meet in a tunnel, and Treasure Island partially obscure the hills of Point Richmond and Berkeley and the Emeryville marina. And the jewel, the Golden City itself, rises in front of you.

Looking out into the Bay from Aquatic Park anchorage

South Beach Harbor and the two anchorages south of the Bay Bridge will not give you quite the same view, lying as they do on the east shore of the City Front rather than on the north shore. You will have an excellent view of the Bay Bridge and, across the Bay, Oakland and Alameda.

SAN FRANCISCO MARINA

This small craft harbor, the first public marina on the City Front inside the Golden Gate, is a legacy of the Panama Pacific International Exposition of 1915.

Approach

West Harbor, one of the two harbors of the San Francisco Marina, is 1.85 miles east of the Golden Gate Bridge. The entrance, marked by a light, is 500 yards east of the cupola on the seawall. Visible among the

San Francisco Marina, West Harbor

trees above West Harbor is the cream-colored octagonal rotunda of the Palace of Fine Arts, designed for the Panama Pacific Exposition of 1915.

The waters outside the harbor are popular for racing sailors and sailboarders, so be on the lookout for racing buoys, flotillas of sailboats, and dozens of colorful sailboards flitting about like butterflies.

Enter cautiously because of shoaling that may extend shoreward from the spit. Dredging usually keeps the shoaling under control, and the marina personnel reset the channel markers as necessary to help boaters avoid the shoal area. Inside West Harbor, Golden Gate Yacht Club is the first building to starboard. St. Francis Yacht Club is at the west end of the harbor on the same side of the channel. Directly across the channel from the Golden Gate Yacht Club is a dock where boaters may tie their boats while they visit the Harbormaster's office to sign in for slips in either West Harbor or East Harbor.

BRIAN BATES

San Francisco Marina, East Harbor

The entrance to East Harbor (also called Gashouse Cove), the second of the San Francisco Marina docks, is 600 yards east of the entrance to West Harbor. This harbor is protected from the wave and surge action by a breakwater running west to east and another running north to south on the east side of the marina. A light marks the end of the pier at the entrance. When abeam of the harbor entrance, you can readily spot the fuel dock at the back of the entrance channel.

San Francisco Marina Harbormaster   415-292-2013

Facilities

At or near San Francisco Marina
 Bus Stop
 Fuel Dock
 Hoist
 Grocery Store
 Laundromat
 Post Office
 Pump Out
 Restaurants
 Showers

AQUATIC PARK

Approach

Just opposite Alcatraz Island on the City Front is Aquatic Park (the San Francisco Maritime National Historic Park), 0.5 mile east of San Francisco East Marina. This anchorage stands out clearly because of the huge 19th century sailing ships at the Maritime Museum dock that forms the east side of Aquatic Park Lagoon. Behind the cove about 200 yards, the Ghirardelli Square sign is prominent. A curved breakwater extending from Black Point protects Aquatic Park. The entrance into the anchorage area is approximately 200 feet wide, but set a course for the center to avoid the fishing lines that always seem to be in the water here.

Ghirardelli sign identifies Aquatic Park, behind the pier.

Anchorage

Aquatic Park has been a favorite location for swimmers from the Dolphin Swimming Club and the Southend Rowing Club for over a century; hence, it is closed to power vessels. Park regulations specify that sailboats can enter the park only under sail to anchor. While rangers understand that some sailboats are more maneuverable under power, they are still worried about a possible injury to a swimmer. Check with the ranger at Aquatic Park for current regulations before entering. Historic Park police patrol the lagoon area.

Though moorings belonging to the Sea Scouts take up the south side of the anchorage, another 10 to 15 boats can anchor in this lagoon without crowding. Although boats rarely anchor bow-and-stern in San Francisco Bay because of the heavy current, be prepared to do so if you anchor near others who have bow and stern anchors down. Anchor in 7 to 14 feet in clay and sand in the center of the lagoon. The breakwater protects anchored boats from much of the motion of San Francisco Bay, but the surge may still keep your boat rolling.

The current in this anchorage is strong at times, causing many boats to drag anchor and thus endanger the historic ships displayed at the Maritime Museum. The Park Service wishes to accommodate boaters, but the Service's first obligation is to protect the irreplaceable old three-masters, paddle steamer, and scow schooner, the *Balclutha*, the *C. A. Thayer*, the *Eureka*, and the *Alma*. The park rangers urge visiting boaters to anchor as far away from these ships as possible, at least 500 feet, to minimize the danger to these treasures of our maritime history.

Sign warning boaters at Aquatic Park

To remain anchored in Aquatic Park for more than 24 hours, boaters must obtain permission from the Aquatic Park Ranger Station.

Landing a dinghy or sportboat on the inviting sand beach on the south shore of the anchorage is simple enough. However, do not leave your tender unguarded while you're ashore.

San Francisco Maritime Historic Park Ranger   415-556-1238

Facilities

Aquatic Park has no facilities specifically for the use of boaters.

Near Aquatic Park
> Bus and Cable Car Stops
> Grocery Store
> Restaurants
> Shops

PIER 39

Approach

Just east of Aquatic Park is the Fisherman's Wharf area, which offers no facilities for boaters, but is the site of a constant flow of ferry traffic. A short distance beyond, 0.75 mile from Aquatic Park, signs designate Pier 39, but it is also easily located by the sailboat masts on either side of the buildings on the pier. In the background, 0.5 mile southeast of the marina, the 210-foot Coit Tower, a slender column built in 1937 as a monument to San Francisco firefighters, stands above the trees on Telegraph Hill. From Pier 39 to the Bay Bridge is another 1.55 miles.

Enter the marina on the east side of the buildings at Pier 39. A breakwater extends from the end of the buildings to the east and then to the south. Lights mark the position of the breakwater. The entrance is back near the shore and leads to the docks immediately below the harbormaster's office.

Pier 39 also has a harbor on the west side of the buildings, but many of the docks in this harbor have been given over to the colony of sea lions that have taken up permanent residence here. Do not enter this harbor unless directed to do so by the harbormaster.

Entrance to Pier 39, East Harbor

DAVID DAWSON

Berthing

Pier 39 Marina gladly caters to guest boaters, but call ahead because demand often outstrips the number of available slips, especially on weekends.

Pier 39 Harbormaster   415-705-5556 or VHF 16.

Sea lions on the docks at Pier 39, West Harbor

Facilities

At or near Pier 39 Marina
   Bus and Cable Car Stops
   Grocery Store
   Laundromat
   Restaurants
   Shops
   Showers

PT. RINCON ANCHORAGE (BAY BRIDGE ANCHORAGE)

Approach

Finding the Point Rincon anchorage is as easy as finding the Oakland-San Francisco Bay Bridge. The anchorage is immediately northwest of the point where the bridge meets the City. The anchorage extends westerly from the bridge to the Ferry Building, a long, low terminal of gray sandstone dominated by a tall clocktower. The cove, easily spotted between the bridge and the clocktower when you're close to shore, once had about ten mooring buoys, but the city removed them some years ago.

Anchorage

Boats can anchor in 12-15 feet of water, with good holding, within 150 feet of shore. Though large enough for about 10 boats, this anchorage is rarely used by cruising boaters because of the wake caused by passing ferries, the pilot boat, and pleasure craft, especially during daylight hours.

Facilities

Point Rincon anchorage has no satisfactory beach or pier for landing a tender. You can land at the inviting concrete ramps by the seawall, but your tender will

Rincon Point anchorage, west of the Bay Bridge south tower

be vulnerable to any of the thousands of passerbys and the ever-present street people in the area. Your dinghy will also be at the mercy of the waves which will be constantly throwing it against the concrete. We would recommend having one crew member take those ashore who wish to explore and then return to pick them up later.

SOUTH BEACH HARBOR

South Beach Harbor gives one a wholly different feeling from the other marinas along the City Front. Near the southernmost extremity of the Embarcadero, this area of the Bay has little tourist activity and traffic. Yet handsome red brick commercial buildings grace this portion of the waterfront, and the marina itself attaches to a grassy park with trees and benches and a long fishing pier at the southern end. Here, you can enjoy the City experience in relative solitude from the City bustle. You can walk to numerous fine restaurants, take public transportation to all points of San Francisco, or simply take advantage of the view from this prime piece of real estate that can be yours for a night at a reasonable cost.

Approach

This modern marina is 0.5 mile southeast of the City end of the Bay Bridge. As you pass under the bridge close to shore, shipping terminals obscure the marina. When you get closer, however, you'll recognize the marina by the breakwater with navigation lights on it and the masts of the sailboats. This harbor can also be identified by the large three-masted schooner (which once served as a restaurant) on the shore.

South Beach Harbor, south entrance

Boaters can enter the marina through openings at either end of the breakwater. Shipping terminal warehouses to the north of the marina protect boaters from the winds and waves, making South Beach Harbor an excellent destination.

Anchorage and Berthing

No anchorage area exists in the marina. Visiting boats can tie up at the long guest dock at the northeast end of the marina or in one of the 700 berths that is vacant. The South Beach Yacht Club is located at the shore end of the guest dock, but it has no guest dock of its own.

South Beach Harbormaster   415-495-4911 and VHF 16

South Beach Yacht Club   415-495-2295

Facilities at or near South Beach Harbor

Banks (1 mile)
Boat Maintenance and Repair
Grocery Store
Haul Out
Laundromat (1 mile)
Launch Ramp
Post Office (1 mile)
Pump Out

Public Transportation
Restaurants
Shops
Showers

CHINA BASIN ANCHORAGE

Before it was largely filled in with the rubble from the 1906 earthquake, China Basin, also called Mission Bay, figured largely in the history of the San Francisco waterfront. In 1776, a few Ohlone villages clustered around a creek emptying into the bay. Mission Dolores, one of the first two Spanish settlements in the Bay Area, sat on the shores of Mission Bay. During the latter half of the 19th century the shores of this then large basin were the site of "greaseways," railways for moving boats into dry dock for repairs. Today you can see a later vintage railway on the southwest shore—a ferry terminal for transporting Santa Fe railroad cars between China Basin and Point Richmond across San Francisco Bay.

At the turn of the century, San Franciscans lined the shores here to watch the rowers who competed in races from Fort Point.

Bascule bridge, south of South Beach Harbor

The creek where the Ohlones lived, later called Mission Creek or Third Street Channel, was dredged in the late 19th century, and its banks were the site of hay and lumber wharves and brickyards. You can take your tender up this channel, today the location of several houseboats. The entrance to the creek is immediately south of South Beach Harbor Marina. You will pass under the old bascule bridge.

Approach

The China Basin anchorage is 0.2 mile south of South Beach Harbor. You can easily spot the huge red crane on the end of the shipping terminal to the north of the anchorage. This pier, the Mission Rock Pier, is the largest on the City Front, extending out from the shore some 0.25 mile and having an end that is approximately 0.15 mile wide. Enter the anchorage area just south of the pier, steering a course for the abandoned railroad ferry landing on the south side at the back of the anchorage. You can see the large cement plant on shore to the southwest and the

Mariposa Hunters Point Yacht Club in the northwest corner near the foot of the pier.

Anchorage

For good holding and excellent protection from prevailing winds, anchor in 25 feet of water in front of the Mariposa Hunters Point Yacht Club, but don't block the passageway for the launch ramp used daily by club members or for boats coming from the Bay View Boat Club dock in the southwest corner of the basin. The anchorage area close to Mariposa Hunters Point Yacht Club accommodates only two or three boats, but you can also find good protection from prevailing winds to the south outside of the abandoned ferry pier.

Looking out toward the anchorage at China Basin

Members of both yacht clubs here are friendly and helpful. Tie up your tender at their docks and visit their clubs when they are open, though the locals caution against leaving either your tender or your boat unattended after dark.

Facilities within Walking Distance

Boat Maintenance and Repair
Haul Out
Launch Ramp
Public Tranportation
Restaurants

CENTRAL BASIN ANCHORAGE

Approach

Approximately 0.3 mile south of China Basin Anchorage, still technically in the China Basin area, is the Central Basin Anchorage. Identify the anchorage area by the large ship repair facilities to the south. Floating drydocks face north, and at the back of the cove are two boat haul-out facilities and two restaurants.

Anchorage

Anchor in 20 feet of water off the fishing pier in the northwest corner of the cove, with good protection from prevailing winds. This anchorage has room for 10 or more boats. To the north of the anchorage

Central Basin anchorage

area is an abandoned pier in an advanced state of disrepair. You can anchor close to the abandoned pier to be sure you are out of the way of the tugs bringing ships in or taking them out of the drydock area (a relatively rare occurrence).

On the water's edge is a small marina. The docks in front of the Mission Rock Restaurant are easily identified by their state of disrepair. The manager of the restaurant keeps two slips open for customers who wish to park their boats and go ashore for breakfast or lunch; however, the condition of the docks might make you unwilling to tie up and leave your boat. Be on the lookout for debris in the water and under the surface in the area of these docks. You can tie up your tender at the docks in front of the restaurant and go ashore for breakfast or lunch.

You can also tie up your tender at the docks in front of the San Francisco Boat Works adjacent to the Mission Rock Resort, but don't block access to a slip. These docks are busy. You can go ashore to get boat parts at the chandlery or to have lunch at the Ramp, the restaurant adjacent to the boat yard.

Facilities

Boat Maintenance and Repair
Chandlery

Haul Out
Launch Ramp
Public Transportation
Restaurants

Attractions of the City Front

The primary attraction for cruising sailors to the City Front is the ready access to the City itself, its multitude of pleasures requiring an entire guidebook to enumerate. And the public transportation in San Francisco gives you access to any of these pleasures. The top tourist draw in the City—and second in all of California—is Pier 39, attracting 10.5 million visitors annually. After savoring the foods, sampling the wares, and admiring (as well as smelling!) the sea lions that have captured several docks in the marina at Pier 39, you may be ready for a bus or taxi ride to one of the country's most accommodating and beautifully landscaped city parks, Golden Gate Park.

Up until the 1850s, the site of this park, now dense with vegetation, was a windy sand dune so inhospitable that neither the native tribes nor the Spanish and Mexican explorers had permanent settlements here. Today, though, this site has something for every cruising sailor: the Japanese Tea Garden; two art museums, the M. H. de Young Memorial Museum and the Asian Art Museum; the California Academy of Sciences, including the Steinhart Aquarium, the Morrison Planetarium, and a natural history museum; Strybing Arboretum; lakes; and walking, biking, and skating paths throughout. In the summer and early fall, drama productions and concerts add to the allure of the park.

Other points of interest near the marinas and anchorages are, of course, the Embarcadero itself, where you can go aboard a restored Liberty ship or a three-masted square-rigger; Fisherman's Wharf; the Maritime Museum; museums at Fort

Cable cars on Hyde Street

Ferry on the City Front

Mason, the Presidio, and Fort Point; and the Palace of Fine Arts (housing the Exploratorium Science Museum, a wonderful hands-on exhibit for children and adults alike).

Chinatown remains one of San Francisco's colorful attractions, where you can experience the flavor of China in the architecture, the food, and the wares for sale along the narrow, crowded streets. From the waterfront, part of the adventure is in the getting there. Two of the three remaining cable car lines run from near Fisherman's Wharf up to Chinatown. Catch a car at either Hyde and Beach or at Taylor and Bay.

Alcatraz, since 1972 a part of the Golden Gate National Recreation Area, is another popular site for boaters. A ferry picks up passengers at Pier 41 and transports them to the island, where they may go ashore and wander around the buildings and through some of the cell blocks on a self-guided tour. You can also take ferries from the Ferry Building to Alameda, Oakland, Sausalito, and Larkspur; from Pier 43 1/2 to Angel Island, Tiburon and Sausalito; and from Pier 39 to Marine World Africa USA. While you can take your own boat to all but Alcatraz, Larkspur, and Marine World, you may find the convenience of the ferries appealing.

Those of you wanting to enjoy the enticements ashore will be best off staying in one of the marinas, where you'll not worry about the security of your tender or your boat if you are away after nightfall. But some cruising sailors like to anchor out for a night on the City Front to partake of the spectacular views afforded of the bridges, the lights of the city, sunset over the Golden Gate, and the parade of other boats, ships, tugs, and ferries on the Bay.

HORSESHOE BAY
Chart #18649 or #18652

If you're entering San Francisco Bay through the Golden Gate, the first anchorage and marina you see will be tiny Horseshoe Bay, 500 yards northeast of the north tower of the bridge. With this strategic location, Horseshoe Bay has had a long history of military presence. At the end of the Civil War, the U. S. Government purchased several hundred acres on the north side of San Francisco Bay and eventually established three forts here and equipped them with heavy artillery to guard the entrance into the Bay. The most easterly of these three, East

Horseshoe Bay with Coast Guard docks in foreground

Fort Baker, sits immediately above Horseshoe Bay. Though a small contingent of military personnel remains, the batteries for guns and the platforms for missiles have become historic landmarks, and the land is now part of the Golden Gate National Recreational Area.

In Horseshoe Bay is a small marina and an anchorage for one or two single boats or as many as six or eight boats rafted together.

Approach

When you approach Horseshoe, turbulent winds exceeding 25 knots in this area can cause problems if you don't lower your sails before entering.

An additional problem is the sometimes 5- or 6-knot current at the entrance. If your boat speed is slow, you can easily find yourself slipping out under the Golden Gate Bridge before you can get into the harbor. Plan to enter the harbor on slack water or with a small ebb or flood tide.

The third serious problem with Horseshoe Bay is also weather related: fog. When a thick fog slides in under the bridge, your best plan is to choose another anchorage. Even if you could find the harbor and get anchored safely inside, the beauty of the anchorage would be minimal in such weather.

As you enter Horseshoe Bay, a fishing pier is on your port. Choose a course midway between the end of the pier and the breakwater on the starboard. The harbor is quite shallow; the average depth at low water is between 5 and 6 feet.

Inside the breakwater, a small marina rings the south and east perimeter of the harbor. The boats in the slips belong to active duty military and government personnel.

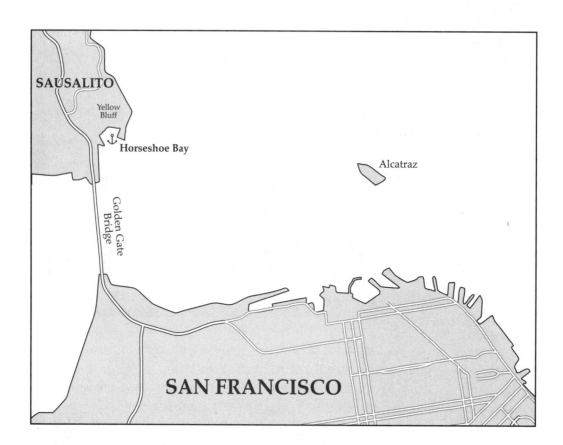

Anchorage

Since Horseshoe Bay is part of a military base, you must have permission from the Presidio Yacht Club to anchor here, but permission is routinely granted. Leave plenty of space around the Coast Guard docks on the west side of the harbor because CG boats arrive and depart regularly on an emergency basis. Although the depth and holding vary little from one part of the harbor to the next, that portion toward the east side near the docks is best because it will keep you comfortably away from the departure routes of emergency craft. The buoy on the east side of the harbor belongs to the Yacht Club, but it is unsafe to use.

Holding in the harbor is good, but not wonderful. Silt covers the bottom, and some anchors do not hold well in such loose material. After your anchor is down and you have let out an appropriate amount of rode, test the anchor's holding by running up your boat's engine to about one-half its normal cruising speed in reverse and keep it there for at least 45 seconds. If your anchor drags, hoist and drop it again and again, until you are confident it will hold if the wind increases.

Facilities and Restrictions

The Presidio Yacht Club has a clubhouse in the northeast corner of Horseshoe Bay and offers reciprocal privileges of the club's facilities, including restrooms and showers, to members of other yacht clubs. You may tie up or anchor here only with permission of the commodore of the Presidio Yacht Club. Visiting boats are limited to a few days' stay, if space is available. Generally, Presidio Yacht Club staff are around the facilities Friday evening, Saturday, and Sunday; at other times, only the harbormaster is there.

A public boat launching ramp is in the northwest corner of the bay. No other facilities are available at this anchorage and marina.

Presidio Yacht Club   415-332-2319

Attractions

Directly up from the beach, shadowed by towering eucalyptus trees, is a row of trimly kept wooden buildings, formerly part of East Fort Baker but now housing a Coast Guard Station. A short walk beyond these buildings takes you to the old administration buildings that are now the Bay Area Discovery Museum. Those of you with youngsters (or the young-at-heart) aboard will want to explore this inter-active display of science and art. As well as exhibits, it has a carousel, a small cafe catering to

Trails above Horseshoe Bay

children's tastes, and special presentations of music and dance on selected nights.

The Museum is open Wednesday through Saturday, from 1000 to 1700, and Tuesday through Saturday during the summer. The entry fee is $5 for all over one year old, but admittance is free to all on the first Thursday of each month. A friendly sign beside the ticket counter also assures all comers: "If our fees pose a problem for you, simply pay what you can."

Horseshoe Bay is an ideal stop for hikers. From the beach area you can pick up trails heading east and north along the shore toward Sausalito, north toward Gerbode Valley, or west along the coastal headlands toward Point Bonita, with its 140-year-old Fresnel lens beacon still flashing a warning to sailors far out at sea. These trails take you past the 130 years of military history of this region, through the grasslands once the grazing pastures for the cattle of Rancho Saucelito, to the shores where Coast Miwoks fished. The miles of trails crisscross the Marin Headlands, velvety green and laden with wildflowers—blue lupine, yellow mimulus, white Queen Anne's lace, orange California poppies—in the spring. And year round, hawks, egrets, terns, and brown pelicans soar above this shoreline.

From Horseshoe Bay on a clear day, you have an unobstructed view of the city of San Francisco; by night the lights of the city and of the Bay Bridge sparkle like the jewels they are. But perhaps the single greatest attraction of this spot is, finally, the magnificent view afforded one of the fabled Golden Gate Bridge. Late in the afternoon you'll watch the coastal fog pushing its way into San Francisco Bay, gradually enveloping all the Golden Gate Bridge except for its two towers pushing their way toward the heavens, bright orange above the white fog. No sight is more quintessentially San Francisco!

SAUSALITO
Chart #18649, #18652, or #18653

Sausalito as a cruising destination is a mixed bag. The anchorages tend toward either frequent turbulence or precarious water depth, and the marinas with guest docks are few and expensive. Yet the town of 7,500 permanent residents is a city with personality.

Sausalito (or *Saucelito*, as Juan Manuel de Ayala reportedly named this site, presumably for the "little willows," or tule grass, growing here) has a long history of human occupation, having been home to perhaps as many as 2,500 Miwoks. Ayala, the first European to explore San Francisco Bay from the sea, anchored his ship in the protected cove near Sausalito in 1775. The first permanent European settlement here began in 1838, when William A. Richardson, an English seaman, obtained a Mexican land grant for Rancho Saucelito. With the coming of statehood, Richardson eventually lost all his holdings; we mark his legacy in the naming of Richardson Bay, the bay just inside and to the north of the Golden Gate Bridge.

This coastal town has been a much favored tourist attraction for a half century, yet it maintains much of its unique flavor. True, its main street, Bridgeway, sports dozens of art, crafts, and toney clothing shops you'll immediately recognize as appealing to those on land tours. Nevertheless, the many businesses offering services necessary for a boating community, from chandleries to machine shops to sail lofts, attest to its nautical orientation. And in the hills above the tourists, and the traffic congestion they bring to Bridgeway Boulevard, lies the other Sausalito with its turn-of-the-century

Anchorage off Sausalito city front

houses, its churches, its commercial enterprises like those of other communities, and its streets lacing through the year-round lushly green cliffside on which the citizens have built their homes.

Approach

Sausalito is easy to identify because of its close proximity to the Golden Gate Bridge. From the north tower of the Golden Gate Bridge,

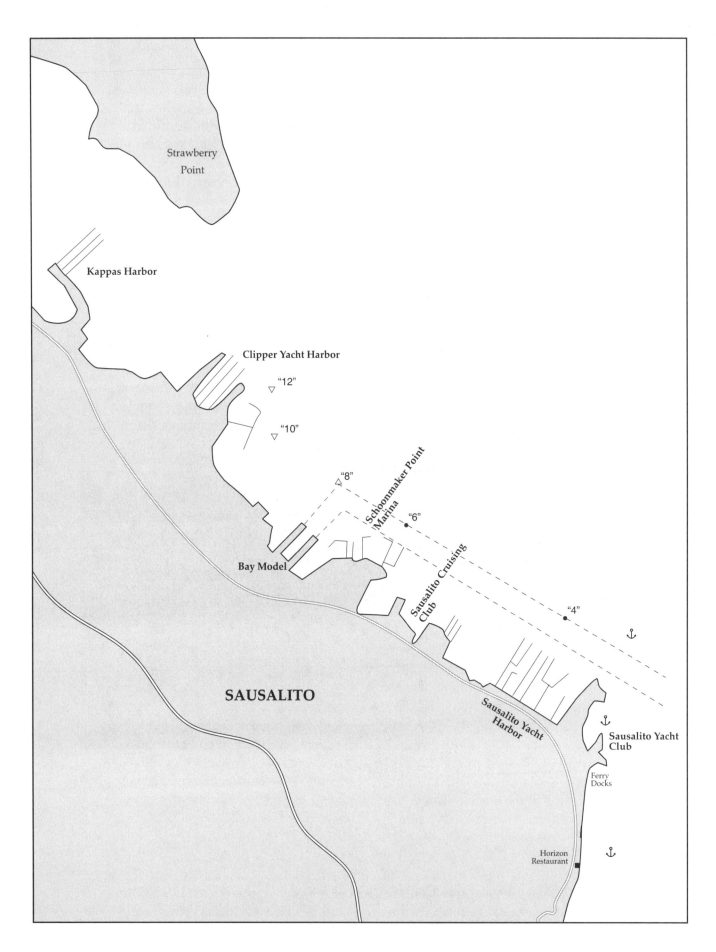

Strawberry
Point

Kappas Harbor

Clipper Yacht Harbor

▽ "12"

▽ "10"

Schoonmaker Point
Marina

▽ "8"

"6"

Bay Model

Sausalito Cruising
Club

"4"

⚓

SAUSALITO

Sausalito Yacht
Harbor

⚓

Sausalito Yacht
Club

Ferry
Docks

Horizon
Restaurant

⚓

go north 1.5 miles, and you will see Sausalito on the hillside. In the early hours of the day, it stands out because the morning sun reflects off its buildings, if there is any sun in the area at all. On summer afternoons the fog rolls inland over the mountains behind the town, engulfing the steets and houses but rarely the boats in the harbors. Both the morning sunshine and the afternoon fog will help you identify the town as you approach.

If you are approaching from the east, 1.3 miles separates Sausalito from Belvedere, the land mass to the east. Halfway between Peninsula Point, the southernmost point of land on Belvedere, and Sausalito, Buoy 2 marks the entrance to the Sausalito channel, which proceeds in a northwesterly direction. Keep the channel markers to your starboard and the town of Sausalito on your port; you will have plenty of water. **Do not stray to the starboard of the channel.** Examine your chart closely before entering Richardson Bay because much of this large bay contains shallow water.

The channel in Richardson Bay

Be cautious, too, of the winds in the Sausalito area. Local sailors often refer to the area just south of the town as "Hurricane Gulch," where winds roar down the canyons in the afternoon hours. Sailboats can be sailing along under full sail in 10 knots of wind one minute and can suddenly be hit with a 30-knot gust, leaving the boat on her beam ends. The closer you are to shore, the greater the impact of these gusts on your boat.

Anchorage and Moorage

If you plan to stay for no more than a few hours to have lunch on your boat, you can anchor off the part of the city facing San Francisco. The holding in this area is good, and the scenery in every direction is spectacular. Anchor off *Old Town City Front* seaward of the Horizon or Scoma's restaurant in 15-20 feet of water. The Horizon Restaurant has three moorings that you may use free of charge. Call the restaurant at 415-331-3232 to obtain permission. While you and your guests will enjoy the beauty of the area, strong wind gusts and a rolling anchorage keep this site from being anything more than a temporary destination.

If you plan to stay for more than a few hours, consider anchoring in the area between the *Sausalito Yacht Club*, adjacent to the ferry terminal on the north side, and the Spinnaker Restaurant. The club also has six buoys that visiting boaters can use if they belong to a yacht club. The club's buoys are frequently reserved months in advance on weekends, but they are normally free on weekdays. Call ahead

Sausalito Yacht Club with moorings in front

to see if one of the buoys is available. The club is open Friday, Saturday, and Sunday, and it offers showers, a bar, and a restaurant. The anchorage and the buoy area also suffer from rolly conditions, but this area is somewhat protected by the ferry terminal. In spite of the uncomfortable motion, this location is a good destination because you can leave your dinghy at the club dock and go ashore for shopping and sightseeing.

Slightly more than 0.5 mile beyond the Spinnaker Restaurant up the Sausalito channel, a smaller channel turns off to the port side, leading to the *Sausalito Cruising Club*. You can recognize the channel because Cass's Marina shares the same channel and has a large sign. Since the depth in the channel at low water is 4 feet or less, enter at high water.

Once you leave the Sausalito channel and head up the channel to the Cruising Club, keep the green markers to your port side. Go all the way to the club before making your turn into the basin in front of the club building. Unlike the anchorage areas by the city front, the water by the Cruising Club is calm. The guest dock at the

Sausalito Cruising Club to left; Cass's Marina to right

club exceeds 100 feet but is often full. Call ahead to be certain space exists for your boat. The club is open after 1600 on Fridays and Saturdays. If you are planning to arrive at a time when the club office is not open, call the Hot Line to get permission to enter and tie up to the guest dock. You can also get permission to leave your dinghy at this dock if you decide to anchor out. A 48-hour limit has been established on the guest dock here to prevent anyone from monopolizing the facilities.

Two hundred yards farther up the Sausalito channel, also on the port side, is *Schoonmaker Point Marina*, located just after Channel Marker 6 and easily spotted from the channel. Schoonmaker is strictly an upscale facility, offering guest berthing, showers, electricity, laundromat, restaurant, groceries, and beautiful, wide concrete docks. All this comfort and convenience come at a price, of course. Call ahead to ask if guest berthing is available.

Almost a mile farther up the Sausalito channel beyond Schoonmaker, *Clipper Yacht Harbor* is easily identified by the large Chevron sign marking the busy fuel dock. While Clipper Yacht Harbor does not have a specific guest berth area, the harbormaster will attempt to provide guest berthing if visitors call ahead. Again, as with all areas in Richardson Bay, be careful to stay in the channel.

For those boaters wishing to anchor out, *Richardson Bay* offers one of San Francisco's best known anchorages. Although the waters are normally shallow, you can still find a good spot for anchoring out. To the east of Clipper Yacht Harbor, depths are about 5 feet at low water. Across from the Sausalito Cruising Club and Schoonmaker, the depths shown on the chart are generally about 4 feet at low water. Back down the channel toward San Francisco, however, the water deepens. Much of the anchorage area in Richardson Bay has a soft mud bottom.

Sausalito Yacht Club	415-332-7400
Sausalito Cruising Club	415-332-9922 or 415-332-9349
Schoonmaker	415-331-5550 and VHF 16
Clipper Yacht Harbor	415-332-3500

Facilities

Within walking distance of all docks:
    Banks
    Boat haul-out (one major one—Anderson's— and three small yards)
    Boat maintenance and repair shops
    Chandleries
    Grocery stores

Launch ramp
Laundromats
Library
Post Office
Restaurants
Golden Gate Transit service (bus and ferry)
Shops

Locations of other services:
Dinghy docks: In front of Caruso's Seafood Deli (public access)
and Sausalito Yacht Club (private)
Fuel dock: Clipper Yacht Harbor
Pump-out: Schoonmaker

Attractions

In the 19th century wealthy San Franciscans built elegant summer homes on the hills overlooking Richardson Bay. Though you can see some of these Victorian beauties from your boats, you may want to get a bit of aerobic exercise by hiking up the hill to get a closer look.

As you walk along the waterfront, notice the huge barn-like buildings left over from Sausalito's boat building days. As early as 1890 boat building was an important enterprise here; this enterprise boomed in the early 1940s with the opening of Marinship, the shipyard that built 93 of the Liberty ships as well as tankers and landing craft during World War II.

From Sausalito a fairly competent hiker can walk to the Marin Headlands of the Golden Gate National Recreation Area. Follow the shoreline south of Sausalito Point for about a mile to the Recreation Area, where a hiking trail veers off to the left just before the Y in the road. This trail connects with the numerous trails of the Marin Headlands. (See section on Horseshoe Bay for more details.)

Save an hour or two out of your sightseeing and hiking day to visit what may be Sausalito's premier attraction for many boaters: the Bay Model Visitor Center, located in the Marinship area. Operated by the U. S. Army Corps of Engineers, the Bay Model is a one-acre scale model of San Francisco Bay and the Delta region. With the use of hydraulic pumps, the model simulates the ocean tides and Delta river flows to demonstrate effects on the Bay that can't be determined mathematically. You'll walk along the shores of the entire Bay and Delta region—in miniature, of course—as the waters slowly rise and then recede in imitation of the ceaseless rhythms of this intricately balanced water system.

TIBURON PENINSULA
Chart #18649, #18652, or #18653

The Tiburon Peninsula comprises two somewhat separate and, in many ways, wholly different cruising destinations. Tiburon (Spanish for "shark"), a waterfront settlement and former railroad town, is a pleasant village of Victorian buildings, expensive private homes and condominiums, and a one-of-a-kind shopping area, Ark Row, which, along with the Boardwalk Shopping Center, sits on filled-in mudflats. Belvedere, once separated from downtown Tiburon by a large lagoon which began to be filled in the 1920s, is an exclusive housing area, where roads too narrow in places for two cars to pass wind around this "island" to houses tucked into the hills above or below the roads.

Approach

Tiburon and Belvedere on approach from the water are hardly distinguishable from one another. Belvedere is that point of land 1.5 miles due east of Sausalito, its southernmost tip called Peninsula Point,

Corinthian Yacht Club and buoys as seen from Raccoon Strait

which is directly across Raccoon Strait from Point Stuart on Angel Island. From the buoy off Peninsula Point, go north into Belvedere Cove. Inside the cove, the San Francisco Yacht Club sits in the back of the cove on the port side, and the Corinthian Yacht Club sits on the point in the center of the cove.

Except for some shallow water near the shoreline in the far back of the cove, the minimum depth here is 5 feet at low water. The entrance into the San Francisco Yacht Club is at the back of the cove.

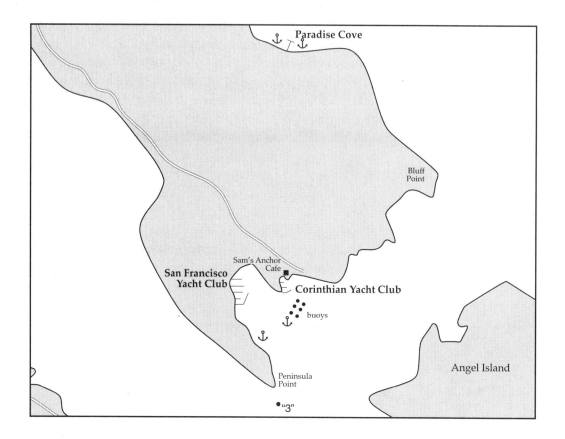

Anchorage and Guest Berthing

The *San Francisco Yacht Club* offers guest docking for yacht club members. *Corinthian Yacht Club*, about 400 yards east of San Francisco Yacht Club, is distinguished by its grand old turn-of-the-century building sitting prominently out in the middle of the cove when you enter. Like the San Francisco Yacht Club, Corinthian offers guest berthing to yacht club members. Call ahead, since both these clubs are quite busy, especially on weekends. If the guest berth facilities at both are full, ask permission from Corinthian Yacht Club to use one of its mooring buoys. Like the guest berthing at both clubs, these moorings are available only to members of other yacht clubs.

Sam's Anchor Cafe, long a favorite destination for Bay Area boaters, has two large docks, one 100 feet long and the other 115 feet long. Boaters can tie up on both sides of these two docks; 15 or 20 boats tie up there on weekend afternoons in the summer and fall. Dock space is free for boaters who wish to tie up and have lunch or dinner at Sam's. Check the tide when visiting Sam's; if your boat has a deep draft, you might come back from dinner to find your boat sitting on the bottom.

The manager of the cafe reports that about four feet of water under the docks is typical at low water.

One other cautionary note: the heavy surge in the marinas in Belvedere Cove mandates the use of strong dock lines and spring lines when you tie up here.

Entrance to Corinthian Yacht Club and Sam's docks

In *Belvedere Cove* boaters can also find an acceptable location to drop a hook just south of Corinthian Yacht Club, being sure to anchor well clear of the permanent moorings. With depths of about 10 feet, you won't have to let out much anchor rode. The bottom in the cove is soft mud. You can leave your dinghy at the docks behind Sam's Cafe while you have dinner or go ashore.

San Francisco Yacht Club	415-435-4202 and VHF 16
Corinthian Yacht Club	415-435-4771
Sam's Anchor Cafe	415-435-4527

Facilities

Within walking distance from all docks:
    Banks
    Bus and ferry service
    Grocery stores
    Laundromat
    Library
    Post Office
    Restaurants
    Shops

Location of other service:
    Dinghy docks: Sam's Anchor Cafe (with permission)

Attractions

The event that changed Tiburon from an insignificant waterfront settlement to a community has left little for the touring sailor to see. In 1884 the branch line of the San Francisco and North Pacific Railroad was completed, bringing passengers to Tiburon, where they could board a ferry to San Francisco. The old depot, now a historic landmark, is about all that remains. A well-used walking and biking path covers the bed of the tracks. This pathway through Shoreline Park provides you a view of much of the San Francisco Bay: Richmond, Red Rock, and the Richmond-San Rafael Bridge with San Pablo Bay beyond it to the north, Sausalito and the Golden Gate Bridge to the southwest, the San Francisco skyline to the south, and Angel Island to the east.

If you're up for a hike of just under 3 miles, continue west along this path to Richardson Bay Park and the Richardson Bay Audubon Center and Sanctuary. This 900-acre sanctuary of tidal baylands, grasslands, woodlands, and a freshwater pond is one of the few remaining San Francisco Bay wetlands virtually unaltered by human development. Here you might see up to 80 species of migratory waterfowl. A man-made treasure of this Park, the Lyford House, is one of the Bay Area's oldest houses, having been built around 1876. This restored Victorian is worth a visit for both its authentic style and for the art and nature exhibits it contains.

Another invigorating hike is the one up the hill to Old St. Hilary's Church, a simple wooden Gothic style built in 1888. This site gives you an even more commanding view of the Bay than the walk through Shoreline Park.

Back down at the waterfront, all you sailors will be intrigued by Ark Row, shops and offices in "arks" that were formerly floating homes in parts of Belvedere Cove now filled in. Some of these arks are over 100 years old. Nearby is another bit of sea history, China Cabin, the social saloon of the *SS China*, removed from the derelict ship in 1886. It is the only surviving social saloon from a 19th century passenger ship.

Even if you don't try the food, treat yourself to a drink on the deck at Sam's Anchor Cafe, where the gulls frequently swoop low over the tables in flocks of 30 or 40 and the waiters and waitresses rush to hide under the umbrellas sheltering some of the tables.

ANGEL ISLAND
Chart #18649, #18652, or #18653

We can't know what vision Juan Manuel de Ayala might have had in August, 1775, that inspired him to name this largest of the islands in the San Francisco Bay *Isla de los Angeles*. Perhaps it was the Western gulls circling overhead, their white wings glittering in the sunlight, or the snowy egrets "got up as angels" (from Elizabeth Bishop's poem "Seascape"). It could have even been the white pelicans skimming along just above the water in Ayala Cove with such grace and dignity in their pure white raiment. This island may have looked heavenly to Ayala simply because the cove now bearing his name gave safe haven to him and his crew after a difficult nine-day passage from Monterey through gales and fog. Whatever Ayala's reasons, visitors to Angel Island today approve the name, and for boaters particularly this is indeed a celestial island.

For as long as 3,000 years previous to Ayala's charting of the Bay, Coast Miwoks occupied Angel Island. In 1775 they were living in four villages on the island, where apparently their idyllic life had not prepared them to resist the European intrusion that followed.

During the almost 200 years between Ayala's naming of the island and its designation in 1962 as a California State Park, Angel Island underwent many mutations: a Russian base for hunting sea otters, a cattle ranch, a rock quarry, a Civil War fort, a U. S. Army Cavalry headquarters, a vegetable farm for the inmates on Alcatraz, a quarantine station, a prisoner-of-war camp, an immigration center, and a Nike missile facility. Today, this island is once again clothed in green, though not all the flora is native, most visibly the gigantic eucalyptus trees but other trees and bushes as well brought here from around the world when Angel Island was a military base. This foliage gives shelter to numerous species of land and sea birds, to deer, and to raccoons.

As a cruising destination, Angel Island is for many sailors ideal. Its seven anchorages (one with buoys) ringing the island promise variety, availability, and at least one protected anchorage in any weather. For day use by boats up to 50 feet long, the dock in Ayala Cove makes going ashore convenient. Once ashore, visitors could spend several days exploring the beaches, the flora, and the fauna along the island's miles of hiking trails and bike paths, the visitor centers, and numerous sites bearing testimony to the many eras of the island's history.

AYALA COVE

Approach

Angel Island is nearly equidistant from the three bridges in the Central Bay. From the south the island is 4.0 miles from the Bay Bridge; from the north, 4.0 miles from the Richmond-San Rafael Bridge; and from the west, 3.0 miles from the Golden Gate Bridge.

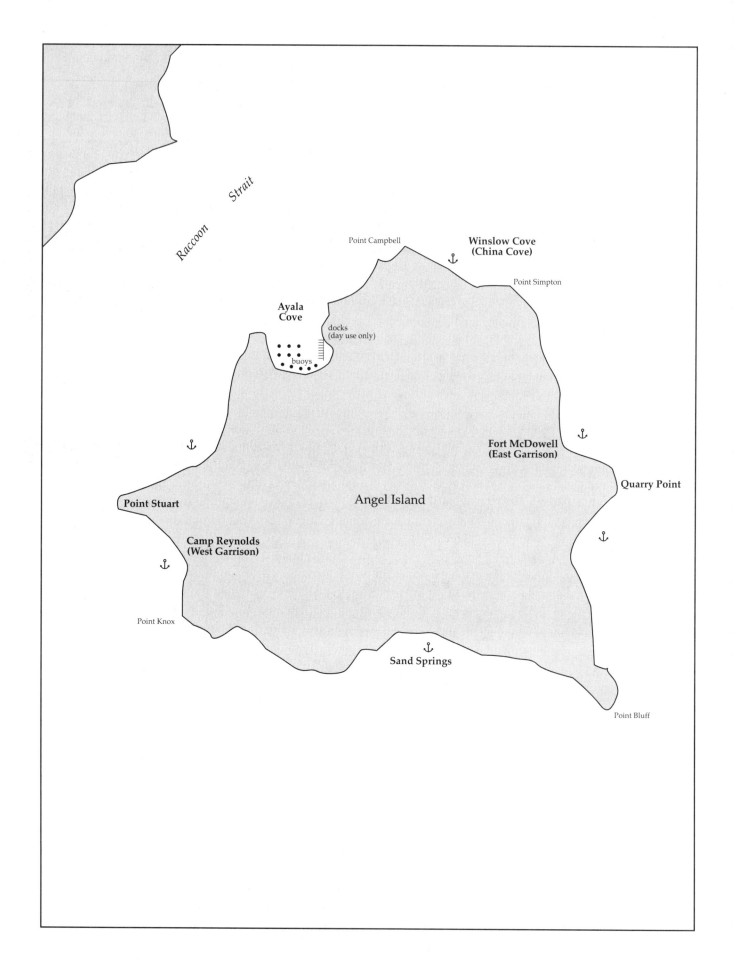

Raccoon *Strait*

Point Campbell

**Winslow Cove
(China Cove)**

Point Simpton

**Ayala
Cove**

docks
(day use only)

buoys

**Fort McDowell
(East Garrison)**

Quarry Point

Angel Island

Point Stuart

**Camp Reynolds
(West Garrison)**

Point Knox

Sand Springs

Point Bluff

Ayala Cove, on the north shore of Angel Island, facing Tiburon, is the first choice of most boaters who visit the island. Identify Raccoon Strait, the body of water between the island and the Tiburon Peninsula. Raccoon Strait runs roughly east to west and has depths in excess of 100 feet in most areas. Ayala Cove is located almost in the center of the south shore of the Strait on the north shore of Angel Island. You can recognize Ayala by the ferry docks on the east shore of the cove, the pleasure boat docks on the southeast shore, the green lawn and two-story white wooden administration building above the lawn, and the mooring buoys in the center.

Ferry leaving docks at Ayala Cove

Anchorage, Berthing, and Moorage

Docks in Ayala can accommodate 47 boats. These docks may be used only between 0800 and sunset; park rangers check daily to be certain all boats have been moved from the docks before sunset, and they patrol the docks in the morning to prevent boaters from tying up before 0800. Rangers collect a fee for each boat using the docks; the fee may be paid at the kiosk at the top of the ramp leading to the docks or to the ranger patrolling the docks.

A cross current in excess of one knot will often be encountered around the docks as you are attempting to tie up. If you are unprepared, the current can slam your boat into the dock or away from the dock and into a nearby boat.

Boaters may use the mooring buoys in the cove during the day or night. Rangers collect a fee in the morning for all boats on buoys overnight. Park personnel recommend boaters use bow and stern moorings because of the frequently changing currents in Ayala Cove. Bring long lines with you if you plan to use these buoys because many are at least 150 feet apart. You can tie one end of a long line to a cleat on your boat, pass the other end through the ring on the top of a mooring buoy, and then bring that end back to the cleat and tie it. If your boat has good maneuverability, you can tie a stern line to a buoy as you pass by and then motor ahead to pick up a buoy for your boat's bow. Make allowances for the current in the cove, however, or you may end up being swept away from the buoy you want. Some boaters prefer to use a tender to take mooring lines from their boats to the buoys.

The mooring buoys in Ayala Cove cannot possibly accommodate all who wish to visit the island, so boaters share the moorings in creative ways. Friends and club members often raft up two, three, and four boats to a pair of mooring buoys. On busy weekends, boaters will tie their bow to the buoy you are using for a stern buoy and then tie their stern to someone else's bow buoy. The situation becomes thoroughly confused when boaters begin mooring their boats across the channel, blocking access and preventing people who wish to depart from doing so. Although boats will ride most comfortably with the bow pointed northward, boaters will often tie every which way, being willing to suffer the rolling just to be at Angel Island.

Boats moored creatively in Ayala Cove

Anchoring is a possibility at Ayala Cove, but the only room for boaters wishing to anchor is outside of the cove to the north. If you choose to anchor, be certain you are far enough away from the boats on moorings so you won't swing into them. Depths here are 20-60 feet, but holding is good. We cannot recommend this area because of the excessive wind and wave action. When Ayala Cove is full, most boaters proceed on around the island clockwise, looking for a good spot to anchor.

WINSLOW COVE (CHINA COVE)

Approach

From Ayala Cove proceed eastward 0.4 mile to Point Campbell and then southward for another 0.2 mile to Winslow Cove. The palm trees at Winslow stand out behind the beach, and the old two-story faded white immigration station building appears on the west side of the cove about 200 feet inshore of the beach. This cove does not provide the protection that

Winslow Cove and Immigration Station buildings

Ayala does, hence the tremendous popularity of Ayala.

Anchorage

Winslow Cove has no docks or mooring buoys. However, boaters regularly anchor here in 20-30 feet of water and gain good holding in mud and clay. A strong tidal current runs through the anchorage; use plenty of scope and set your anchor carefully. The best anchorage area is between the beach below the old immigration station and Point Simpton.

EAST GARRISON

Approach

South from Point Simpton 0.5 mile, East Garrison anchorage is easily recognized by the buff-colored barracks, hospital, and mess hall remaining from Fort McDowell, the world's largest military induction center during World War I and World War II. Quarry Point marks the south extremity of the anchorage area. The recently rebuilt ferry dock is just north of Quarry Point.

East Garrison anchorage

Anchorage

Anchor well clear of the dock because of the ferries that arrive and depart regularly on weekends. The best anchorage is in 20-35 feet of water. The mud and clay bottom insures that holding is good. As with Winslow Cove, a strong tidal flow runs through this anchorage, so set your hook well.

QUARRY BEACH

Approach

The anchorage at Quarry Beach is 0.2 mile south of Quarry Point. This anchorage is the largest on the island, extending 0.4 miles to the island's southernmost point, Point Blunt. The anchorage area is off the sand beach below the East Garrison buildings.

Anchorage

Anchorage is in 15-30 feet of water with mud and clay bottom. Choose a protected spot as far inside the cove as possible. Waves wrap around Point Blunt and keep boats in the anchorage moving. Although this anchorage can be uncomfortable, many boaters return again and again because it is so beautiful and so spacious.

Quarry Beach anchorage

DAVID DAWSON

SAND SPRINGS BEACH

Approach

From Quarry Beach anchorage, go around the buoy at Point Blunt (0.4 mile) and then go west 0.5 mile. Stand at least 0.5 mile offshore when rounding Point Blunt because the area between the point and the buoy has numerous rocks above and just below the surface. A small white sand beach denotes the anchorage.

Anchorage

Anchor off the beach at Sand Springs in 20 feet of water with mud and clay bottom. Use the Sand Springs Beach anchorage only when the north winds blow and make Ayala Cove, Winslow Cove, East Garrison, and Quarry Beach unsafe. **If the winds are from the south or west, this anchorage is not only rough but unsafe. This anchorage is temporary only; do not plan to go ashore from here or to anchor here overnight**.

WEST GARRISON

Approach

From Sand Springs proceed clockwise around the island 0.5 mile to Point Knox; West Garrison anchorage is 0.25 mile beyond. Only a few pilings remain of the old wooden pier, but they serve nicely as a landmark for the anchorage. On the island 100 feet from the water's edge is a large two-story brick structure that reportedly saw service as a schoolhouse and as an ordnance storehouse. This and the remainder of the buildings in the background were part of Camp Reynolds, a U. S. Army installation built in 1864.

Anchorage

When you have identified the old pier and the brick building, proceed to a position 200-300 feet south of

West Garrison anchorage

the old pier and about the same distance from the beach. Anchorage is in 12-20 feet of water with good holding in clay bottom. **This anchorage is secure when an east or south wind is blowing. When the prevailing west or northwest wind is blowing, this anchorage is on a lee shore and must be avoided**.

POINT STUART

Approach

From the West Garrison anchorage to Point Stuart is 0.15 mile, and from the Point on to the anchorage is another 0.25 mile. The anchorage begins where the shoreline, which is basically east-west after Point Stuart, turns northerly for the 0.3 mile run to Point Ione.

Anchorage

Drop anchor in 15-25 feet of water with typical mud / clay bottom and good holding. Anchor 100-200 feet from shore, and expect strong currents in the Point Stuart anchorage. This anchorage gets overflow boaters from Ayala Cove. **Consider this anchorage temporary. Do not leave your boat untended, and do not stay overnight here**.

Angel Island Facilities

> Ferry Service between Angel Island and Vallejo, Tiburon, Sausalito, and San Francisco
> Restrooms
> Snack Bar
> Angel Island State Park info 415-435-1915

Angel Island Attractions

Many boaters settle into one of the anchorages off Angel Island and never go ashore, finding the natural beauty and wildlife activity to be all the entertainment they need. We have done just this many times. But for first-time visitors, we suggest you spend some time getting acquainted with this loveliest of islands.

Once ashore, you have three options for transportation: hiking, biking, or taking a TramTour. (You can rent bikes or take the tram daily May through September and on weekends October through mid-November and March through April). Hiking will, of course, give you access to the most locations. On the dirt trails you can circle the island or ascend to its summit, Mt. Livermore (781 feet above sea level); a less strenuous hike along the paved perimeter road, at about 200 feet above sea level, will give you 5 miles of outstanding views of the Bay. If you have your own bicycle aboard, you can take it ashore and ride on the perimeter road.

Whether hiking or biking, you'll be able to review the history of

Commanding officer's home at West Garrison

the previous 150 years on Angel Island. For an overview of the island's geography and history, stop first at the Visitor Center, housed in the administration building of the San Francisco Quarantine Station (1892-1952) in Ayala Cove (formerly Hospital Cove). The four primary sites of significance in U. S. history—Ayala Cove and North, East, and West garrisons—were also the sites of the four Coast Miwok villages noted by the first European explorers. You can take either direction from the Visitor Center to these other historically significant sites—the Immigration Station (North Garrison), Fort McDowell (East Garrison), and Camp Reynolds (West Garrison)—and to Mount Livermore, the island's pinnacle.

Ayala Cove and Quarry Beach at Fort McDowell both have sandy beaches protected from the cool afternoon winds and therefore are suitable for playing in the water or swimming, though the strong currents make venturing beyond the beach area risky. No lifeguards are on duty on the island.

PARADISE COVE
Chart #18649, #18652, or #18653

Paradise Cove, often called Paradise Park, has perhaps the greenest site above any anchorage in the Central Bay. The bright, manicured lawns framed by darker green oaks and redwoods coupled with this well-protected and generally uncrowded anchorage make it a particularly peaceful destination.

The U. S. Navy had as many as 2,000 men stationed nearby during World War II; one of their primary functions was to set nets beneath the water's surface under the Golden Gate Bridge to snare any enemy submarines that might try to slip into San Francisco Bay. Some of the 2-ton concrete weights used to keep the nets submerged remain on the beach just north of the pier at Paradise Cove. The large iron rings on the tops of the weights, where the nets were attached, look like sturdy mooring rings.

Approach

Paradise Cove is on the east side of the Tiburon Peninsula, 1.5 miles northwest of Bluff Point, the southeast corner of the peninsula. When you approach the anchorage from the south, the Romberg Tiburon Centers will appear on the shore .75 mile northwest of Bluff Point. This is the location of the original U. S. Navy coaling station and the assembly site of the submarine nets during World War II. Steel pilings where ships were tied remain 200 feet

Concrete weights for sub nets

offshore; stay at least 300 feet offshore as you pass. You can easily identify the remains of the massive concrete coal bunkers 150 feet inland of the seawall.

Coaling station pilings offshore of Romberg Tiburon Centers

At Point Chauncey, 0.25 mile beyond the Romberg Centers, you have your first view of the green lawns at Paradise Beach County Park. Steer for a point just off the end of the concrete pier at the park.

Approaching from the north, set a course of 180° mag. from the center span of the Richmond-San Rafael Bridge. The anchorage is 2.5 miles from the bridge.

From Richmond to the east, set a course of 240° mag. as you go past Buoy 4. You will first see the bright green lawn of the park shortly after you depart from the Richmond Channel. From Buoy 4 to the Paradise Cove anchorage is 2.75 miles.

The T-shaped pier extends 320 feet from the shore and has a 200-foot-long end. Boaters may not tie up at the pier; it is strictly for fishing.

The park is heavily used on weekends. Swimmers often venture 400-500 feet out into the Bay, so you must be particularly careful when operating a boat in the area.

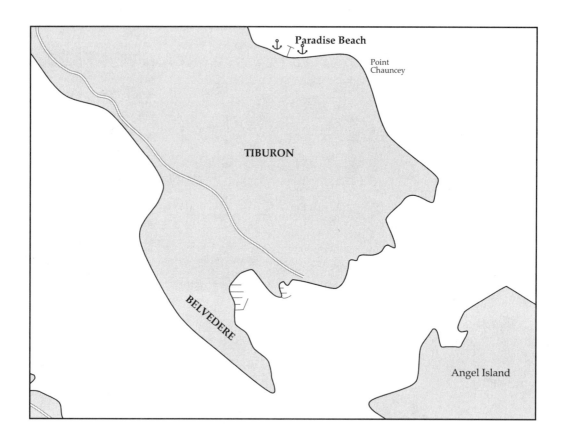

Anchorage

The best anchorage is found at least 200 feet from the end of the pier and to the north, but boaters commonly anchor to the south of the pier when the favored area to the north becomes congested. The depth is about 10 feet, and the clay bottom provides excellent holding, although it also produces a muddy mess when you hoist anchor.

Boat in anchorage off pier at Paradise Cove

Facilities and Restrictions

No facilities are available at this county park except for restrooms and a freshwater shower (but no hot water) at the entrance of the pier.

You may row a dinghy or sportboat in; a park ranger will come down and collect a fee for each person who goes ashore. **Park administration rules strictly prohibit operating any boat motor closer than 320 feet from shore.** In other words, you cannot operate an outboard-powered sportboat, dinghy, or jet ski closer to the shore than the end of the pier. Boaters are welcome to land their tenders on the beach, but they must row ashore. This restriction is strictly enforced!

Attractions

Paradise Cove enjoys many beautiful warm, sunny days in the spring and summer, and it has a solid, if somewhat rocky, beach and bottom to attract both sunbathers and swimmers. Up the hill above the beach are dozens of picnic tables, many tucked in among the oaks and redwoods. A woodsy trail winds through these areas.

For a longer hike, go up to the paved road, turn left, and walk about a mile, past the Bay Conference Center and the Romberg Tiburon Centers on the left. After another 100 feet, a sign on the right points you to the Tiburon Uplands Trail, a 0.7-mile climb through woods and meadows.

Cruisers who anchor at Paradise Cove regularly explore the surrounding areas by sportboat. Mike Ransom, a cruising friend who has spent many days and nights here, tells us he has gone up into the beautiful marina and housing area at Paradise Cay on occasion. When he feels more adventurous, he continues on up Corte Madera Creek, passing under the Highway 101 bridge, into the lagoon area behind the homes. He has gone far enough into the lagoon so that he has been almost behind Marin Community College.

The 5-mile trip up Corte Madera Creek offers an excellent adventure, but we recommend making the trip only early in the day to avoid a wet, uncomfortable ride back to your anchored boat. The winds pick up to 20 knots or more in the afternoon; you won't enjoy this trip nearly so much then.

Another sportboat trip boaters anchored at Paradise enjoy is a trip across the Bay to Red Rock, which is just south of the Richmond-San Rafael Bridge. This island is privately owned, so you must take that into account if you decide to explore the island. You should also

DAVID DAWSON

Red Rock Island, with Richmond-San Rafael Bridge

consider that the island is totally undeveloped and has no vegetation worth mentioning. Having said that about the island, we must also note that we know a number of boaters who have made the trip. Be sure you time your trip across the Bay shortly after daybreak to avoid a wet, dangerous return ride. Red Rock is 2.5 miles from the anchorage at Paradise Cove, and the prevailing winds during the cruising months could leave you making an upwind return trip if you depart from Red Rock after about 1000 hours.

Another boater, Matt Morehouse, reports he has anchored his boat to the north of Red Rock Island a few times. He considers it a good day anchorage but not one for an overnight stay. The island does provide good protection from the prevailing winds, however, for boats anchored between it and the Richmond-San Rafael Bridge.

RICHMOND and POINT RICHMOND
Chart #18649, #18652, or #18653

Richmond and Point Richmond, though incorporated as one city, have maintained their separate identities. Richmond is a large industrial city that was especially prosperous during the first half of this century, through World War II. Point Richmond, which takes its name from the point about a mile south of the town, began the modern era as a small island and, in many ways, has retained its small, isolated status. Unlike the Richmond commercial district, which has spread out for miles beyond its Old Town, Point Richmond's downtown is still two or three blocks of businesses and services built around the original triangle.

Both communities were a part of Rancho San Pablo, a Mexican land grant given to the Castro family. Later, a U. S. citizen named Tewksbury bought 2,200 acres of the Rancho at Point Richmond. He built a dike and a road out to the point, and gradually the land filled in to make the island and mainland one.

The Richmond-Point Richmond area will greet you most of the year with warmer and sunnier days than almost any other destination on the Bay. The fog, when it does get in this far, burns off early in the morning and comes in late in the afternoon. The wind here is usually more moderate than on other Bay waterfronts.

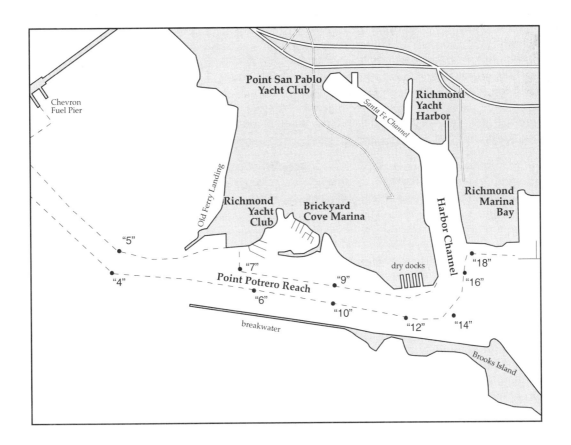

Approach

The channel into the Richmond marinas, Point Potrero Reach, exits San Francisco Bay 2.5 miles southeast of the east span of the Richmond-San Rafael Bridge. The channel is easy to spot when you approach from the north or west because channel markers and buoys outline it clearly for the large cargo ships that dock in Richmond.

When you approach from the south, set a course for Southhampton Shoal light. From the light, proceed north for 1.5 miles, keeping a sharp lookout for the jetty extending westerly for 1 mile off Brooks Island. To enter Point Potrero Reach, you must clear the west end of the jetty. At night or in foggy weather, the breakwater is difficult to spot because it barely rises above the surface of the water. Identifying this obstruction are a marker on a pole at the end of the jetty and two range markers on poles, the closest only 350 yards southeast of the end of the breakwater.

Anchorages and Marinas

The Richmond area has four possible destinations if you wish guest berthing, but it offers no anchorage area. Inside the Reach, navigation aids designed for commercial ship traffic clearly mark the 35-foot-deep channel. Do not stray outside the channel markers on the starboard side, where water depths are as low as 2 feet in some areas.

Brickyard Cove Marina and *Richmond Yacht Club* share Brickyard Cove, entered from Point Potrero Reach, on the port side 0.5 mile beyond the end of the jetty. You will pass Buoy 7 some 200 yards before you reach the entrance to the cove. The landmark for Brickyard Cove is the row of dark brown condominiums with green roofs snug in against the hillside behind the marina. Both the yacht club, with docks to the port just inside the breakwater, and Brickyard Cove Marina, on the south end of the cove, try to provide guest berthing for visiting boats, but call ahead.

Entrance to Brickyard Cove

Brickyard Cove Marina   510-236-1933

Richmond Yacht Club   510-234-6959 and VHF 16.

One mile beyond Brickyard Cove, Point Potrero Reach makes an abrupt turn to port. Five hundred yards after the turn, the entrance to *Marina Bay* exits to the starboard, proceeding in an easterly direction for 0.3 mile. With 758 slips, this is the largest marina in the Richmond area and can provide guest slips. Use caution entering this marina as the depth is only 5-6 feet at low water.

Richmond Marina Bay   510-236-1013 and VHF 16

The channel, at this point called the Harbor Channel, continues in a northerly direction for 0.5 mile past the Marina Bay entrance, then bears off to the port and becomes the Santa Fe Channel. The *Point San Pablo Yacht Club* is on the port side at the far end of the Santa Fe Channel, 0.6 miles beyond the Harbor Channel. Although the club is comparatively small, club members try to accommodate visiting boaters.

Point San Pablo Yacht Club   510-235-1176

Facilities

At Brickyard Cove Marina
     Bus Stop (0.5 mile)
     Hoist
     Laundromat
     Showers
     Restaurant
At Richmond Yacht Club
     Boat Maintenance and Repair
     Bus Stop (0.5 mile)
     Chandlery
     Hoist
     Pump Out
     Restaurant
     Showers
At Marina Bay
     Bus Stop
     Convenience Store
     Launch Ramp
     Laundromat
     Pump Out
     Restaurant
At Point San Pablo Yacht Club
     Showers
In either *Richmond or Point Richmond, accessible by bus from all marinas:*
     Banks
     Boat Maintenance and Repair
     Chandleries

Fuel Dock
Grocery stores
Haul-out
Laundromat
Post Office
Restaurants

Attractions

Brooks Island, just across Point Potrero Reach from Point Potrero, has recently become part of the regional park system. This small, uninhabited island, once home for the Ohlones, is a short ride by dinghy from any of these marinas. With permission from the East Bay Regional Parks, you can go ashore to watch some of the over one hundred species of sea and shore birds sighted here or to hike around the approximately 2-mile-long island, but you'll want your boots. At low tide you'll be hiking in the mud!

As you walk out of the Brickyard Cove Marina parking lot, notice the two large kilns in front of the condominiums. Many of the bricks used for the reconstruction of San Francisco after the 1906 earthquake were fired here and then taken by ferry to the City.

On Dornan Road, south of the tunnel that was built in 1915 to accommodate the traffic to and from the Richmond-San Francisco ferry at Point Richmond is the Miller-Knox Regional Shoreline Park. It has paved walkways around a small saltwater lake seasonally populated by Canadian geese, snowy egrets, mallards, wood ducks, phalaropes, American coots, sandlings, and gulls of several species. At the north end of the park is a small swimming beach, heavily used on warm summer afternoons. Across from the park a nature trail climbs steeply to the ridge of the hill. But watch out for the poison oak thriving in this sunny terrain.

Across the street, too, is the Golden State Model Railroad Museum, 10,000 sq. feet of operating model trains of all major scales.

On Garrard Street, immediately north of the tunnel is the Richmond Plunge (or "Natatorium," as it is named above the entrance), built in 1924-25. Turn west in front of the natatorium, cross the railroad tracks laid down in 1895 by Santa Fe Railroad to ferry trains by barge from Richmond to San Francisco, and you'll be in downtown Point Richmond, where you will think you've taken a turn back in time.

Marina Bay, the most recent addition to this area's marine developments, has a history worthy of note. This complex of marina facilities and condominiums sits where once the world's largest shipyard sat, the Henry J. Kaiser Shipyard, which built over 500 Liberty ships during World War II.

BERKELEY
Chart #18649, #18652, or #18653

Berkeley is undoubtedly better known for its location as the first campus of the University of California, dating from 1873, than for its marina. But it does also have quite an inviting marina, and certainly the opportunity to spend time wandering around this unique city adds to the appeal.

Some citizens argued that the city should be named Peralta, for Luis Maria Peralta, whose 1820 Spanish land grant that he named Rancho San Antonio encompassed all this area, from San Leandro to El Cerrito.

Perhaps an even greater claim could have been made for naming the city for the Huichuins, earlier native residents who spoke one of the eight Ohlone languages. After the scout Ortega saw these shores, he reported back to Portolá that he saw smoke rising from countless villages. In fact, one of the area's largest middens, 300 feet across and over 20 feet deep, lies buried under the site of Spenger's restaurant on the north side of University Avenue.

But some citizens liked so well what George Berkeley, an English bishop, said—"Westward the course of empire takes its way"— that "Berkeley" the city was named.

Anytime the fog comes into San Francisco Bay, it eventually comes to rest up against the Berkeley hills. Hence, Berkeley has an abundance of foggy days. Still, residents echo what Mayor Stitt said in 1911: "Any kind of a day in Berkeley seems sweeter than the best day anywhere else."

Berkeley pier and the UC Berkeley campanile, two excellent landmarks

Approach

If you approach Berkeley from the south, go around the end of the old Berkeley pier before setting a course for the marina. The 3-mile-long Berkeley pier, now in ruins, is a navigational hazard. The city rebuilt a section of the pier extending 0.5 mile from shore, but the more than 2-mile section remaining, abandoned for over 50 years, is now only a row of pilings with gaps in it. Some boaters with local knowledge go between some of the visible pilings, but we strongly advise against this practice because other pilings remain upright below the water's surface.

Although the old Berkeley pier is a hazard, it is also an excellent navigational asset for first-time visitors to the Berkeley marina regardless of direction of approach. When you have identified the old pier, and have taken up a position on the north side of it, run in an easterly direction parallel to the pier. Stay at least 100 yards off the restored section of the pier because of the numerous fishing lines in the water; this is a well-used fishing pier.

The only other navigational hazards are the unlighted racing buoys in the area and Berkeley Reef. The nine unlighted racing buoys are easily visible during daylight hours but difficult to see at night except in bright moonlight. The location of these buoys is marked on your charts, of course, but essentially they are within 3 miles of the marina, extending from the Berkeley Pier almost to Brooks Island. Berkeley Reef is located 0.5 mile north of the entrance to the marina and 0.3 mile out from shore. It is marked by a lighted piling.

Local boaters often use Sather Tower, or the campanile, as a landmark when going to Berkeley Marina. The campanile is on the UC Berkeley campus, 3 miles almost directly east from the marina. From 5 miles out this tower stands out distinctly, and the marina is directly in a line between the southeast corner of Angel Island and the tower.

Berkeley Marina has well-lighted breakwaters at the entrance to minimize the effects of the constant waves that pound the east shore of San Francisco Bay in this area. Local boaters enter and exit the marina on either side of the breakwater located immediately at the entrance.

Berkeley Marina entrance, with campanile in background

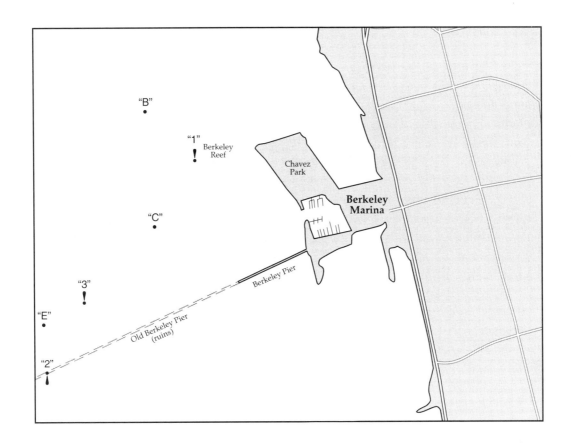

Anchorage

Berkeley Marina has no anchorage. The Berkeley Yacht Club has a guest dock at the Marina for reciprocal use by members of other yacht clubs. Otherwise, guest berthing is available from the Berkeley Marina Harbormaster by phone or VHF channel 16. The Marriott Inn also has a large amount of guest dock space available for restaurant customers.

Berkeley Yacht Club   510- 540-9167

Berkeley Marina Harbormaster   510-644-6376 and VHF 16

Marriott Inn   510-548-7920

Facilities

At the marina:
Boat Maintenance and Repairs
Bus Service
Chandlery
Fuel Dock (gasoline and diesel)
Grocery Store
Haul Out
Launch Ramp

Pump Out
Restaurants
Showers

All other services are available in the city of Berkeley, with excellent bus service at the marina.

Attractions

Berkeley Marina has three primary attractions: the pier, the 90-acre Cesar Chavez Park, and the Shorebird Nature Center. Berkeley has had a pier of some sort since Jacob's Landing, constructed in 1853. In 1926 the Golden Gate Ferry Company built a wooden automobile pier 3 miles long, where ferries picked up vehicles and their passengers to take them across the Bay. On the 0.5-mile concrete fishing pier that has replaced the old wooden pier, you can fish without a license. Smelt, striped bass, perch, sharks, skates, and rays are common here. Or you can get your aerobic exercise by walking out to the end of the pier against the fierce winds that often blow from the Bay into the marina.

The Cesar Chavez Park has a large central green where you can watch the kites flying. Circling this green is a 1-mile paved shore walk, along which wild flowers bloom in profusion in the spring.

The Shorebird Nature Center comprises The Adventure Playground, where children learn to create using hammers, saw, and nails, and The Nature Center, which has a 100-gallon aquarium, a touch table, and a cormorant display. The Playground is open daily in the summer between 1100 and 1600. The Center is open Tues.-Sat. 1000-1600.

Despite its relatively small size, the city of Berkeley has a large number of attractions because of the University of California campus. The campus itself is worth a walk around. Take a bus at the foot of University Avenue, ride about 3 miles, and you'll be at the campus. On this nearly 1,200-acre campus are a botanical garden, exhibits of art, anthropology, and science, and many striking and historically interesting campus buildings.

Stop at the Chamber of Commerce office, 1834 University Avenue, for a detailed map of the city and the campus.

EMERYVILLE
Chart #18649 or #18652

The two marinas at Emeryville—Emery Cove and Emeryville City—both welcome visiting yachts. Constructed between 1971 and 1974, the man-made spit of land sheltering these two has been turned into the national award-winning Waterfront Park, with a spectacular view of the San Francisco City Front and of sunsets over the City and Golden Gate Bridge.

Entering Emeryville Marina: Stay between the markers.

Approach

The entrance to Emeryville Marina lies between the east span of the Bay Bridge and the old Berkeley pier. When approaching from the west or north, identify the buoy 0.5 mile off the end of the Berkeley pier and set a course of 078° mag. The channel into the Emeryville marinas begins 2.0 miles from the buoy.

When approaching from the south, steer to the east of Yerba Buena Island and pass under the span of the Bay Bridge closest to the island. After clearing the bridge, set a course of 026° mag. for 2.2 miles to arrive at the Emeryville channel.

The entrance channel into Emeryville requires caution. Stay carefully inside the clearly marked channel, which has a depth of 6.0 feet at low water. When you reach the last two buoys, 5 and 6, make a hard starboard turn. From that last buoy to the seawall of the marina is only 150 yards. Do not turn before Buoy 6, or you will almost certainly run aground.

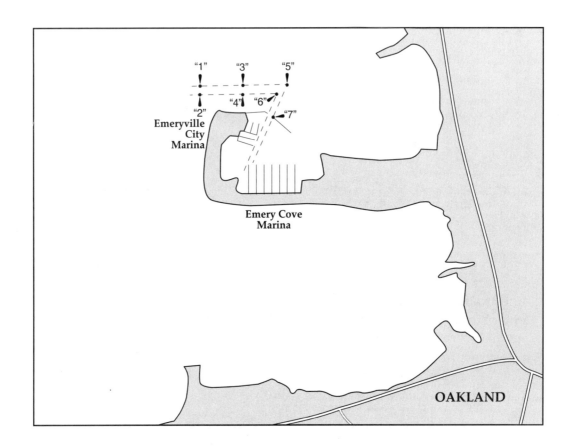

Anchorage

Emeryville has no open anchorage area. Emeryville City Marina, with 404 slips, is on your right as you pass through the breakwater. Ahead and to port as you pass the City Marina is Emery Cove Marina, with 430 slips. Observe the markers closely, and do not attempt to cut across from the breakwater to the Emery Cove Marina as that area is shallow.

Emeryville City Marina   510-654-3716 and VHF 16

Emery Cove Marina   510-428-0505

Facilities

At the marinas:
- Boat Maintenance and Repair
- Bus Service
- Chandlery
- Fuel Dock (gasoline and diesel)
- Launch Ramp
- Laundromat
- Pump Out
- Showers

Nearby:
- Bank
- Grocery stores
- Movie theatres
- Restaurants
- Shops

Piling sculpture in Emeryville

Attractions

Emeryville provides a low-key, peaceful, and quiet spot within a few hundred yards of most of the services boaters might need. A paved and board walkway traces the shoreline from Interstate 80 out to the end of the spit and then back up the other side. Walk through the parking lot at Trader Vic's restaurant to gain access to the boardwalk behind the condominiums on the north side of the spit. Along the boardwalk near the frontage road of I-80 is a row of whimsical sculptures on pilings in the shallow water.

Piling sculpture in Emeryville

A sidewalk passes under the freeway at the frontage road. Take this walk for one block (on Powell Avenue); then turn left on Christie, and after one more short block, you'll see the old Pacific Linen building on the right. The ground floor is a public market, with about 20 international food merchants, several small shops, a large bookstore, and two night clubs, one featuring live jazz music and the other Caribbean dance music. Across the street is a complex of 10 movie theatres.

CLIPPER COVE AND TREASURE ISLAND MARINA
Chart #18649 or #18652

Clipper Cove lies between Yerba Buena Island and Treasure Island, directly below the northeast span of the Bay Bridge as it disappears into the Yerba Buena tunnel. Yerba Buena (Spanish for "good herb") is a natural island, called "Goat Island" on earlier charts. The name "Yerba Buena" was given first to the cove that lay across the channel to the south on the peninsula, in that part of San Francisco known as the Embarcadero and bordered by Broadway and Harrison. Yerba Buena village was a busy landing, the settlement being renamed San Francisco in 1847. This once important cove had been largely filled in by 1851.

Lighthouse on south shore of Yerba Buena

Today, Yerba Buena Island is the site of a Coast Guard station. The Coast Guard has an installation on the east end of the island. You will see rescue boats tied up at the docks there.

Clipper Cove, sometimes called "Treasure Island" or "T. I.," is named for the China Clipper airplanes that used this cove as a base for their transPacific flights from 1939 to 1946. Fifty or more boats can anchor here in comfort, upwind of the traffic noise from the bridge high overhead. Frequently, groups of as many as 8 or 10 yachts raft together in these calm waters.

The Treasure Island Naval Base closed in September, 1997, and the City and County of San Francisco has assumed ownership of the

Approach to Clipper Cove from north

Treasure Island Marina. The marina, since renamed Treasure Isle Marina, is currently operated by Almar Marinas. As a result, the 100-berth marina is now open to the boating public.

Approach

The entrance to Clipper Cove is immediately north of the point at which the Bay Bridge meets Yerba Buena Island on the east side. The anchorage itself is approximately 0.25 mile wide and 0.50 mile long, but you won't see the anchorage until you are at the entrance.

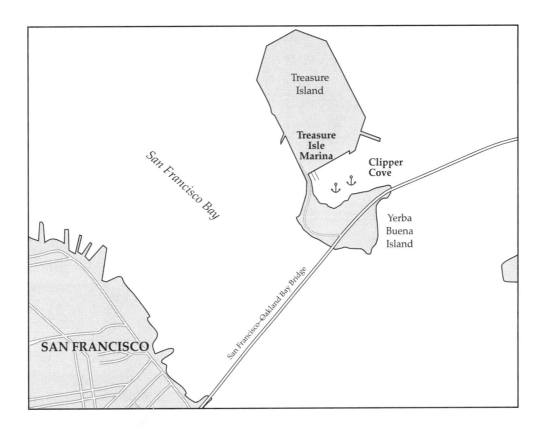

From the South Bay, pass under the bridge in the ship channel, which is below the first span east of Yerba Buena Island. The anchorage will appear to port immediately after you pass under the bridge, the Treasure Island marina being at the far end of the cove on the north side.

From the north, pass east of Treasure Island, steering for the same Bay Bridge span. The anchorage opens to starboard just after the Navy ship docks on the east side of the island.

Anchorage

A low spit connects Yerba Buena and Treasure islands, forming the west end of the anchorage. The entrance to the anchorage is

Anchorage at Clipper Cove

approximately 400 yards wide, but stay 300 yards from the Yerba Buena shore when entering because of shoaling. Anchor in 5 to 15 feet (blue-gray clay bottom). Lie to a single anchor here.

The shallowest water and best anchorage is on the southwest side of the cove, where you will have some shelter from the strong prevailing winds that blow over the spit to windward. If this favored spot is congested, select a spot well clear of the crowd. You can anchor safely anywhere in the cove in good holding and still water under most conditions. If the winds blow in excess of 30 knots, post an anchor watch because many anchors will refuse to hold, especially in the center of the anchorage area. The best holding in the cove appears to be along the north shore of Yerba Buena Island, which is the most protected area along the southern portion of the anchorage.

Facilities

At present, all the slips are rented out at Treasure Isle Marina, but the harbormaster will accommodate visiting boaters when space is available. Although construction has yet to begin, the marina plans to have a large guest dock in place this year and to enlarge the marina within the next two or three years.

Ashore from the marina is a modular head with showers for boaters docked at Treasure Isle. The Delancey Street Cafe is now open a short walk from the marina.

Treasure Isle Marina   415-981-2416 and VHF 16

Attractions

Treasure Island was constructed for the 1939 Golden Gate Exposition to celebrate the completion of the Golden Gate and San Francisco-Oakland Bay bridges. Some say the island's name derives from the title of Robert Louis Stevenson's adventure novel, others say from the traces of gold in the fill used to make the island, and still others say the name refers to the treasures from the Pacific Rim displayed in the Exposition. Three art deco buildings remain from the Exposition, one of them a museum which tells the story of the Exposition, of the China Clippers that used the Cove, and of the Navy's personnel and equipment. The original Farallon Island light, with its Fresnel lens, is displayed here. The museum closed recently but should reopen soon. Before planning a visit to the museum, call the harbormaster to be certain it has reopened.

If you're anchored in Clipper Cove, you may land a dinghy on the beach at the SW corner of the cove. Do not take your dinghy to the marina dock if you want to go ashore without first checking with the harbormaster (call on VHF 16). Since the gate providing access from the marina to the island is locked, you will need a key to get out of the marina as well as to get back to your dinghy.

8 THE SOUTH BAY

The horizon's edge, the flying sea-crow, the fragrance of salt marsh and shore mud. . . .
    —Walt Whitman, "There Was a Child Went Forth"

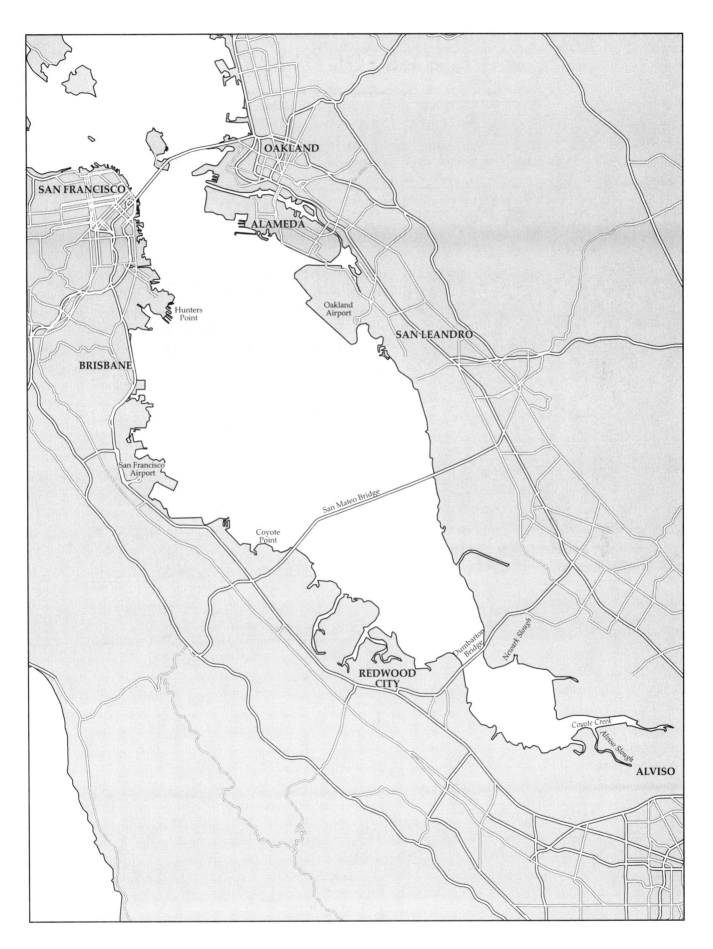

SAN FRANCISCO

OAKLAND

ALAMEDA

Hunters
Point

Oakland
Airport

SAN LEANDRO

BRISBANE

San Francisco
Airport

San Mateo Bridge

Coyote
Point

Dumbarton
Bridge

Newark Slough

REDWOOD
CITY

Coyote Creek

Alviso Slough

ALVISO

OAKLAND/ALAMEDA ESTUARY
Chart #18649, #18650, or #18652

Gantry cranes on the Estuary

As their names suggest, Oakland and Alameda ("poplar grove" in Spanish) attracted the attention of the European settlers in San Francisco Bay because of the abundance of trees. Redwoods covered the hills behind Oakland, and oaks, some reportedly spreading over half a city block, shaded the lower lands. Oakland's thriving lumber industry was made possible by the ease of transportation across the Bay to San Francisco. After the trees were gone, long before the end of the 19th century, the waterfronts of Oakland and Alameda grew even more fiscally prominent. Passenger ferries, railroad ferries, whalers' docks, shipyards, and military installations figured largely in the prosperity of these two cities. Today, towering white gantries stand like skeletons of Trojan horses along the Oakland shore, and through their innards pass thousands and thousands of containers, making this the largest container port on the Pacific Coast.

Plenty of harbor space remains for pleasure boaters and fishermen. The Port of Oakland boasts eight public marinas, and the Alameda shoreline has seven marinas and five yacht clubs, two with their own marinas.

Approach

Getting to the Oakland/Alameda Estuary is easy: just follow the boats. More boaters call the Estuary home than any other area in the Bay. The closest major point of reference is the Bay Bridge and Yerba Buena Island. The entrance to the Estuary is 1.1 miles almost due east of the southeast corner of Yerba Buena Island. Buoys show the limits of the channel. The only possible confusion is distinguishing the channel into the Estuary from the channels into the outer harbor and the middle harbor. Look closely at your chart, however, and the correct channel, the most southerly of the three, is easy to see.

For the first 2.5 miles of the channel, you will see huge ocean-going container ships loading and unloading. This is a busy harbor indeed. After that you will find seemingly endless marinas. The

Oakland/Alameda area contains more than 20 marinas, public and private, with well over 5,000 slips. Distinguishing one marina from another is difficult.

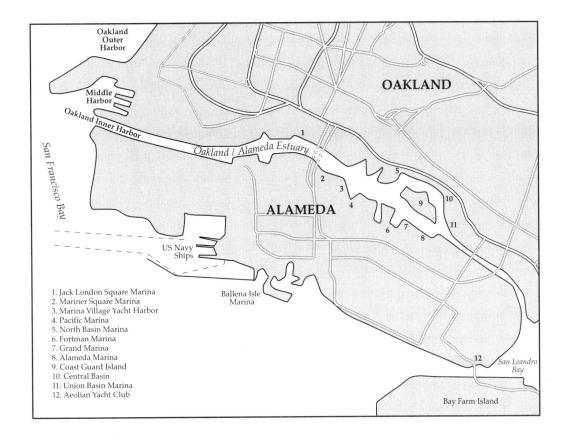

1. Jack London Square Marina
2. Mariner Square Marina
3. Marina Village Yacht Harbor
4. Pacific Marina
5. North Basin Marina
6. Fortman Marina
7. Grand Marina
8. Alameda Marina
9. Coast Guard Island
10. Central Basin
11. Union Basin Marina
12. Aeolian Yacht Club

Anchorage and Berthing

No recognized anchorage area exists in the Estuary. Some boaters occasionally anchor out for a night in the area, but they run the risk of interfering with the heavy ship and boat traffic or anchoring in water that is too shallow. The better option is to get a guest berth at one of the marinas or yacht clubs.

OAKLAND

The eight public marinas on the Oakland side of the Estuary are all under the aegis of the Port of Oakland. The location of each offers access to a different part of the city of Oakland.

JACK LONDON SQUARE MARINA
(PORT OF OAKLAND)

Jack London Square Marina is the first marina in the Estuary, 2.5 miles from Marker 6, the entrance into the Estuary. The marina begins immediately after the last of the large gantry cranes on the port side of the Estuary. Another excellent identifying feature is the huge American flag behind Scott's Seafood Restaurant that can be seen for 2 miles. Scott's is located in the middle of Jack London Marina.

Scott's Restaurant

DAVID DAWSON

This marina has four parts—West Basin, guest berths behind the Waterfront Hotel and Scott's, Central Basin, and East Basin. Call ahead to the Port of Oakland harbormaster to arrange guest berthing.

You can tie up without charge at the 150-foot-long guest dock behind Scott's Seafood Restaurant and go ashore for 4 hours maximum, on a first-come, first-served basis, without permission from the Port of Oakland harbormaster. The harbormaster frequently puts visiting boaters in the berths behind the Waterfront Hotel while they go on a 4-hour tour ashore. The harbormaster also assigns boaters to these slips on an overnight basis. The 4-hour stay is free but carefully monitored; the Port of Oakland charges a reasonable fee for overnight accommodations.

The *Potomac* under way on the Bay

Attractions

Jack London Square Marina is, as the name implies, at the center of the activities in Jack London Square. You can sit in your cockpit and watch the parade of boats on the Estuary or the parade of pedestrians on the sidewalks. Ashore, you can visit the relocated Jack London Klondike Gold Rush cabin; one of his Oakland haunts, the

Fruit market on Webster Street in Oakland

First and Last Chance Saloon, still welcomes patrons. Jack London Village, farther south, has a small museum devoted to London memorabilia.

You can also tour the *USS Potomac*, Franklin D. Roosevelt's presidential yacht that was rescued from the bottom of San Francisco Bay, restored to its former presidential but spartan style, and now permanently moored here. Another attraction for those who like boats is the largest Northern California boat show, held here twice a year, in January and in April.

Early every morning produce vendors bring fresh fruits and vegetables to warehouses along Webster Street, just up from the waterfront. They sell primarily wholesale, although retail customers are welcome to purchase wonderfully fresh produce here.

Numerous restaurants and shops occupy the waterfront, but if you want to venture farther ashore, you'll find public transportation to both Oakland and San Francisco. If you choose to wander even farther afield, Amtrak has a station close by.

Facilities

Bank
Boat Maintenance and Repair
Fuel Dock (gasoline and diesel)
Grocery Store
Launch Ramp
Public Transportation
Pump Out
Restaurants
Showers

EMBARCADERO COVE (PORT OF OAKLAND)

To get to the four marinas and the dock at Embarcadero Cove, proceed eastward down the Estuary 1 mile from the fuel dock at Jack

North Basin seen from the Estuary

London Marina to Coast Guard Island, and turn to port into Embarcadero Cove. The first marina, *North Basin II*, is located on the port side 0.3 mile from the entrance to the cove, and *North Basin I* is just beyond on the same side of the channel. North Basin guest docks are located between North Basin II and North Basin I. You can tie up at these guest docks without charge for 4 hours on a first-come, first-served basis.

Central Basin Marina (Embarcadero Cove Marina) is 0.35 mile beyond North Basin I in Embarcadero Cove. This is a particularly modern marina with great protection from the wind and surge. Visitors who stay at Central Basin can walk to West Marine, Quinn's Lighthouse, and other businesses.

Union Point Basin, although only 0.3 mile from Central Basin, cannot be reached directly because of the causeway connecting Coast Guard Island to Oakland. To get to Union Point Basin Marina, you must go back to the Estuary, turn to port, and go 0.8 mile. Union Point is located east of Coast Guard Island on the Oakland shoreline.

All the Embarcadero Cove marinas come under the jurisdiction of the Port of Oakland harbormaster. Guest berthing can be arranged in most of these marinas. Visitors receive free berthing for 4 hours at the North Basin Guest Docks. If you wish to stay longer, make arrangements with the Port of Oakland harbormaster.

Port of Oakland Harbormaster   510-272-1586 or
                                1-800-675-DOCK

Facilities

      Boat Maintenance and Repair
      Grocery Store
      Launch Ramp
      Public Transportation

Pump Out
Restaurants
Showers

Note! *Quinn's Lighthouse,* a restaurant located immediately east of Central Basin, provides guest berthing for lunch or dinner patrons at the dock on the east side of Quinn's. Call ahead to reserve space.

Attractions

The atmosphere at the Embarcadero Cove marinas contrasts sharply with that at Jack London Square. The marinas here are small and secluded, away from all the bustle of the Square, with little traffic, either boat or foot. A picnic area ashore is in keeping with the less urban feel of these marinas.

ALAMEDA

Alameda, in 1795 a grove of trees in the southern part of Contra Costa County, was part of Rancho San Antonio, the enormous Peralta rancho that covered much of the *contra costa,* that is, the coast opposite San Francisco. Like all the *contra costa,* Alameda was first a source of wood for the San Francisco market. The hamlet of Alameda began in 1850, when two men leased 160 acres for peach orchards. Two other hamlets, Encinal and Woodstock, arose to become eventually one with the city of Alameda, by the end of the century a popular resort area because of its sandy beach and sunny days. San Franciscans rented cottages here for the summer, many of them spending their days at the "Coney Island of the West," Neptune Beach, where they could swim in one of the country's largest swimming pools, thrill to carnival rides, or watch prize fights and baseball games.

Before 1902 Alameda was a peninsula, its marshy eastern shore connecting to the mainland where the Estuary today flows into San Leandro Bay. The opening of the Tidal Canal elicited a two-day carnival. Contemporary boaters circumnavigate Alameda each New Year's Day.

The island of Alameda is particularly accommodating for cruising sailors. In addition to its seven marinas (six on the Estuary) and five yacht clubs, Alameda has a wide array of marine shops and chandleries. The compactness of the city facilitates your getting about on foot to visit one of the city's many parks, view some of the 3,500 Victorian homes, or shop along Park Street. Ten 19th century "Red Train" stations scattered around the island are commercial centers today, housing shops and service centers of various sorts. The "Red Trains" circled the island, taking commuters to the ferry boats on the west end. The surviving stations vary from several buildings at an intersection to twenty buildings comprising two blocks.

MARINER SQUARE MARINA

Mariner Square Marina, the marina on the Alameda shoreline nearest the mouth of the Estuary, is almost directly opposite Oakland's Jack London Square Marina. Locate the marina by identifying the Rusty Pelican, a one-time favorite eating establishment that closed its doors a few years ago. The brown building with its name emblazoned in huge white letters stands out clearly. Mariner Square Marina's 132 docks almost completely surround the Rusty Pelican building.

Mariner Square Harbormaster 510-521-2727

Facilities Nearby

    Boat Maintenance and Repair
    Grocery Store
    Haul Out
    Laundromat
    Launch Ramp
    Public Transportation
    Pump Out
    Restaurants

Rusty Pelican Restaurant at Mariner Square

MARINA VILLAGE YACHT HARBOR

If you continue eastward 0.5 mile from the Rusty Pelican, you will come to Marina Village. Marina Village Yacht Harbor has 744 berths, making it the largest marina on the Estuary. Guest berthing is available in front of the Tied House, a popular waterfront restaurant.

Marina Village Harbormaster   510-521-0905 and VHF 16

Attractions

The site of this marina has a long nautical history, having been occupied by the Bethlehem Steel Company, Shipbuilding Division for many years. This extensive and attractive complex is now the setting for commercial establishments, apartments, and condominiums. A shoreline park with good hiking and biking trails is nearby.

Facilities Nearby

> Grocery Store
> Laundromat
> Public Transportation
> Pump Out
> Restaurant
> Showers

PACIFIC MARINA

Immediately east of Marina Village, Pacific Marina has 210 berths, all owned and managed by the Oakland Yacht Club. The club welcomes visiting boaters from other yacht clubs.

At the eastern end of Pacific Marina, Encinal Yacht Club, one of the oldest in the Bay Area, having incorporated in 1890 to cater to the owners of boats smaller than those prevailing at the San Francisco Yacht Club, has a club building and dock. The club has no slips, but visiting club members are invited to stay on the guest dock in front of the yacht club.

> Pacific Marina (Oakland Y C) Harbormaster   510-522-6868
>
> Encinal Yacht Club   510-522-3272

FORTMAN MARINA

Eastward beyond Pacific Marina another 0.3 mile, past Encinal Basin, is Fortman Marina. Fortman Marina has a history almost as lengthy as that of Encinal Yacht Club, though its inception was in response to the needs of commercial fishing boats rather than those of pleasure boats. From 1904 to 1929 the Alaska Packers Association had a yard ashore of Fortmann Basin and had laid up here between seasons the last great West Coast fleet of square riggers.

Marina personnel provide guest berthing when they have empty slips.

Alameda Yacht Club is located in Fortman Marina. The harbormaster will provide guest berthing for visiting yacht club members if slips are available.

Fortman Marina

Fortman Marina Harbormaster   510-522-9080 and VHF 16

Alameda Yacht Club   510-865-KNOT

Facilities

> Launch Ramp
> Laundromat
> Mini-mart
> Public Transportation
> Pump Out
> Showers

GRAND MARINA

Grand Marina is 300 yards east from Fortman Marina. Grand has two easily identifiable landmarks for boaters visiting for the first time: The name *Grand Marina* has been painted on the warehouse and is clearly readable from the Estuary. The second landmark is the fuel dock with the two-story office and small market over the water.

The Estuary's newest marina, Grand is in many ways grand indeed: It has more facilities than any other marina on the Estuary. A former tinned-salmon warehouse, the last surviving building of the Alaska Packers Association, houses shops and reminds one of the grand and varied maritime past of the Estuary.

Grand Marina Harbormaster   510-865-1200 and VHF 71

Facilities

> Boat Maintenance and Repair
> Deli / Mini-mart
> Fuel Dock (gasoline and diesel)
> Haul Out
> Launch Ramp
> Laundromat (restricted use)
> Public Transportation
> Pump Out
> Restaurants
> Showers

ALAMEDA MARINA

Since Alameda Marina is immediately east of Grand Marina, you can use the same landmarks that make Grand Marina easy to find—the fuel dock and the words *Grand Marina* on the Warehouse. In addition, the name *Svendsen's* on a warehouse behind the marina gives boaters one more landmark.

Island Yacht Club has facilities in Alameda Marina, immediately in front of Svendsen's Boat Works.

Alameda Marina

Alameda Marina Harbormaster   510-521-1133

Island Yacht Club   510-521-2980

Facilities

Boat Maintenance and Repair
Grocery Store
Haul Out
Laundromat
Launch Ramp
Public Transportation
Pump Out
Restaurants

AEOLIAN YACHT CLUB

Aeolian Yacht Club is unquestionably the most difficult destination to reach in the estuary. If you continue eastward down the Estuary, through the Park Street, Fruitvale, and High Street bridges, you will eventually arrive at Aeolian Yacht Club. Be very careful if you decide to visit Aeolian, however, because the channel shown on the decide to visit Aeolian, however, because the channel shown on the charts must be followed exactly or you will certainly go aground. Aeolian normally has empty slips for visiting yacht club members.

Aeolian Yacht Club   510-523-2586

Facilities

Grocery Store (about 1 mile)
Showers

Attractions

This small, friendly yacht club will afford you an opportunity to explore Bay Farm Island (not an island at all but a peninsula). A footbridge immediately south of the yacht club crosses over to the island, where you can hike along a trail tracing the waterfront to the northeast. At the terminus of this trail begins the Martin Luther King Jr. Regional Shoreline, which runs for several miles along the shore of San Leandro Bay.

The footbridge also leads to Island Drive, where the Alameda Municipal Golf Course extends for several blocks on the left side. A turn to the right on Bridgeway and then a second right on Packet Landing Road will take you to Shoreline Park. A fair-sized shopping center is about a mile from the yacht club on this street.

BALLENA BAY (Ballena Isle Marina)
Chart #18649 or #18652

Ballena ("whale") Bay, on the south shore of the island of Alameda, today bears few signs of its namesake. The whaling industry that figured prominently in the early European settlement of Alameda started in California during the mid-1850s, when two stations, one at Monterey and one at Crescent City, began operations. By the 1870s seventeen whaling stations were operating along the California Coast. Whaling ships laid up between seasons in the Oakland Estuary, on the opposite side of Alameda from Ballena Bay.

Approach

Whether boaters approach Ballena Isle Marina from north, south, or west, the Alameda Naval Air Station simplifies identification. The ships, especially the aircraft carriers, and the large buff-colored buildings make the NAS easily recognizable. Coming from the north or west, identify the Buoy 2 at the entrance channel into the NAS, set a course of 90° mag. from that buoy, and go 2.85 miles to the marina. On this approach, avoid getting too close to the shore. The area within 0.4 mile of now closed Alameda Naval Air Station is no longer off limits, but the area close to the breakwater of the marina has shoal water.

Just south of the base is a small boat launch ramp beside the Encinal High School ball field. South of the high school a large housing complex with two- and three-story beige-colored buildings

Ballena Bay tower at entrance

stands out. The canal beside the housing is not the entrance into Ballena Isle, but rather the entrance into another housing development. The entrance into Ballena Isle is south of the breakwater that encloses the marina. A tower is located in the water 0.35 mile southeast of the harbor entrance.

Those boaters approaching Ballena Isle from the south can use the Oakland Airport to help them identify the marina.

Ballena Bay approach

The entrance is 4.5 miles northwest of the Oakland Airport hangars and control tower. To avoid shoaling and underwater obstructions, boaters should stay at least 1.25 miles offshore when coming north from San Leandro.

The breakwater on the port side as you enter the marina has markers and lights. On the starboard side four red buoys indicate the right side of the channel. Shoal water awaits those who go outside the channel.

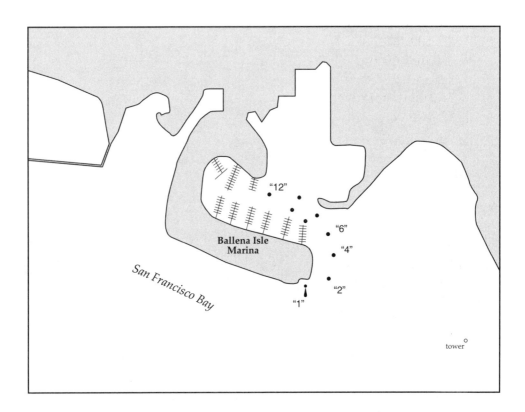

Anchorage and Berthing

No adequate anchorage area exists in the immediate area. Sailboats do occasionally anchor in the small bay just inside the harbor, but shallow water and poor holding make this anchorage untenable. Recently some boats in here dragged anchor and were badly damaged or destroyed.

Ballena Isla Marina is modern, and the harbor personnel are accommodating. The guest dock is at the extreme west end of the harbor, adjacent to the fuel dock. Many boaters consider the weather at Ballena Isle the best in the Bay.

Boaters can get free guest berthing at the marina while they have lunch or dinner at the Whale's Tail Restaurant, and those belonging to a yacht club can use reciprocal privileges to stay overnight if they arrange ahead with the harbormaster.

Harbormaster   1-800-675-SLIP or VHF 16

Ballena Bay Yacht Club   1-510-523-2292

Facilities

At the Marina:
    Boat Maintenance and Repair
    Deli / groceries
    Fuel dock (diesel and gas)
    Haul Out
    Launch Ramp
    Laundry
    Public Transportation
    Pump Out
    Restaurant
    Showers
In Alameda, approximately 1 mile, all other facilities available.

Attractions

Like the Estuary, where the whaling ships of the last century laid up, sunny Ballena Bay makes an excellent layover spot for cruising pleasure boats. It's far enough away from town to be relatively quiet, yet all the city facilities of Alameda are easily accessible by moderate walks or short bus rides.

Directly east of the marina are the sandy beaches of the Crown Memorial State Beach, formerly the site of Neptune Beach. The city restored the beach, badly eroded by wind and water, in 1982. You will spot people here several hundred yards offshore, walking in the warm, shallow water. This beach is a fairly easy and certainly a most pleasant walk from the marina. Walk up to Central, turn right, and then on your right, just before Crown Drive, take the public shore walk (0.6 mile from the marina). Another five-minute walk along the water will afford you a view of the shorebirds on the rocks and of the attractive landscaping of the condominiums.

Just inside Crown Memorial State Beach, the Crab Cove Visitors Center has some fine exhibits of both the human and the natural history of Alameda. Farther on, you'll find playground equipment, tennis and basketball courts, barbecue pits and picnic tables, and extensive trails. On a low-tide Saturday in June, the Sand Castle and Sand Sculpture Contest takes place in front of the bathhouse on the beach.

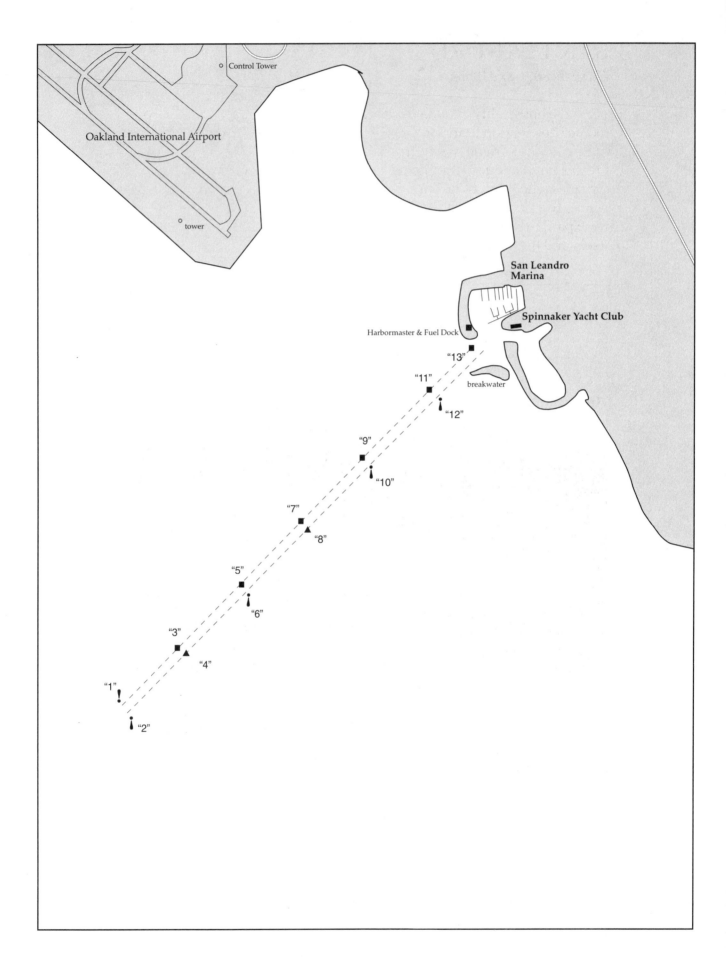

Control Tower

Oakland International Airport

tower

San Leandro
Marina

Spinnaker Yacht Club

Harbormaster & Fuel Dock

"13"

"11"

breakwater

"12"

"9"

"10"

"7"

"8"

"5"

"6"

"3"

"4"

"1"

"2"

SAN LEANDRO
Chart #18651 or #18652

If hospitality is what you're looking for, you'll scarcely find a likelier destination than San Leandro. Named after St. Leander, a bishop of Seville, this friendly city has retained many of its links to the past. Oyster shell mounds, some as old as 3,000 years, remind us of the Ohlones who hunted the once-plentiful game, trapped fish in nets strung across the sloughs, and dug oysters in the mud flats. The heritage of the Spaniards remains in the names of streets, parks, schools, the city itself, and the historical landmark homes. The names of Don Luis Peralta

Spinnaker Yacht Club dock with guest boats

and Don Jose Joaquin Estudillo, who camped here in 1772 and who later established land grant ranchos, are particularly prominent in San Leandro. Roberts' Landing and Mulford Point signify the arrival of European Americans who prospered in the freighting, grain, and oyster businesses in the second half of the 19th century.

Today, San Leandro has one of the most modern and accommodating small boat harbors in the Bay. The public marina gives guest boats the first night free, with subsequent nights for a nominal fee. This welcoming attitude carries over to the marina personnel, who walk the docks and generally make themselves accessible to both permanent and visiting boaters. The Spinnaker Yacht Club members are no less hospitable. When we came alongside the club's guest dock,

Shallows await those who stray at San Leandro.

two club members hustled down to the dock to help us tie up (a bit of a challenge in strong prevailing afternoon wind blowing us away from the dock) and to warn us we'd be sitting in the mud at low tide (a condition which sailors in this part of the Bay take as a matter of course, not a cause for alarm). The next morning we had breakfast in the cockpit, our boat listing slightly in the mud. As we watched a mallard hen and her ten ducklings feeding in the shallows, a club members came down to tell us he had opened the club so we could take showers.

Approach

With the haze and fog that often obscure vision in San Francisco Bay, you may be unable to see the markers into San Leandro Marina until you are within 1 mile. We used GPS to help us locate the entrance. The crew of *Maluhia,* a boat cruising with us at the time, used radar and located the channel markers from 5 miles away. Loran and SatNav can also be effective. If you rely on a compass and a knotlog, plot a course that keeps you well clear of danger, and steer carefully.

One natural obstruction in the approach to this marina is the San Bruno Shoal. Boaters have been going aground on this shoal for years. Its approximate location is halfway between the entrance to San Leandro Marina and the San Francisco Airport. Identify it on the chart before you depart.

Boaters generally use three reference points to plot a course to San Leandro. Coming from the north, identify Buoy 1 approximately 1 mile off San Francisco's Central Basin and set a southwesterly course for 8.7 miles. Another course is the ship channel 1.5 miles south of Hunters Point Naval Base. From buoys 1 and 2, set an easterly course to the marina and go 5.7 miles. The third approach is from the entrance buoy at Coyote Point Marina. The entrance into San Leandro Marina is 6.3 miles on a 030° mag. course. All these courses skirt the dreaded San Bruno Shoal.

A number of objects on shore help identify the marina. To the south of the entrance rise the buff-colored Coyote Hills; some boaters find them most distinctive and helpful. The huge hangars and control tower of the Oakland Airport 1.5 miles north of San Leandro Marina are easily visible from 3 miles offshore, long before the channel markers. Watch the depth as you approach San Leandro. If you fail to make a visual identification of the entrance and are off course, you will go aground.

Although the entrance to San Leandro Marina is bounded by shallow water, the 2-mile long channel has a depth of 7 feet. Stay in the clearly marked channel. We saw one boater who had wandered out of the channel; he was standing alongside his listing boat in ankle deep water for a long while waiting for the tide to come back in and float the boat off the mud.

Anchorage and Berthing

Shoals build up on both sides of the entrance, so stay in the center of the channel. At the end of the channel, the Spinnaker Yacht Club is directly off your port bow. The open basin to the south of the yacht club might appear to be an anchorage, but the depths are not adequate. You will need to tie up at a dock for your visit to San Leandro.

The Spinnaker Yacht Club has a long guest dock on the south side of the south dike protecting the marina. The San Leandro Marina is on the north side of this dike, to your port after you pass Mulford Point on West Dike. This large, modern marina has 455 berths, and the harbormaster welcomes guest boaters. Maximum liveaboard time in the marina is 2 days; if you plan to stay longer and want to stay on your boat, consult the harbormaster. San Leandro Yacht Club has a guest dock and club house in the northeasst corner of the harbor.

Harbormaster	800-559-7245
Spinnaker Yacht Club	510-351-7905
San Leandro Yacht Club	510-351-3102

Facilities

At the Marina
Fuel Dock (gasoline and diesel)
Hoist
Launch Ramp
Pump Out
Restaurants
Showers

Nearby (0.5-1.0 mile)
Bank
Grocery Store
Laundromat
Post Office
Public Transportation

Attractions

Two public golf courses on the east side of the San Leandro Harbor effectively constitute a greenbelt, lending the harbor a pastoral atmosphere despite its proximity to a busy city of over 70,000 people. On both the West Dike and the narrow grassy finger of land ending in Faro Point, at the south entrance to the harbor, are sections of the Bay Trail. On this south finger of Marina Park are 18 fitness stations. Hikers may walk for miles north or south on this trail. South along the shore past marshes filled with American avocets, black-necked stilts, snowy plovers, and Forster's terns, follow the San Lorenzo Trail to Roberts' Landing, in the late 19th century one of the South Bay's most important ports for scow schooners that transported hay and produce to San Francisco. To the north the trail leads to Neptune Street, then continues through the Oyster Bay Regional Shoreline, a 157-acre park atop a former garbage dump. Don't be put off by the site's past. The hillside now hosts fields of wild fennel and mustard, swallowtail and painted ladies butterflies, and soaring black-shouldered kites and red-tailed hawks. Those fascinated by aviation can sit in the grass and watch the planes coming and going at Oakland International Airport.

A long walk (about 4 miles) or a short bus ride will take you to the heart of town, where you can stroll along a portion of the original El Camino Real and through a neighborhood settled by Portuguese immigrants who had cherry orchards here. Check out Little Shul, built in 1889, the oldest synagogue still standing in Northern California, and visit the Southern Pacific Railroad Station built in 1898, twenty-nine years after the first transcontinental railroad went through San Leandro. You can also locate several other sites of historic interest—homes, parks, churches—clustered around the downtown area.

NEWARK SLOUGH

Chart #18651 or #18652

Newark Slough, now part of the 23,000-acre San Francisco Bay National Wildlife Refuge, was during the 1800s an important access route for Mission San Jose and then later for the town of Newark. In the

1850s John Johnson built a system of levees through these marshes to contain the salty water from the Bay in evaporation ponds. He began what remains a thriving industry in the South Bay, the production of salt. Previous to Johnson's enterprise, salt was a precious and expensive commodity in this part of the world. The Refuge still leases some of these wetlands as salt evaporation ponds.

Sign at Newark Slough

Newark Slough has long been a destination for boaters in the South Bay. However, as the natural sedimentation continues, the water depth becomes increasing suspect for boats with drafts of 5 and 6 feet. Without local knowledge, you may decide to do as we did and anchor outside the mouth of the slough and take a small boat up the slough.

Approach

After you pass under the San Mateo Bridge and then the Dumbarton Bridge (85 feet vertical clearance), you will pass through the old abandoned railroad bridge, now locked in the open position. From the Dumbarton Bridge, 0.65 mile away, the passageway through the railroad bridge looks minimal, but it has a horizontal clearance of 125 feet.

Dumbarton railroad bridge

After clearing the railroad bridge, set a course for Marker 16, approximately 090° mag., and go 1.1 miles. If you elect not to take your larger boat into the slough, anchor out of the channel near the marker in 10-12 feet of water. Holding is good, but you are in a somewhat exposed position. If the winds pipe up, you could have a rough anchorage.

South Bay boaters have taken their boats into Newark Slough for years and consider it one of the finest anchorages in the area. To get to the entrance of the slough from Marker 16, set a course of 300° mag. for approximately 0.35 mile. A piece of 4-inch PVC pipe sticking out of the water designates the entrance to the channel between the mudflats. Keep this pipe to port as you navigate this narrow channel. Water depth at low water is a scant 1 foot, so the only time to enter with a deep-draft boat is at high tide, and then you'll be trapped until the next high tide.

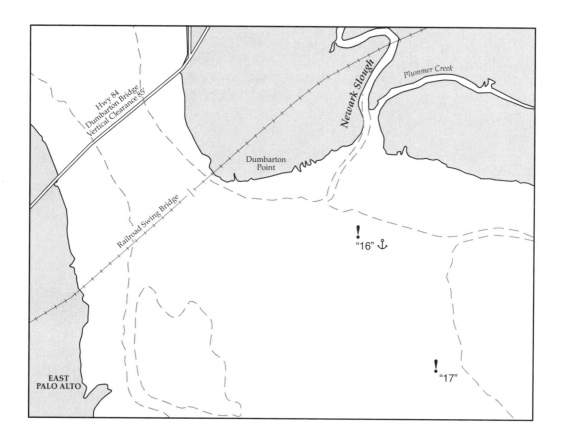

Anchorage

If you decide to anchor inside Newark Slough, the best anchorage area in the slough is about 0.7 mile up the slough from the PVC marker. When you travel from the PVC marker at the entrance of the channel, the area on each side of the channel will be under water, so it will appear to be almost a mile wide. But be aware that the channel is no more than 50 feet wide in most places. We recommend taking a sport boat in ahead of the larger boat if you decide to anchor in Newark Slough, sounding as you go. We use a Depthstick (a portable depth sounder) to determine the deepest area when we are in waters we know are shallow.

You can easily recognize the best anchorage area by studying your chart carefully. The water depths increase as you go farther up the slough. As you proceed, it narrows until you are traveling up a slough that is no more than 200 feet from the tule bank on one side to the tule bank on the other. While the depths near the marker at the entrance to Newark Slough are about 1 foot at low water, the depths in the anchorage area are closer to 7 feet.

Although the channel from the Bay into Newark Slough looks easily recognizable on the chart, you will find it totally invisible from the Bay or from inside the Slough. The only time you will be able to see the channel will be at extreme low water when the mudflats on either side of the channel are exposed, and then the channel will be too shallow for you to make the passage. The narrowing tule grass at the back of the bay will give you an indication of where to go up the channel. Another problem that convinces many people not to attempt this anchorage is the difficulty of finding the channel when they are returning to the South Bay. Without binoculars, the PVC marker is invisible until you are far down the channel toward the Bay.

CAUTION! If you decide to take your deep draft boat up the slough, do so just before high water. There is not enough water to enter the slough except at high water, and in case you go aground, you will want to have enough time to get off before the tide goes out. Experienced cruisers warn that you should proceed at a dead slow speed to avoid driving your boat hard aground in case you get out of the channel.

Facilities

None

Attractions

For many sailors from either the San Francisco Bay Area or outside the area, exploring these waters near the southernmost terminus of the Bay is a treat in itself. Little traffic passes this way now, though such was not the case when Moffett Field, across the Bay and south of Newark Slough, had a busy port where barges transported aircraft fuel up Guadalupe Slough. Pleasure and fishing boats that were moored in the Palo Alto Yacht Harbor, no longer accessible to boats because the city has ceased dredging the channel, also kept these waters busier than they are today.

Other than the tranquility and isolation of this anchorage, the great attraction is the excursion up the slough. You'll see seals by the hundreds, sunning in the cordgrass at water's edge, an unusual sight to those accustomed to seeing seals on rocks or sand beaches. Large flocks of willets stand in the marshes nearby and fly up in dizzying M. C. Escher patterns of black and white as you pass. American avocets, blacknecked stilts, and Forster's terns nest here. In the fall and winter, you'll see migrating waterfowl, such as greater scaups, surf scoters, Northern pintails, ruddy ducks, and Northern shovelers. Dilapidated hunting blinds visible above the pickleweed attest to the popularity of this site for waterfowl hunting. (Waterfowl hunting is still permitted in Newark Slough south of the Hetch Hetchy aqueduct, roughly from mid-October to mid-January.)

Seals in Newark Slough

ALVISO
Chart #18651 or #18652

     This port, on the National Register of Historic Places and adjoining the extensive San Francisco Bay National Wildlife Refuge, certainly merits a visit, but some of you more conservative boaters may elect to make that visit by land rather than by water. The slough leading to what was the port of entry to San Jose before the coming of the railroad, and therefore once one of the busiest ports on the Bay, is now a challenge for even the smallest of pleasure boats. A combination of natural sedimentation and the loss of industrial importance has rendered the Alviso waterfront a relic of its busy past.

     In 1840 Ignacio Alviso moved from Santa Clara Mission to the site of the present day Alviso, then a part of his 6,353-acre Rancho de los Esteros. From this port beaver pelts, cattle hides, and tallow went to San Francisco. In 1851 four U. S. citizens purchased the land surrounding the port and named their nascent city "Alviso." For the next 35 years this active port supplied redwood, grain, and produce to Northern California. The railroad completed in 1884 between San Francisco and San Jose bypassed Alviso and thus effectively ended this port's commercial usefulness. Between 1907 and 1936 the Bayside Cannery brought renewed prosperity to Alviso. By 1920 this cannery was the third largest in the country.

     Many wells were dug near these shores of the South Bay in the late 19th century to irrigate the orchards and fields and to provide water for the burgeoning population. The result was land subsidence averaging 11 feet. Flooding became commonplace for Alviso. Cord-weed surrounds the remnants of the docks and the derelict boats sinking into the silt at the defunct marina. The South Bay Yacht Club maintains its docks (though the boats sit in the mud at low tide) and continues with an active membership.

Alviso Marina

Approach

A cruise to Alviso, at the southernmost end of San Francisco Bay, offers all the adventure many boaters could ask for. To get to Alviso, pass under the Dumbarton Bridge, go through the old railroad bridge one mile east, and proceed down the Bay, carefully observing the channel markers. The first marker, #16, marks the entrance to Mowry Slough, to your port about 0.65 mile east of Marker 16.

From Marker 16, change course to approximately southeast and proceed past markers 17 and 18 to Marker 20, where Guadalupe Slough exits from the San Francisco Bay. Water depths are 10 feet or more in the channel as far as Marker 20, where the Bay becomes Coyote Creek. Continue northeast for 1.3 miles to the intersection of Alviso Slough, which exits to starboard immediately after you pass under the overhead power cables. Local boaters state that Alviso Slough exits from Coyote Creek 50 feet from the southernmost tower in the creek. The area by the old pier to starboard is shoal. Look carefully at your chart before entering.

Some boaters choose to anchor west of the intersection and use their tenders to make the 3.3-mile trip to the town of Alviso, tying up at either the South Bay Yacht Club dock or alongside the launch ramp at the marina. One member of the yacht club had had his 100-foot boat anchored at this intersection for six months when we recently visited Alviso.

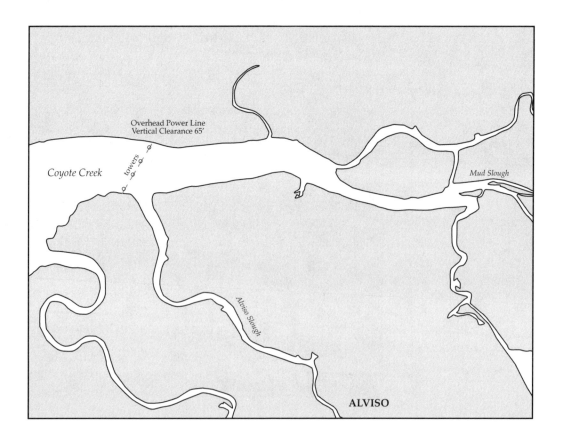

If you decide to take your boat to Alviso, plan your trip to coincide with a high tide; some locals suggest making the trip only when the tide is 6 feet or greater. Then, boats with even a 7-foot draft can make the trip without difficulty. (Though plans are on the table to dredge the slough into Alviso, a date for the dredging has not been set, so don't postpone your trip waiting for that date.) Follow the slough slowly, watching your depth. As if you were transiting a river, swing wide at the turns, which tend to silt on the inside. Going aground and getting off quickly are commonplace on this trip. We recently spoke with members of the Peninsula Yacht Club in Redwood City about their club cruise to Alviso. Apparently, only one of the boats, a sailboat with a 6-foot draft, went aground on the trip. Club members reported they got the boat off the soft mud easily and continued on with their great adventure.

Anchorage and Berthing

You can anchor along Alviso Slough almost anywhere between Coyote Creek and the town of Alviso, but expect to sit in the mud, particularly at low tide. South Bay boaters experience neither surprise nor alarm when they feel their boats settle into the mud at low tide when they are at anchor. The closer you get to Alviso, the shallower the water in the slough. For that reason many boats with deep drafts anchor a mile or more from the docks in Alviso.

Few remaining slips in Alviso

If you wish to tie up to a dock, you can stay for two or three days at South Bay Yacht Club. The guest dock there has enough space for two or three boats, and many more can be accommodated by rafting up. Be sure to call ahead to reserve space.

South Bay Yacht Club   408-263-0100

Facilities

Chandlery
Grocery Store
Launch Ramp (at high tide only)
Laundromat
Post Office
Restaurants
Showers

Attractions

The history of Alviso lives in the several buildings remaining from its glory days. And they're all within easy walking distance of the dock. Several buildings are reminiscent of this port's earlier prosperity, including the old Wade warehouse, cannery buildings, and the Tilden House. The town has numerous seafood and Mexican restaurants to sample as you walk around the streets of Alviso.

Shorebirds feeding in Alviso Slough show shallows.

The serious hikers will find a real treasure of a trail here: the 9-mile loop on levees along the east side of Alviso Slough, along the south side of Coyote Creek, and across Triangle Marsh back to Alviso. From this trail you can see great egrets, blue herons, white pelicans, and dark-crested night herons that nest here. Avocets, stilts, and willets feed in the exposed mud at low tide. You can also get a good look at the geography of the area, with views of the salt ponds and salt "mountains," of the Santa Cruz Mountains to the west and the East Bay hills to the north, and tiny Station Island (or Drawbridge Island) to the northeast. Pick up this trail at the east end of the marina parking lot.

You may prefer to explore with your boat's tender or the increasingly popular sea kayak. If you've brought your boat all the way up Alviso Slough, you can take the smaller boat back out the slough to Coyote Creek, turn to the starboard and go over to Station Island, the setting for the ghost town of Drawbridge, where two hand-operated drawbridges built by South Pacific Coast Railway in 1876 were the seeds of a town. Hunters soon discovered this paradise of waterfowl; and hunting, along with fishing, swimming, and boating, led to the development of a small town by the turn of the century. Today, no permanent residents remain on the island. Ranger-led tours during the summer months provide the only access for visitors onto the island. You can see the town from Coyote Creek, but be aware that the water in the creek is too shallow for even a sportboat or sea kayak unless you stay in the channel or make the trip at high tide.

One other worthwhile destination for those who cruise to Alviso is the San Francisco Bay National Wildlife Refuge Visitor Center. The Visitor Center is a good place to get on the trails out into the Refuge. The Center is a healthy walk, almost 2 miles from town, but the naturalists there will willingly provide you with information about the wildlife in the area.

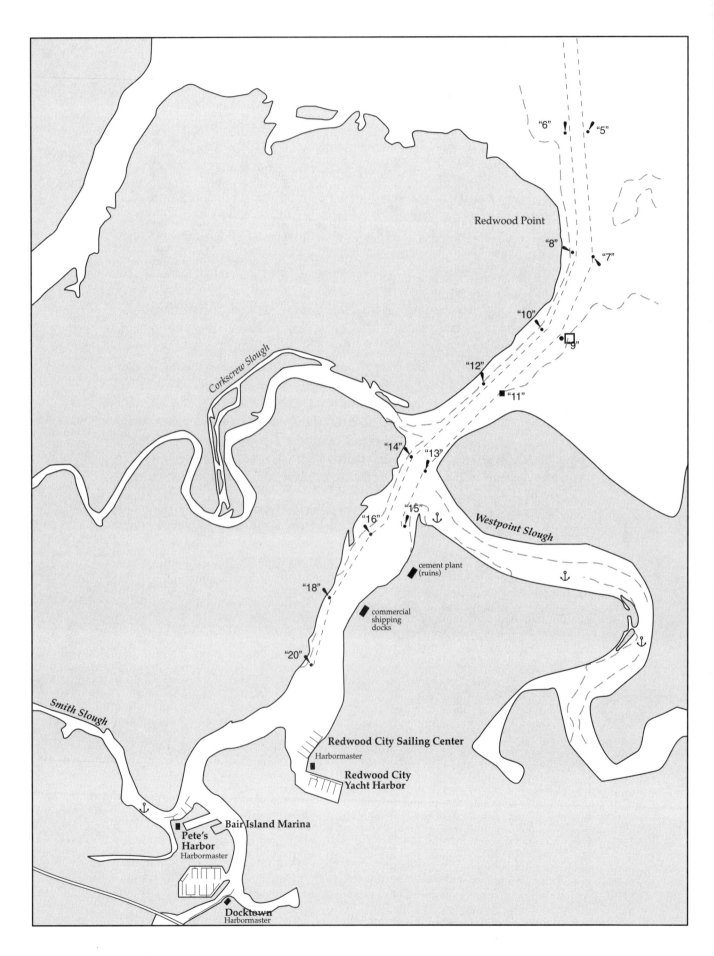

"6"
"5"

Redwood Point

"8"
"7"

"10"
"9"

Corkscrew Slough

"12"
"11"

"14"
"13"

Westpoint Slough

"15"
"16"

cement plant
(ruins)

"18"

commercial
shipping
docks

"20"

Smith Slough

Redwood City Sailing Center
Harbormaster

Redwood City
Yacht Harbor

Bair Island Marina

Pete's
Harbor
Harbormaster

Docktown
Harbormaster

REDWOOD CITY
Chart #18651 or #18652

Rancho Las Pulgas ("the fleas"), comprising the land between the Bay and the coastal range bounded by San Mateo Creek and San Francisquito Creek, was the Spanish land grant of Jose Dario Arguello. Cattle—with fleas that didn't always confine themselves to the cattle—cropped the grasses growing below the redwood forests on the mountainside. The redwood trees gave impetus to the building of the Port of Redwood City.

Redwood City continues to be the site of an important commercial port in San Francisco Bay. Whereas its earliest commercial purpose was for the shipment of redwoods, first to San Francisco and up the river to Sacramento and later overseas, primarily to Japan, today the chief cargo leaving here is scrap metal and salt processed by Cargill Salt from its 32,000 acres of evaporation ponds nearby. Long before the 1850s, when John Johnson built the first system of levees through the Hayward marshes to collect

Salt ready for shipment at Redwood City

water from the Bay for salt production, the Ohlones had gathered salt along the shores of these marshes. Conditions here are ideal for the accumulation of salt: shallow salt water; flat, dense soil; meager rainfall; and abundant sun and wind.

This port is also a busy place for pleasure boaters. It has five marinas and two anchorages.

Approach

Because ocean-going vessels enter this port, you'll find a well-marked, wide, deep channel to navigate—a genuine treat in this region of the Bay, where water depths average 6 feet and often disappear during low tides.

Whether coming from north or south, boaters will find excellent landmarks for Redwood City: two major bridges. Boaters approaching from the north will pass under the San Mateo Bridge and continue for 3.1 miles, staying in the ship channel, following a SW course. The entrance markers, a channel marker on a piling to starboard and a buoy to port, are in water over 40 feet.

The few boaters approaching from the south will go under the

Dumbarton Bridge and follow the ship channel for 4.5 miles, holding a NW course.

The Redwood Creek channel has excellent depths for the first 3.25 miles, but boaters who stray out of the well-marked channel may quickly find themselves aground.

Anchorages and Berthing

The options for boaters visiting the Port of Redwood City include a range of marinas—from the recently renovated Municipal Marina to the funky Docktown Marina and the marina with character, Pete's Harbor. The two anchorages are easily as varied. The Smith Slough anchorage gives one the sense of being in the middle of the marina activity. Westpoint Slough, conversely, at the east end of the harbor complex, gives boaters a retreat.

The first anchorage area after entering the channel, *Westpoint Slough*, to port off the Redwood Creek channel 2.0 miles from the entrance, defines the western side of Greco Island, part of the San Francisco Bay National Wildlife Refuge . Turn to port 20 yards south of Marker 13, and set a course for an imaginary point just off the east end of the old pier at the abandoned cement plant on the starboard side of the channel. Proceed slowly as sand bars form in unusual places. Some boaters anchor 75 yards off the old pier in 10-15 feet of water. Mud bottom here offers good holding, and the protection from the prevailing winds is excellent.

Other boaters anchor 0.5 mile farther in the slough off the second abandoned pier, this one on the port side of the channel. Anchor about 75 yards off the pier in about 8 feet of water. Watch your depth sounder as you anchor to make certain you are in the deepest part of the channel.

The favorite place of the local sailors is around the corner beyond the second of the abandoned piers. You will encounter a buoy set by local yacht club members in the middle of the turn. Anchor in 10 feet of water on the south side of the buoy. Don't get too close to the eastern shore of the slough. We did and went aground (though going aground in this soft mud causes little concern among the local sailors).

A second slough where local boaters anchor is **Smith Slough**, just beyond Pete's Harbor. In fact, from Pete's restaurant you can see the slough and many of the boats anchored there. Boats anchor in Smith Slough in about 5 feet of water at low tide, but that is enough. This slough has become so popular recently that some boaters have anchored there more or less permanently. The local sheriff and the Coast Guard, however, are in the process of clearing the slough of derelict boats.

We recommend entering sloughs in the area at low water or when the tide is coming in. If you go aground, you want to be sure your boat will float off soon and not be there for a week. Also, you'll be able to locate the numerous sunken boats that are submerged except at low water.

Anchoring in the Redwood City area sloughs can be an absolute pleasure, as long as you are careful and watch the tides, . Dick Honey, a long-time sailor of this area, told us, "When we're sailing this area, our tide books are our bibles."

Those boaters wishing to visit Redwood City or enjoy the security of being tied to a dock can go into one of the five marinas. *Redwood City Sailing Center* is the first marina down the channel beyond the

Entrance to Redwood City Yacht Harbor

pier where the ships load. It is to the port of Marker 21. The *Redwood City Yacht Harbor* is just beyond the ship docks where the freighters load salt and scrap metal. Turn to port before Marker 21 and enter the marina. Guest docks are between the first two docks next to the seawall. The Sequoia Yacht Club is here.

The third marina southward into the channel is *Pete's Harbor,* on the starboard side of the intersection of Smith Slough and Redwood Creek, about 0.5 mile beyond the Redwood City Marina. Pete actively participates in the operation of his marina and in the welfare of boaters in the South Bay generally. He has a store of both current and historical information to share with boaters.

The fourth marina, *Bair Island Marina*, is immediately adjacent to Pete's Harbor. This new marina with concrete docks can accommodate boats up to 60 feet. Within easy walking distance is the San Francisco

Bay National Wildlife Refuge with a three mile trail from which visitors can enjoy the variety of wildlife.

The last marina up the channel is *Docktown,* a row of slips along the edge of the slough just beyond the entrance to Peninsula Marina. This marina also has shallow water, causing boats docked here to sit in the mud at low water.

Harbormasters:

Bair Island Marina	650-701-0382
Docktown Marina	650-365-3258
Pete's Harbor	650-366-0922
Redwood City Sailing Center	650-363-1390
Redwood City Yacht Harbor	650-306-4150 & VHF 16
Sequoia Yacht Club	650-361-9472

Facilities

None of the marinas or anchorages is in an area of the city that has a variety of markets and shops. Bair Island, Pete's, and Docktown are the closest to commercial districts, these three being about 0.5 from a marine and RV supply house, a dive shop, a canvas shop, and movie theaters; 1.0 mile from service stations, banks, and a post office; and 1.5 miles from a mini-market and a laundromat.

At Docktown Marina
    Boat Maintenance and Repair
    Haul Out
    Launch Ramp
    Showers
At Bair Island Marina
    Pump Out
    Restaurant
    Showers
At Pete's Harbor
    Restaurant
At Portside Marina
    Restaurants
At Redwood City Yacht Harbor
    Launch Ramp
    Laundromat
    Pump Out
    Restaurants
    Showers

Attractions

If you anchor in Westpoint Slough a mile or so beyond the channel, you may never see another boat, seeing, instead, a spectacular shorebird show, especially when the tide recedes to expose the shoals extending into the slough on either side. Feeding on the invertebrates here are

Derelict boat in Westpoint Slough

American avocets, willets, long-billed curlews, snowy and common egrets, blue herons, dunlins, and marbled godwits. And if you don't see all these species feeding alongside your boat, you'll be sure to see them if you take your tender farther up the slough.

The Smith Slough anchorage will appeal more to those of you who want access to some of the appurtenances of civilization: restaurants, shops, theaters, and the like. This anchorage is in the middle of the marina activity and thus has many of the same attractions as the marinas.

From any of the marinas and anchorages, you can take your tender up Smith Slough, then to Steinberger Slough, and to Corkscrew Slough to explore the shorelines of Bair Island, some of which is a part of the San Francisco Bay National Wildlife Refuge.

For hikers, a 3-mile trail along the levee system east and north of Pete's Harbor circles marshes rich with shorebirds. The eastern leg of this trail running parallel with Highway 101 connects both to the north and south with the Bay Trail, which in turn connects to many side trails. Thus the Redwood City marinas and anchorages are an ideal destination for those of you wanting to experience some of the marsh lands remaining in San Francisco Bay. The Refuge has protected these marshes, and trails exist to take you to them.

COYOTE POINT
Chart #18651 or #18652

Coyote Point Marina is on the opposite side of Highway 101 from the city of San Mateo, yet so remote does it seem that it might as well be on the other side of the Bay from the city. The marina is part of a large San Mateo recreation area, with an expansive eucalyptus-tree-covered picnic area, acting as a buffer between the city and the marina.

Approach

Approaching Coyote Point Marina from any direction, use the San Francisco Airport as a convenient landmark. The tower, the beacon, the hangars, and the continuous flow of aircraft taking off and landing make this a great landmark. The entrance to Coyote Point is just over 2.2 miles east of the end of the runway. You can also use as a landmark the tree-covered Coyote Point, which extends out into the Bay at this point.

The 0.25 mile channel into the marina is clearly marked. Markers 1 and 2 are easy to identify. Shoal areas extend out from the breakwaters, and harbor personnel have placed conspicuous signs to warn boaters.

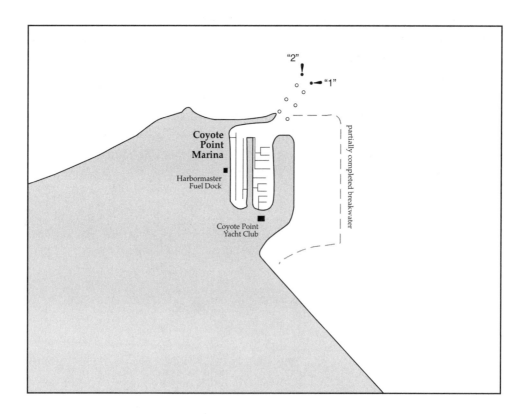

Coyote Point channel behind the masts

Anchorage and Berthing

No anchorage areas exist in the harbor or in the immediate vicinity outside the harbor.

The Coyote Point Marina, with 580 slips, can offer guest berthing accommodations for many boats. This marina allows no liveaboards, but visiting boaters can stay on their boats for a few days.

Coyote Point Yacht Club has a long guest dock for members of other yacht clubs. The restaurant serves lunch and dinner Friday, Saturday, and Sunday.

Harbormaster   650-573-2594 and VHF 16

Coyote Point Yacht Club   650-347-6730

Facilities

Fuel Dock (gasoline and diesel, Friday and Saturday only)
Launch Ramp
Public Transportation
Pump Out
Showers

Attractions

The Coyote Point County Recreation Area inland of the marina has a 2.5-mile hiking trail around the park, leading to the Coyote Point

Museum for Environmental Education "devoted to the wildlife and ecosystems of the Bay Area." Farther along the trail are an elegant restaurant on the water, a sandy beach, and a well-equipped children's playground. The San Mateo Municipal Golf Course lies at the southern end of the park. A rifle and pistol range is open on weekends.

You can also hike or bike on another trail, part of the Bay Trail planned to follow the entire shoreline of San Francisco Bay by the year 2000. It goes south from Coyote Point Recreation Area to Third Avenue, past marshlands alive with waterfowl, and north to Burlingame Shoreline Park, along the shores of some great windsurfing waters.

While none of the city amenities are on the marina side of Highway 101, an overpass on the other side of the park from the marina will take you across the freeway and onto Peninsula Street, past immaculately kept homes and yards for about 0.5 mile, where you'll find a shopping center with a supermarket and other small shops. To reach the overpass, take the path that traces the southern perimeter of the park, above and alongside the golf course, for close to 1.0 mile. Though this walk will take you about a half hour each way, it's such a scenic trip you'll not mind the length.

BRISBANE and SOUTH SAN FRANCISCO
Chart #18651 or #18652

The three marinas along the Bay shores of Brisbane and South San Francisco—the Brisbane Marina, Oyster Cove Marina, and Oyster Point Marina—entice boating visitors with their modern docks and facilities, security, ease of access, and generally quiet isolation on the edge of the urban growth spreading south from San Francisco.

The shoreline where these marinas are located has been shaped by human intervention as much as any other shoreline in the Bay. Before the turn of the century San Bruno Mountain rose abruptly from the Bay shore to its 1,314 feet. Today, as a result of silting, it begins its ascent almost 3 miles west of the marinas. For hundreds—perhaps thousands—of years, Ohlones harvested oysters and other mollusks here. The shellmounds testifying to this enterprise once lined the shores of both the Bay and the creeks; none of those mounds has survived the expansive urbanization and industrialization. Catching on to the suitability of these waters for oysters, American entrepreneurs set up oyster beds at the end of the 19th century. Their enterprise was much shorter lived than that of the Ohlones: by 1905 polluted waters from raw sewage and insufficient tidal flushing caused by the diversion of freshwater streams for agricultural use had a deleterious effect on the oysters. By World War I Oyster Cove teemed not with boats harvesting oysters but with transport ships carrying pipes and steel from the heavy industries ashore and with ships newly built for service in the war.

Today you'll see little that is reminiscent of the oyster harvesting and/or cultivating that prospered for centuries or of the shipping industry that thrived for three-quarters of this century.

All three marinas sit on landfill, with office buildings nearby. The only activity on the water now is that of the pleasure boats, whose owners enjoy hearing the splashes of California brown pelicans diving for dinner and the squawks of Forster's terns sitting on the breakwater.

Approach

When you're approaching these three marinas from the north, Point Avisadero is the first major waypoint. Although it can be difficult to identify, Avisadero denotes a minor course change. You'll know you've passed Avisadero when you identify the Navy ships, ocean-going tankers, and huge cranes at Hunters Point Naval Shipyard on the starboard side approximately 0.25 mile beyond Point Avisadero.

The entrance channel to Brisbane and Oyster Cove marinas is 3 miles from the center of the Hunters Point complex on a course of 178° mag. Do not stray off course to starboard as the water shoals abruptly between Hunters Point and Brisbane. Notice on your chart that the water shallows from 20 feet or more to 4 feet just starboard of your course.

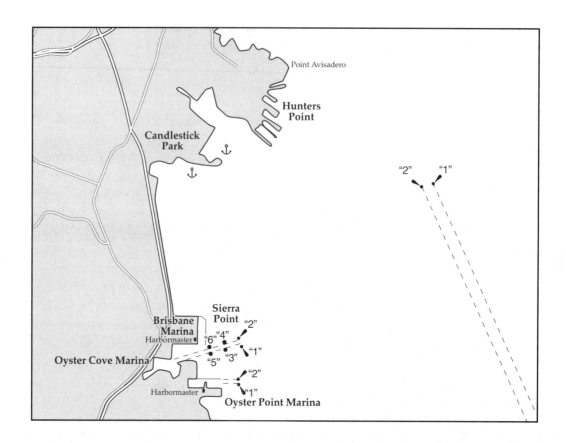

Boaters approaching Brisbane, Oyster Cove, or Oyster Point marinas from the south or east can use the San Francisco Airport for a landmark. From the northern terminus of the airport, the entrance to Oyster Point Marina is 2.1 miles farther north, and to Brisbane and Oyster Cove, 2.85 miles.

Channel markers 1 and 2 identify the channel into Brisbane and Oyster Cove. A series of 10 pairs of markers clearly outlines the boundaries of the mile-long channel. Stay carefully between the markers as the water shallows quickly outside the channel. Turn to starboard just past Marker 6, 0.5 mile up the channel; the entrance into Brisbane Marina at Sierra Point, only 250 yards from the channel, is easy to see.

If you're going to Oyster Cove Marina, continue up the channel rather than turning right into Brisbane Marina. Oyster Cove Marina is just over 0.5 mile beyond Brisbane.

Oyster Point Marina is adjacent to Oyster Cove Marina, but the entrance is on a separate channel, 0.75 mile south of the Brisbane-Oyster Cove channel. The Oyster Point channel has markers that identify it, and, like those in the earlier channel, these markers are numbered 1 and 2. Unlike the Brisbane-Oyster Cove channel, the Oyster Point channel is short, only 0.20 mile.

Anchorage and Berthing

The most colorful anchorage local boaters use is in the lee of Candlestick Park. Members of Peninsula Yacht Club in Redwood City

Brisbane Marina entrance

refer to this anchorage as "Friday Harbor" because they regularly anchor here on Friday nights when they're bound for the Central Bay. They report it offers good holding even though the wind often screams through the rigging during the night.

During the fall months when 49er football games are played at home, boats raft up in this anchorage for foredeck parties. They watch the game on a television set on deck while listening to the broadcast over the loudspeakers at Candlestick Park. Recently, one of the boats anchored here had a huge 49er flag spread out on top of the boat, and the camera crew on a blimp overhead showed the anchored football fans on national television.

Enter the anchorage from the east 100 yards off the south side of the peninsula at Candlestick. Identify the two piers extending southward from the shoreline. The best anchorage is between these two piers within 100 yards of shore in 6 to 10 feet of water.

Some boaters have anchored in the small cove directly east of the peninsula at Candlestick in 5 to 10 feet of water and reported having good protection from the heavy winds that roar across the Bay just south of Candlestick. We have not dropped anchor in this area and cannot recommend the anchorage.

San Francisco Bay boaters who sail the area regularly warn that the protected cove between Candlestick Point and Hunters Point, called South Basin, should be avoided because the bottom is foul and shallow.

A second anchorage area in the Brisbane/Oyster Point area is located at the end of the channel, immediately beyond Oyster Cove Marina During World War II, a shipyard was located at this point. Pilings and other remains of this yard are visible along the south shoreline. Boaters familiar with the area warn that the cove is foul toward the back of the anchorage. During herring season, fishing boats occasionally use this anchorage. As with all of this area, the wind strength often exceeds 25 knots during the afternoons in spring and summer.

The three modern marinas in the area readily offer guest berthing accommodations. Oyster Point Yacht Club will arrange guest berthing for individual boats or cruise-ins from other yacht clubs; Sierra Point will make such arrangements with the harbormaster for cruise-ins.

Harbormasters

Brisbane Marina	650-583-6975 and VHF 16
Oyster Cove Marina	650-952-5540 and VHF 16
Oyster Point Marina	650-952-0808 or 650-871-7344 and VHF 16

Yacht Clubs

Sierra Point Yacht Club	650-952-0651
Oyster Point Yacht Club	650-873-5166

Facilities

At Brisbane
Pump Out
Showers
At Oyster Cove
Laundromat
Pump Out
Showers
At Oyster Point
Boat Maintenance and Repair
Fuel Dock (gas and diesel)
Haul Out (power boats only)
Launch Ramp
Pump Out
Restaurants
Showers

Attractions

Bird watching, fishing, and walking are the primary activities in these somewhat isolated marinas. Short segments of the Bay Trail have been completed nearby. From Brisbane Marina, the trail to the south leads to an exercise station and to the north to a wooden fishing pier and along the western shore of Brisbane Lagoon, a cove before the construction of Highway 101, for excellent viewing of shorebirds. From Oyster Point Marina, the trail winds along the shoreline almost to Oyster Cove Marina to the northeast and, to the south, to San Bruno Point (with a short portion necessitating a walk along city streets).

The Cabot, Cabot & Forbes Park, with 33 acres for picnicking, hiking and jogging, is close by Oyster Point Marina, as are a 2.5-acre sandy beach (with lifeguards from Memorial Day to Labor Day) and a 300-foot concrete fishing pier. With a walk of approximately 2 miles along city streets and across Highway 101, you can reach San Bruno Mountain County Park from Oyster Point and Oyster Cove marinas.

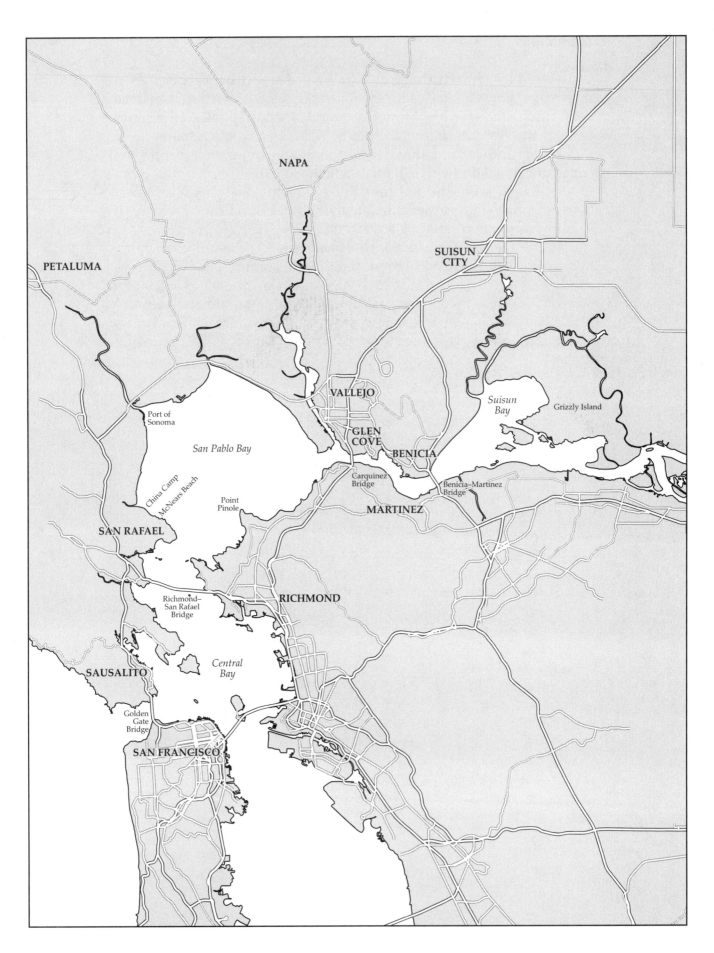

9 THE NORTH BAY

It was kind of solemn, drifting down the big still river, laying on our backs looking up at the stars, and we didn't ever feel like talking loud, and it warn't often that we laughed, only a little kind of a low chuckle. We had mighty good weather, as a general thing, and nothing ever happened to us at all, that night, nor the next, nor the next.
　　　　　　　—Mark Twain, *Huckleberry Finn*

SAN RAFAEL
Chart #18652, #18654, or #18649

The oldest city in Marin County, San Rafael has today the same asset that attracted the first Spanish to settle here: in the lee of Mount Tamalpais it thrives in a Mediterranean-like climate, with warm, sunny days throughout a long summer. And we can safely assume the Coast Miwoks who lived here for thousands of years before the Spanish came appreciated this place they called "Nanaguani" for the same reason. What a paradise it must have been! Antelope and elk grazed on the grassy hillsides made verdant by the combination of the sunny summers and rainy winters. Salmon spawned in the creeks, and mussels and abalone were abundant along the rocky shoreline. Sea otters were so numerous in the Bay they were said to form islands of fur over which canoes could skim.

The padres at *Misión San Francisco de Asís*, or Mission Dolores, had grown concerned with the mortality rate among the Natives at the mission, a rate higher than at any of the other California missions. They began looking for a spot around the Bay with a climate less severe than that of San Francisco, where they could establish an *asistencia* (hospital). In 1817, *Misión San Rafael Arcangel* became that site, having been named, appropriately, after the healing messenger of God, archangel Rafael. With this new establishment, to become number twenty among California's twenty-one missions, the padres would also be able to attract a large number of new converts among the Miwoks living in what is now Marin County.

Establishing the *asistencia* in this part of the Bay Area also served a political purpose: it served as a warning to the Russians, who were beginning to look south of Fort Ross for new sea otter hunting grounds, that San Francisco Bay and all its contiguous lands belonged to the Spanish crown.

Mission San Rafael Arcangel

The padres at Mission San Rafael apparently realized all their goals. The converts brought here from Mission Dolores were healthier, new Miwok converts flocked to the mission, and the Russians did not encroach on the Spanish territories. Succeeding far beyond their dreams, the padres, with the invaluable labor supplied by the converts, turned the mission farmlands into highly productive fields of wheat, corn, barley, beans, and peas. Later, after Mexico gained independence from Spain and, thirteen years later, secularized the missions, General Mariano Vallejo had a cattle and sheep ranch here. Mission San Rafael also became noted for the quality of its grapes.

During the Bear Flag Rebellion of 1846 John Fremont and Kit Carson used the mission as a barracks. The reconstructed mission standing today replaces the original adobe that was dismantled in 1861.

John Reed started up a ferry service in the 1830s to transport the padres and their charges between Mission Dolores and Mission San Rafael and also to take the whalers and seamen anchored in Richardson Bay in Sausalito to San Francisco. In 1907, the Northwest Pacific Railroad, bought by Southern Pacific in 1929, began to run trains down to the waterfront to meet the ferries.

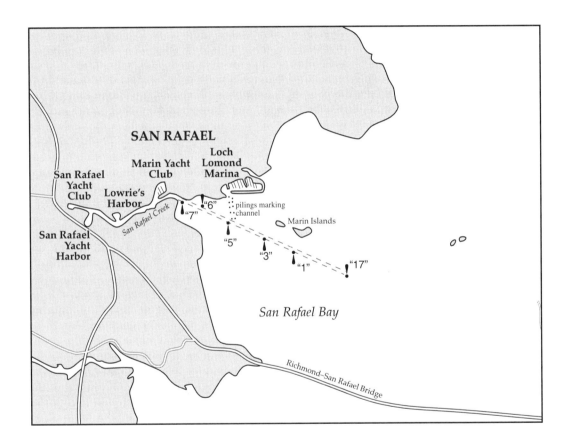

Approach

Approaching San Rafael from either north or south, you will be in the ship channel. Enter San Rafael Channel at Marker 17, 1.4 miles northwest of the Richmond–San Rafael Bridge. Boaters transiting San Rafael Channel must use caution because the channel suffers from chronic shoaling. Stay inside the channel that is 100 feet wide and less than 5 feet deep at low water; those who stray outside the boundaries of the channel regularly go aground. The channel has large markers that identify the port side of the channel as you proceed from San Rafael Bay to San Rafael.

Loch Lomond channel markers

Vessels with a deep draft should not enter at low tide. If you wish to cruise to San Rafael and are not confident about the water depths in the channel, call one of the local marinas for an update on conditions and for advice on navigating the channel. Though shoaling is a continuing problem, the hundreds of boats moored in San Rafael furnish testimony that you can find enough water in the channel.

The *Loch Lomond Marina* channel exits to starboard from the San Rafael Channel 1.35 miles from the entrance marker. This channel also suffers from shoaling problems and must be dredged regularly to allow boaters to enter the marina without going aground. When we visited the marina recently, marina personnel cautioned that we should enter only at high water until the channel was dredged, a major event scheduled annually. Pilings on the port and starboard mark the channel. With 500 slips, Loch Lomond is the largest marina in the area.

The San Rafael

Marin Yacht Club channel

Channel continues 0.65 mile beyond the Loch Lomond channel, passing through mud flats before joining San Rafael Creek. When you join the creek, you will change course, coming about to a SW course. The entrance to *Marin Yacht Club* exits to starboard from the creek 300 yards after the intersection of the channel and the creek.

Up San Rafael Creek 0.4 mile beyond Marin Yacht Club, *Lowrie's Yacht Harbor* is also on the starboard side of the creek

Another 0.25 mile up the creek from Lowrie's is the *San Rafael Yacht Harbor,* on the port side of the creek. The *San Rafael Yacht Club* building is at the far west end of the navigable creek (just before the Grand Avenue bridge). Again, be cautious because shoaling is particularly evident at the upper end of San Rafael Creek.

Anchorage and Berthing

No anchorage exists in the San Rafael area. If you plan to cruise to San Rafael and are a member of a yacht club, call ahead for a guest berthing at any one of the yacht clubs. If you're not a member of a club, call Loch Lomond Marina, Lowrie's Yacht Harbor, or the San Rafael Yacht Harbor for guest berthing.

Marina Harbormasters
Loch Lomond Marina   415-454-7228

Lowrie's Yacht Harbor   415-454-7595

San Rafael Yacht Harbor   415-456-1600

Yacht Clubs
Loch Lomond Yacht Club   415-459-9811

Marin Yacht Club   415-453-9366

San Rafael Yacht Club   415-459-9828

Facilities

At Loch Lomond
Boat Maintenance and Repair
Chandlery
Fuel
Grocery Store
Launch Ramp
Pump Out
Showers
Snack bar
At or near Lowrie's

At or near Lowrie's
  Grocery Store
  Laundromat
  Restaurants
  Showers
At Marin Yacht Club
  Showers
  (1 mile to Grocery Store and Laundromat)
At or near San Rafael Yacht Club
  Boat Maintenance and Repair
  Grocery Store
  Laundromat
  Post Office (1 mile)
  Restaurants

Attractions

San Rafael is a particularly satisfying cruising destination because it has a variety of attractions clustered within a few blocks. The heart of the downtown area is only four blocks from San Rafael Creek. You can take five walking tours through historic San Rafael, guided by a brochure available from the San Rafael Chamber of Commerce, 818 Fifth Street.

The "Downtown San Rafael" walk begins at Courthouse Square, where the Marin County Courthouse formed the "heart of the county" until 1969, when the county offices moved to the Civic Center, the last structure designed by Frank Lloyd Wright. Hotels, commercial buildings and private residences remain from as early as 1859. The "Mission and Early Mansions" walk will take you past the reconstructed mission and what is said to be the oldest building in San Rafael, the Coleman House, built between 1849 and 1852. One of the most interesting buildings on the third walk, the "Forbes Addition" walk, is one of the two remaining buildings from the 1915 Panama Pacific Exposition in San Francisco. The Victrola building that had housed the Victor Talking Machine Company was dismantled at the end of the exposition and barged across the Bay as a gift to Leon Douglas, who coined the slogan "His Master's Voice." Southwest of the harbor is a fourth walking tour, "Short's Tract: The Gerstle Park Area." Finally, the Dominican tour is a bit of a distance from the harbor—10 or 12 long blocks—but well worth the walk. The Dominican College campus has long been renowned for the architectural excellence of many of its buildings. One of the most significant historically is the Mother House, the 1889 convent house built for the Dominican Sisters when they moved to San Rafael from Benicia. The tiles around the front entrance of the Mother House are by the Italian Renaissance sculptor Luca della Robbia. On campus, too, dating from 1888, is Meadowlands, the summer house of Michael H. deYoung, one of the founders of the *San Francisco Chronicle*. The Dominican Order purchased the house in 1918 and added a dormitory wing in 1924.

If outdoor adventuring is more to your taste than historical walks, you can pick up a section of the Bay Trail at Pickleweed Park, on the south shore of San Rafael Creek near its mouth. Then walk along the Shoreline Park trail, with an excellent view of the Marin Islands just across San Rafael Bay. Take binoculars along to view the snowy and great egrets and the black-crowned night herons building nests, caring for their young, and feeding around the islands. You can continue south to Point San Quentin, named for Chief Quentin, who, along with Chief Marin ("el marinero"), led an uprising against the Mission in 1824. San Quentin State Prison is on the southwest side of this point.

Marin Islands, north of San Rafael Channel

MCNEARS BEACH and CHINA CAMP
Chart #18652 or #18654

The anchorages off McNears Beach, a county park, and China Camp State Park promise boaters some of the best weather in the Bay Area, with more than 200 fog-free days recorded each year. In both anchorages you'll find good protection from the westerlies; China Camp usually attracts more boats, perhaps because it is more distant from the rock crushing plant at Point San Pedro and has a greater variety of attractions ashore.

Approach

From San Francisco Bay, go under the Richmond-San Rafael Bridge to enter San Pablo Bay. Heading due north from the main span of the bridge for 2 miles, pass the Brothers Islands on your starboard, just offshore at Point San Pablo. You can clearly identify East Brother because of the sparkling refurbished lighthouse keeper's house. Directly off your bow about 2 miles are the Sisters Islands, which rise no more than 20 feet above the water's surface. These two islands have no buildings, though barges to haul gravel from the crushing plant are usually anchored nearby. Use caution when passing these barges: tugs are often moving them around.

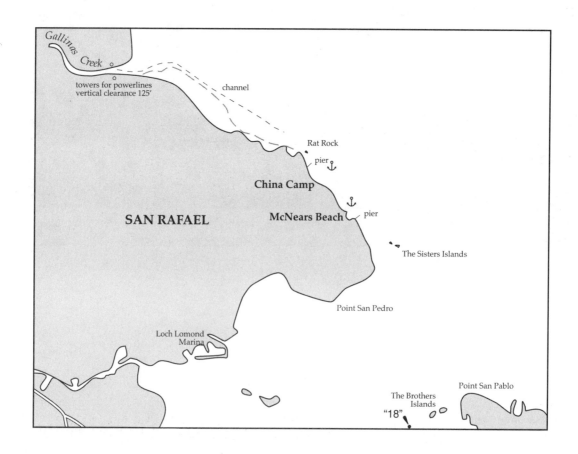

You can safely pass on either side of the Sisters, with about 10 feet of water on the west and 50 feet on the east. Immediately beyond the Sisters, a pier just north of Point San Pedro marks the southern end of McNears Beach.

Anchorages

Prevailing winds come over the land mass to the west during the afternoon, but winds frequently come from the south early in the day or even from the north during the afternoon. Even though the varying wind direction is unsettling, both anchorages are secure and comfortable in moderate winds from any direction but the east. A current, often in excess of 1 knot, runs through both anchorages. Although the wind may blow 15 knots, the strong current can hold your boat beam to the wind. Despite these peculiarities of wind direction and current, both McNears and China Camp are comfortable anchorages. The two can accommodate 50 boats, but rarely will you see more than a dozen on a summer weekend.

McNears Beach Anchorage. Most cruising boats anchor at least 400 yards north of the pier and at least 600 feet from shore because of shallow water. Because of the current and the wind strength, be sure to let out sufficient scope and dig in your anchor by backing down before leaving your boat or settling in for the night.

McNears Beach pier with anchorage to north

China Camp anchorage

China Camp Anchorage. One mile north of McNears and less than 0.5 mile south of Rat Rock is the dilapidated 300-foot-long China Camp pier. Ashore here are several weathered wooden buildings from the days when China Camp was the site of a shrimp drying and packing plant and home to as many as 300 residents. As at McNears, the desirable spot for anchoring is at least 600 feet from shore—but south or east of the pier.

Facilities Ashore

The only facilities at McNears Beach and China Camp are a snack bar and a small restaurant. The nearest fuel and supplies are available at Loch Lomond, 1.5 miles on the road to San Rafael.

Attractions

At McNears, you may land a dinghy or sport boat ashore on the rocky but accessible beach, where you can walk or swim. The rocks in the silt bottom make a pair of water shoes desirable. Above the beach are lush green lawns, picnic tables, and a snack bar. Farther up the hill is Point San Pablo Road, which will take you north to China Camp State Park or southwest for a 3-mile jaunt into San Rafael, where you can find a full range of facilities.

At China Camp, going ashore is a bit easier than at McNears, for you can tie up at the pier if the gate is unlocked, or you can land a dinghy or sportboat on the sandy beach. A few picnic tables are near the water on the north side of the pier, and the small restaurant/

concession stand is open on weekends.

For many visitors the main attraction is the small museum (open only on weekends) chronicling the lives of the Chinese families who settled here in the late 1800s to harvest and process the plentiful grass shrimp in San Pablo Bay. Most of these shrimp were sold in China. The crumbling pier, the old processing plant (now the museum), the kiln and drying racks, the restaurant, and a handful of houses are all that remain today.

A paved road leading away from the museum will take you to numerous well-marked and well-tended trails in this 1,640-acre park. These trails wind through stands of oak trees (and healthy stands of poison oak!) and across the meadows, where Coast Miwoks had settlements until the early 19th century.

On the other hand, you can explore the area by sportboat. North of the anchorage and around Rat Island are a dozen or so duck blinds perched on stilts in the water. To the south and west of these blinds is a channel marked by pieces of PVC pipe stuck in the mud bottom; this channel leads to the mouth of Gallinas Creek, named for the Spanish ranch located here in the 19th century, *Rancho San Pedro, Santa Margarita y las Gallinas*. From Rat Island to the entrance is about 1.5 miles; from the entrance to the first major fork is another 2 miles. At the fork you may go to the right for about 1.5 miles, ending up behind warehouses in east San Rafael, or to the left for almost 2 miles to the back of the Marin Civic Center, designed by Frank Lloyd Wright. Because the creek wanders among thick stands of swamp grass and pickleweed, the water remains fairly calm even on the windiest of days.

PETALUMA
Chart #18652 or #18654

Deer swimming beside boat in Petaluma River

Lakeville, up the Petaluma River

"Up the lazy river" captures exactly the ambience of a cruise up the Petaluma River (in fact, a tidal estuary). After leaving San Pablo Bay, you'll meander along with the river past housing developments, small marinas, undulating pastures dotted with oak trees, and dairy barns. Now and then you may meet a boat coming down the river, but the serenity today belies the busy past of this waterway, once the third most heavily used in the state.

Beginning in 1775 with a band of sailors on a small boat from Juan Manuel de Ayala's ship, looking for a route into Bodega Bay, the Petaluma was a much used waterway for the small boats of Spanish explorers as well as of Russian sailors and game hunters from San Francisco. Paddle-wheel steamboats, cargo sloops, and scow schooners plied the river when the town of Petaluma was the supply center for inland gold camps and later a busy port for the shipment of manufactured goods.

Some of those San Francisco hunters settled in camps that became the town of Petaluma, which has gone from being one of California's largest cities in the 1860s to the world's egg basket in the early 1900s and the current wrist wrestling capital of the world.

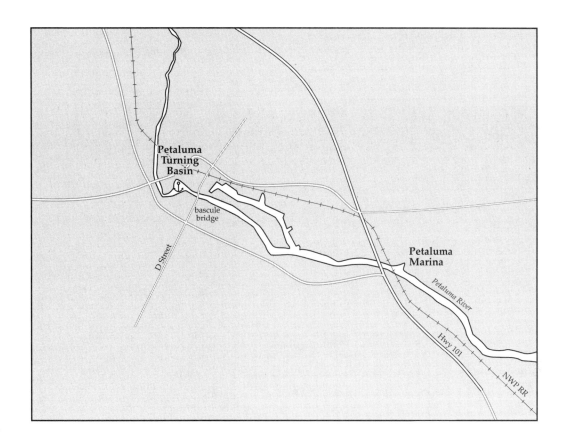

PETALUMA MARINA

Approach

While the Petaluma is a placid river, navigating the channel to the river demands your full attention. On the approach from San Francisco Bay, the last easily recognizable point of reference is the Richmond-San Rafael Bridge. From the bridge, the Brothers Islands are easily visible 1.8 miles to the north.

Once abeam of the Brothers, follow a course of 346° mag. for 6.55 miles, passing buoys 1, 2, 3, and 4 enroute to the Petaluma channel entrance, which is at Channel Marker 5, topped by a green dayboard, and at Marker 6, identified by a red dayboard and a light. The depth will decrease steadily on this course until you have only about 8 feet of water at the channel entrance at low water.

Approaching from the east, follow the ship channel 6.15 miles from the Carquinez Bridge to Buoy 9. At Buoy 9, steer a course of 280° mag. for 4 miles to the Petaluma channel entrance, markers 5 and 6. Just prior to the channel, you'll find only 6 feet of depth at low water. If your boat has a deep draft, steer a more southerly course.

Stay carefully within the channel, well marked to the railroad bridge. The depth in the channel is 8 at low water. The depths outside the channel are in places no more than 1 foot. In the 4.7 miles from the entrance to the railroad bridge, the channel makes a number of course changes to port.

The railroad bridge remains open except when trains are crossing the river. If the bridge is closed, you may have to wait as much as 30 minutes.

On the starboard just past the railroad bridge, Port Sonoma Marina has berthing for 282 boats and a fuel dock (gas only). The Highway 37 overpass (70-foot vertical clearance) is 0.25 mile upriver from the railroad bridge. North of the Highway 37 overpass the river cuts through the countryside for 11.0 miles to the Petaluma Marina. Stay in the middle of the river all the way to Petaluma except for one section 0.7 mile above Lakeville, at Cloudy Bend. Because of shoaling, steer wide to the port here to Buoy 5 at Cut B. Be sure to pass buoys 2 and 4 on the starboard. After you pass Buoy 5, maintain a course up the center of the channel.

Anchorage and Marina

Anchorage opportunities abound along the river. The Petaluma is wide enough in most locations for you to anchor safely out of the way of river traffic. Over the years we have frequently seen boats at anchor just north of the Highway 37 bridge. We assume boaters who anchor here go ashore at the Port Sonoma Marina.

Farther north up the river, most of the anchored boats you pass are fishing boats.

The Petaluma Marina, with its new docks (196 berths), fuel dock, and office buildings, is modern and inviting. The marina has no anchorage but plenty of guest slips for visiting boaters. Boaters here who are reluctant to walk the 1.25 miles into town can take their sportboats on an easy and interesting 1-mile trip to the Turning Basin. They can then tie up their sportboats at the end of the dock in front of the Petaluma Yacht Club.

Petaluma Marina

Petaluma Marina   707-778-4489

Facilities

> Fuel Dock (unleaded gas only)
> Grocery Store (0.5 mile)
> Laundromat (1 mile)
> Launch Ramp
> Pump Out
> Restaurant (0.5 mile)
> Showers

PETALUMA RIVER TURNING BASIN

Approach

The Petaluma River continues beyond the Petaluma Marina to the center of town, just over 1 mile. You must pass through another railroad bridge 100 feet north of the Petaluma Marina. This bridge, like the earlier one, stands open except when a train is passing. Beyond the railroad bridge 150 yards is another highway overpass (70-foot vertical clearance). In 1 mile after this overpass, the D Street bridge will block your entry to the Petaluma Turning Basin. Boaters must make an appointment at least 4 hours (but preferably 24 hours) before they wish the bridge opened. The bridge tender will then be waiting on VHF Channel 09 for a call at that appointed hour. You must follow this procedure for both entering and departing the Turning Basin.

Line of boats at the D Street Bridge

Bridge Tender   707-778-4395 or 707-769-0429

Anchorage

The Turning Basin has 875 feet of dock space for visiting boaters, most of it with power and water. Petaluma is a popular destination, so boaters must call the Petaluma Visitor's Program to reserve dock or anchoring space. On a summer weekend, more than 50 boats in the Turning Basin are not uncommon. Power boats generally tie stern to the dock or raft up. Sailboats raft up or anchor in the Turning Basin once the docks are full. Like the channel, the Turning Basin has a depth of about 8.0 feet at low water.

Petaluma Visitor's Program   707-769-0429

Facilities

No facilities are available on the dock unless you can obtain reciprocal club privileges at the Petaluma Yacht Club. Since the public dock is in the heart of downtown Petaluma, you will be in easy walking distance of the following:

Banks
Boat Maintenance and Repair
Grocery Stores
Haul Out
Laundromat
Movie Theatre
Post Office
Restaurants
Shops

Attractions

The adjective used frequently to describe Petaluma is "charming." The charm lies in its history, its architecture, its riverfront, but, even more than these, in its small-town atmosphere.

In 1830 General Vallejo built California's largest adobe, now called the Old Adobe, here. After viewing the Adobe, step forward in time a few years with a walking tour of Victorian homes in the "A" Street Historic District. A leaflet to guide you on this tour is available from the Petaluma Visitor's Program. Also of architectural interest downtown, on Western Avenue, is the row of commercial buildings with cast iron fronts, these iron fronts mistakenly thought at the time to make structures fireproof.

Petaluma's riverfront is, of course, the reason for the city's existence. The Turning Basin, where pleasure boaters now dock or anchor, was an ox-bow bend in the river dredged to facilitate shipping. This basin is today the centerpiece of the Petaluma River Walk. Many restaurants and cafes, shops, and a brew pub line the banks of this wide spot in the river.

Save time to take a casual stroll through one of the town's 33 parks, two of which are quite close to the Turning Basin. Or you may want to wander about the town, talking with the friendly residents or enjoying the quiet of the residential streets.

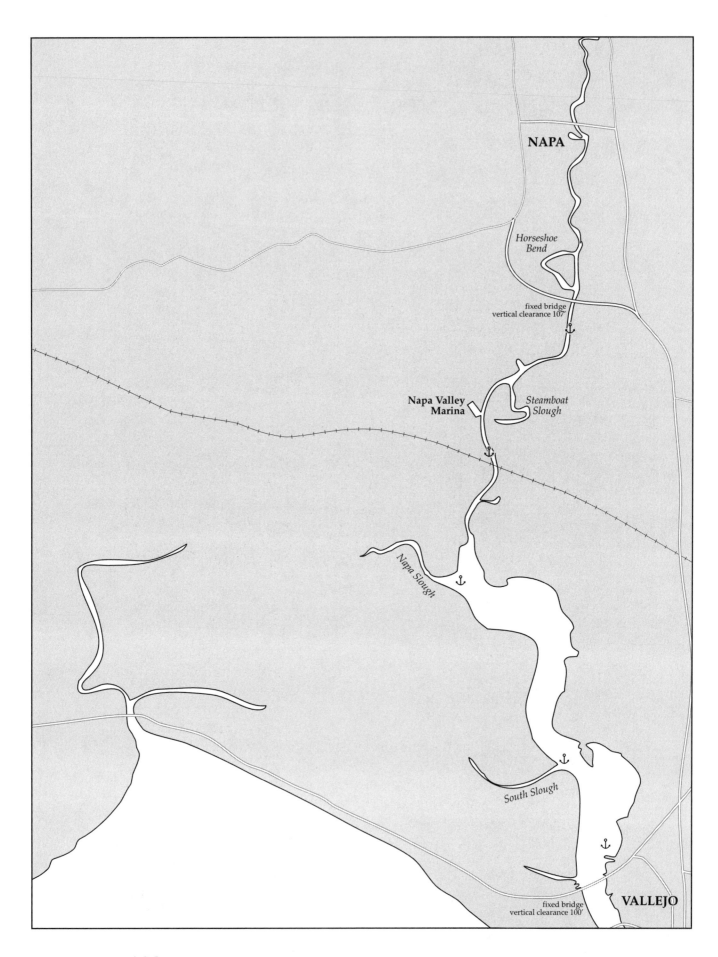

NAPA

Horseshoe Bend

fixed bridge
vertical clearance 107'

Napa Valley Marina

Steamboat Slough

Napa Slough

South Slough

VALLEJO

fixed bridge
vertical clearance 100'

NAPA
Chart #18652 or #18654

Much of the pleasure of the trips up the rivers that pour their waters into the San Francisco Bay comes from the passage itself. On a summer's day you leave the cool, sometimes overcast and windy, Bay to pass through another one or two (or more) climate zones, each

Cruising the Napa River

successively warmer than the last. (By the way, these are trips you might choose to make in the spring or fall if you're adverse to heat but in the summer if you want this abrupt change from the San Francisco chill.)

Going up the Napa River, you soon enter a world of flat sloughs covered with dark green pickleweed punctuated now and then by a snowy egret or a flock of willets. Shortly after, grassy rolling fields appear, golden brown from the dry summer heat, some of them populated with grazing dairy cattle. Farther along, orderly rows of grapevines march up the undulating slopes of the vineyards that have made Napa so prosperous. And then come the bridges, some of them fixed with clearance for sailboats and other ocean-going vessels, others, swing bridges or drawbridges that must be moved before vessels can continue up the river.

Such a trip is also an exploration of history as you pass dilapidated docks, half-sunken barges, and hulls of fishing boats and abandoned cargo ships, reminding you the Napa River was once an important route of commerce between San Francisco and the gold mines of the Mother Lode and the farms and towns of the Sacramento and Napa valleys.

Scow schooners and barges carried grain, lumber, furs, and fish down the Napa to San Francisco and returned with manufactured products. Some commercial traffic still travels this river, but the majority of the boats seen today are private fishing boats and pleasure crafts.

Approach

All boaters cruising to Napa depart from Vallejo. (See the section on Vallejo for directions to Vallejo Marina.) Immediately north of the Vallejo Marina is the Mare Island Causeway Bridge. Bridge tenders monitor VHF channels 13 and 16, and they will also open the bridge if you give them one long and one short blast on your horn. Plan on arriving at the bridge at some time other than peak traffic hours to avoid an excessively long wait. (Bridge tenders will not open the bridge between 6:30-7:30 a.m. or 3:45-4:45 p.m.) Of all the bridge tenders we've encountered in this area on our cruises, the Vallejo tender is unquestionably the friendliest and most willing to help the boaters traveling up the river.

After you clear the Mare Island Bridge, travel 0.6 mile to the Highway 37 bridge, a fixed bridge with a 100-foot vertical clearance. Past the highway bridge, the scenery changes dramatically, with few signs of civilization for the 12 miles from the bridge to the Napa Marina.

The Napa River channel has at least 9.0 feet of water for the entire distance between Vallejo and Napa, if you stay in the channel. And that's the problem. The water just outside the channel is often no more than 1 or 2 feet deep. While making this passage, keep your chart in the cockpit and your eyes on the channel markers. Local boaters warn that you must swing wide at Marker 7 because of shoaling. Looking at your chart, you'll see that in some instances you'll not be able to go directly from one marker to another but will have to make a curve to stay in the channel. As you transit the Napa River, watch your depth closely to keep from drifting out of the channel. When the depth begins to shallow significantly, slow down and find the channel again by moving very slowly to port or starboard.

You will pass through a railroad bridge 6.5 miles north of the Highway 37 bridge; it remains open except when a train is approaching. The Napa Valley Marina is on the port 0.75 mile above the railroad bridge. Edgerly Island is on the left for the last 1.5 miles before you arrive at the marina; this island has numerous homes on the port side of the river.

The Imola Bridge is another 4.5 miles north of the railroad bridge. The bridge tender will open the Imola Bridge if given a 72-hour notice. Immediately above the Imola Bridge on the port side is the Napa Yacht Club, beyond which you'll have little reason to venture except in a tender. A few docks are farther up the river, one being the Sea Scouts dock with its large ex-Coast Guard craft, but fixed bridges and shallow water will prevent you from taking a larger boat farther than the Sea Scouts dock. And you will find no place to go ashore as you proceed up the river.

Even the small dock that was along the river near downtown Napa was washed away by a recent storm.

Anchorage and Berthing

Visiting boaters who like to anchor out can find many good spots in the area. Local sailors recommend a site 1.75 miles north of the Napa Valley

Anchored bow and stern near the eucalyptus trees

Marina, on the west side of the river near the eucalyptus trees. Be sure not to anchor in the center of river because tugs bring barges up the river occasionally. You should show an anchor light at night because of river traffic. Observe the signs warning of cable and gas pipelines crossing the river in the area; anchor between the signs. The current can be strong here, so anchor securely. To avoid being swept into shallow water or into the middle of the channel as the tide changes, boaters use two anchors or tie to a tree on shore and put out a stern anchor.

The Napa River offers many other possible anchorages. Boaters have anchored just north of the Highway 37 bridge on the outskirts of Vallejo for years. The preferred spot is just south of Marker 2. If you choose to anchor here, anchor out of the channel to avoid the tugs in the river but not so far that you end up aground at low tide.

Local boaters also anchor at the entrance of both South Slough and Napa Slough. In both cases you can anchor just out of the Napa River channel or a short distance up inside the sloughs. Notice that the Napa Slough has markers indicating the center of the slough. These sloughs can be wonderful anchorages in the fall when the winds are non-existent, but the winds blow strongly during the spring and summer, making them uncomfortable even though the vegetation along the banks of the sloughs keeps the water relatively calm.

When we were cruising the Napa River recently, we also saw boats anchored in a the wide spot just north of the railroad bridge at Edgerly Island on the east side of the river. This should be a good anchorage because the wind doesn't blow so strongly as in the South and Napa sloughs. In addition, the marina, where you can purchase supplies, is a short run from here.

Boaters also anchor at other places along the west side of the Napa River north of the Napa Valley Marina, taking advantage of the shelter afforded by the eucalyptus trees that line the bank.

Most cruisers stop at the *Napa Valley Marina* on the port side just above the railroad bridge. The harbormaster can usually accommodate cruising boaters if they call ahead two days. Guests are normally directed to tie up at the long dock in front of the haul-out facility.   No restaurants are in the marina, but if you have a tender along, you can use it to get to a restaurant less than a mile away. The store by the marina office is one of the most complete we've seen near a marina in the area. In addition to provisions, it also carries boat equipment and supplies. The marina is well run, and the people are friendly, making this a pleasant cruising destination.

Yacht club members can tie up at the 200-foot guest dock at the *Napa Valley Yacht Club.* To get to the club, you must call ahead 72 hours to have CalTrans open the Imola Bridge. The club is 0.25 mile above the bridge. Boaters who tie up at the Napa Valley Yacht Club can take a pleasant 0.5-mile walk into the town of Napa. Don't confuse the Napa Valley Yacht Club with the Napa Yacht Club. The Napa Yacht Club is an up-scale, on-the-water housing development 0.25 mile below the Imola Bridge on the west side of the river. It has a private marina reserved for tenants but does not welcome visiting boaters.

Napa Valley Marina Harbormaster	707-252-8011
Napa Valley Yacht Club	707-252-3342
CalTrans Imola/Maxwell Bridge	707-762-6641 or 510-286-0315

Facilities

At Napa Valley Marina
> Chandlery (in the marina store)
> Fuel Dock (gas and diesel)
> Grocery
> Haul Out
> Pump Out
> Restaurant
> Showers

At Napa Valley Yacht Club
> Showers

Attractions

For boaters anchoring out, the attractions are the peaceful nights and the days of watching the waterfowl and the boats going up and down the river. You can take your tender up the river for a look at the river side of the town of Napa; tie up at the city dock during summer months and go ashore to explore the city. South of the Highway 12 winter floods. South of the Highway 12 bridge you can take a trail along the levee for a couple of miles, with a good view of the fields and hills to the west and the river to the east. Just north of the bridge is Horseshoe Slough, an ideal vantage point for viewing egrets and herons roosting in the trees. Or you can go into the Napa Valley Marina fuel dock and go ashore for supplies or tie up at one of the docks at the public park just north of the marina, where nearby is the one accessible restaurant in this immediate area. The John F. Kennedy Memorial Park, north of the marina on the east side of the river, also has a dock. Here, you can go ashore for picnics and hikes both north and south along the levee.

This destination has such a quiet, restful atmosphere you'll regret when your allotted time to spend here has passed.

VALLEJO
Chart #18652, #18654, or #18655

"Damn the torpedoes! Full speed ahead!"

David G. Farragut had the good luck to utter (in the presence of someone standing by to record it) one of those immortal lines that express the emotions of a people at a time of crisis, in this case the Civil War. Scarcely remembered, though, is Farragut's naval role in the decade before the Civil War, when he served as the first commandant of the U. S. Government's first navy yard, and the first Pacific naval installation, at Mare Island. During the next 117 years, from 1853-1970, the Mare Island Shipyard built more than 500 Navy ships. Closed in 1996, Mare Island leaves behind the legacy of a prosperous community: Vallejo, with a population of 112,000.

The native Suisuns occupied these grassy hills and marshy shores before 1835, when General Mariano Guadalupe Vallejo came to colonize his land grant, which he called Suscol and which encompassed what is now Vallejo, Benicia, Napa, and Sonoma. In the 1840s the settlers called their new home "Eden." The city of Vallejo was at one time, like Benicia, a capital of California. Vallejo was the state capital for part of one year in 1852-53. Living and working aboard the steamer *Empire*, members of the legislature met in Vallejo in January, moved to Sacramento for four months, and returned to work in Vallejo until early 1853.

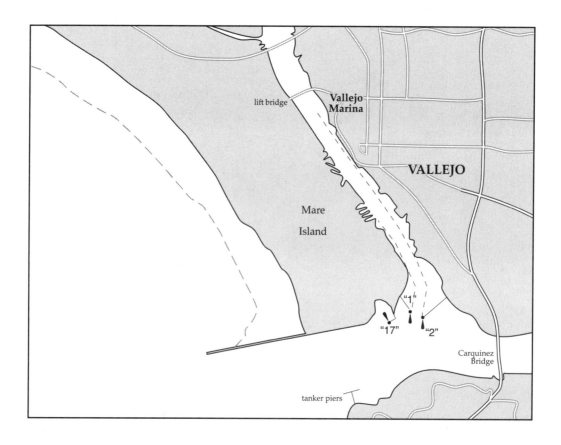

Approach

A cruise to Vallejo from the Bay or Delta makes a good weekend adventure. Those coming from the Bay can depart early in the day, slip under the Richmond-San Rafael Bridge before noon, enjoy the 13.4-mile run across San Pablo Bay, and arrive at Vallejo Marina mid-afternoon. They can enjoy the evening in Vallejo and return to the Bay early the next day. If you want a faster ride under sail and enjoy making a fast passage, then plan to pass the Richmond-San Rafael Bridge early afternoon on a flood. From the Delta, the 23-mile trip from Pittsburg to Vallejo across Suisun Bay, through the Carquinez Strait, and up the Mare Island Strait is a good day's run. A non-stop passage from the Delta to the Central Bay, with 25-knot winds blowing across Suisun and San Pablo Bays, doesn't make good sense. That explains why so many boaters stop in Vallejo.

Plan your departure with a tide guide in hand. From the Bay, pass under the Richmond-San Rafael Bridge just before maximum flood and let the current speed you along. From the Delta, depart just before

The Vallejo Municipal Marina

maximum ebb and ride the current across Suisun Bay.

Whether coming from San Francisco Bay or the Delta, the trip requires only that boaters follow the ship channel. To get to the Vallejo Marina, enter the Mare Island Strait 1 mile west of the Carquinez Bridge on the north side of the Carquinez Strait. Mare Island Strait is a well-marked ship channel. A dike extends from both shores to control waves and swell inside the Strait. The dike on the east side extends 700 yards into the channel, and the west dike extends 500 yards out from Mare Island. The outer 110 yards of the western dike is submerged. Lights mark the ends of the dikes.

Anchorage and Marinas

Vallejo Marina is on the starboard side of the channel, 2.6 miles from the entrance to Mare Island Strait. The blue-roofed white buildings of the marina office are easily visible from the channel.

Immediately south of the Vallejo Marina is the *Vallejo Yacht Club*, fourth oldest yacht club in Northern California. This club offers privileges to members of other yacht clubs.

Even though Mare Island is no longer a U.S. Naval shipyard, private boaters may not anchor off its shores nor land on the island. Because of the private ship repair and dismantling facilities now there, boaters should be cautious when navigating waters around the island.

No anchorage area exists inside or near the Vallejo Marina.

Having more than 800 slips, Vallejo Marina is certainly one of the largest in the San Francisco area. The new portion of the marina has concrete docks and excellent facilities.

Vallejo Municipal Marina   707-648-4370 and VHF 16

Vallejo Yacht Club   707-726-1254

Facilities

At the Vallejo Municipal Marina
   Boat Maintenance and Repair
   Fuel Dock (gasoline and diesel)
   Haul Out
   Laundry
   Pump Out
   Restaurants
   Showers
At the Vallejo Yacht Club
   Showers
Within walking distance of both
   Bank
   Grocery Store
   City Bus Service
   Ferry Service to Angel Island and San Francisco (Ferry Bldg.,
      Fisherman's Wharf, and Pier 39)
   Laundromat
   Restaurants

Attractions

One great attraction of Vallejo, in addition to the exhilarating run across San Pablo Bay or Suisun Bay, is the waterfront along the Vallejo shore of Mare Island Strait. The spiffy new Municipal Marina, with spacious concrete docks and some of the best shower and laundry facilities in the entire Bay Area, is a draw in itself. Combine that with the enhancement the city has added to the waterfront: a wide paved walking/biking path that courses along the water's edge for miles. Vallejo's temperate weather is ideal for outdoor activities.

To make the transition from the waterfront to downtown Vallejo, stop next at the Vallejo Naval and Historical Museum on Marin Street in Old Town. Here you can view the city and Mare Island through a working submarine periscope extended through the roof of the museum.

In the city's beautifully restored Old Town is a Heritage Homes District, one of only four nationally recognized districts west of the Mississippi. This District has over thirty architecturally noteworthy Victorian residences, in a range and mixture of styles, this mix sometimes called the "Working Man's Victorian." All these homes are occupied and not open to the public. A walking tour through the neighborhood will arouse your appreciation for the skills and imagination of the architects and the craftsmen.

Old Town has a practical attraction: you can lay in a fresh store of produce with a visit to the Farmers Market on Georgia Street every Saturday, 900-1300.

If you've come to the Bay Area with the idea of doing most of your sightseeing from your boat, the Vallejo Transit provides bus service to Marine World Africa USA, a wildlife park especially stimulating to sailors of all ages.

GLEN COVE
CHART #18652 or #18657

For the Bay Area boater who wants to get way away—and have the twin stimulants of traversing San Pablo Bay and trying to avoid going aground on the shoals once at the destination—Glen Cove Marina is just the ticket. Up until the late 1980s, this was an isolated cove linked to nearby highways by a dirt road to the old Glen farm. Now, houses cover the hills, but Glen Cove Marina still seems far removed from civilization. A hill obscures the view of the houses and blocks any noise from the paved road that has replaced the winding country road we once bumped along. Adding to the isolation is the tranquil atmosphere of the small marina of 209 slips. With no liveaboards, not much happens during the week.

Glen Cove Marina

The harbormaster's office is in a building built in 1910 as a lighthouse and lifesaving station. It was brought by barge from the breakwater at Vallejo to Glen Cove in 1957. Except for the removal of the lighthouse tower, it is in its original configuration. To see how it looked as a working lighthouse, observe the refurbished lighthouse, now a bed and breakfast, on East Brother. The two lighthouses share a common design.

The pilings west of Glen Cove are remnants of a grain dock, one of the many that once lined the banks of Carquinez Strait to load ships with wheat and barley bound for ports around the world.

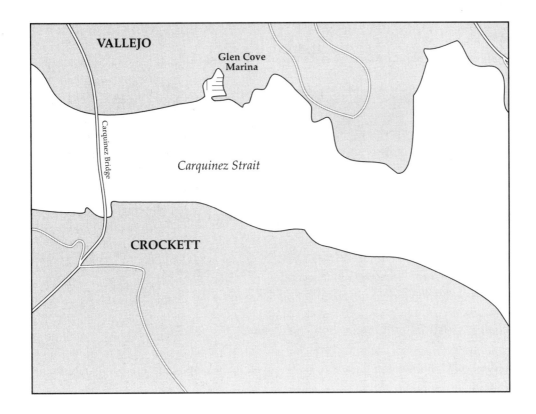

Approach

Plan for the trip to Glen Cove to offer a little of everything. Coming from the Bay, don't choose your departure time casually. First, choose a time that will allow you to arrive at the marina at high tide. Second, depart to take advantage of a flood or slack tide to avoid battling a 4- or 5-knot ebb tide. And finally, choose a departure time to take advantage of the kind of winds that are best for your boat. During the morning hours, you will generally encounter light winds and calm seas. Afternoon winds often blow at 20 knots or more, creating lumpy seas.

The distance between the Richmond-San Rafael Bridge and the Carquinez Bridge is only 14.4 miles, so that part of the trip is relatively short if you take advantage of tide and wind.

Glen Cove is easy to recognize from the Strait. As you pass under the Carquinez Bridge (134 feet clearance), proceed 0.6 mile east. The entrance to the marina appears suddenly. Identify the metal roofing of the many covered powerboat slips and the large 25-room white lighthouse and lifesaving station tucked back inside the cove. No sign identifies the marina, but it is the first marina on the port side after the Carquinez Bridge.

If you are approaching from the Delta, pass under the Benicia-Martinez Bridge and proceed west through the Carquinez Strait for 5.1 miles.

Entering Glen Cove Marina offers as much excitement as most boaters need. Like all other marinas in the Carquinez Strait, Glen Cove Marina personnel struggle to keep ahead of the shoaling. At high water, most boats will find enough water to go in without going aground, but enter only after checking with the harbormaster.

Be especially observant of the currents when entering the marina. With a strong ebb or flood, you will encounter a number of changes in the direction of the current as you enter. This erratic current can turn around a slow-moving light boat.

Anchorage and Marina

Glen Cove has no anchorage area. Boaters wishing to anchor out in the Carquinez Strait area should refer to the Benicia section for suggestions.

Glen Cove Marina has a fine new 100-foot concrete dock just north of the fuel dock that can accommodate a number of guest boats, and the harbormaster will gladly put guests in any empty slips.

Harbormaster   707-552-3236

Facilities

You probably won't be tempted to walk to town from Glen Cove Marina since the nearest town is Vallejo, about a 3-mile trek up a steep hill.

Laundromat
Public transportation
Pump Out
Shower
Small store with drinks and snacks

Attractions

Glen Cove has only itself to attract boaters. Steep hills carpeted with wildflowers in the spring cradle this diminutive cove. Across the Strait the lights of the sugar refinery at Crockett gleam at night, but you hear only the sounds of the water lapping at high tide or of the geese and ducks talking overhead.

BENICIA
Chart #18652 or #18657

A weekend cruise to Benicia has grown popular with Bay Area boaters looking for a relaxing two- or three-day cruise. The run north through San Francisco Bay, across San Pablo Bay, and then down Carquinez Strait can be boating at its best, and Benicia gives one a sense of being in another world and time. It has wonderful weather: sunny summer days cooled by the breeze off the Strait. In some ways, Benicia reminds you of a town in the Mother Lode: small, quiet, and clean, and on every corner a building or a site that figured in the town's lively past.

Founded in 1847 on land deeded to Dr. Robert Semple by General Mariano Vallejo, Benicia was named after Vallejo's wife. The town soon became one of the most important towns in the Bay Area as a point of departure for gold prospectors traveling from the San Francisco Peninsula to the Mother Lode. In 1849 the U. S. Army established Benicia Barracks (later renamed the Benicia Arsenal), one of the strategic forts for the defense of San Francisco Bay. In 1850 Benicia and Monterey were the first two California cities to incorporate. Benicia's enduring claim to a place in California history is its short tenure as the state's capital. For thirteen months in 1853-54 the legislature met here in what had been the city hall. However, Sacramento's larger size and proximity to the gold fields attracted the legislators, and the governor had a home there. So the capital was moved once again.

Greater promise for Benicia's economic future came in 1879 when it was designated as the

Historic State Capitol at Benicia

site of a transcontinental railroad depot. Trains were loaded onto the then world's largest ferry and taken across Carquinez Strait to Port Costa, where they continued on to San Francisco. During this same period, Benicia was the principal tanning center of the Pacific Coast and the site of numerous canneries to process both fish and produce. Then in 1882 one of San Francisco's most successful shipbuilders, Matthew Turner, moved his shipyard to Benicia, where he turned out more than 115 ships in the next twenty years. Turner designed the famous *Nautilus* and the

Galilee. (The stern of the *Galilee* is on display in the San Francisco Maritime Museum.) Benicia's boom days had come indeed!

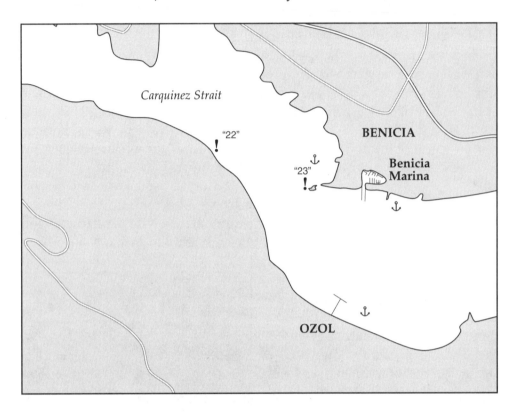

Approach

The trip to Benicia can be quick and exhilarating, depending on your time of departure and the tide state. From the Richmond-San Rafael Bridge to the Carquinez Bridge is14.4 miles, and Benicia is only another 3.6 miles, making a trip total of 19 miles. Use your tide book to plan your trip. If a 4.6 knot flood tide is running when you make the passage, you can easily cut two hours off the usual time. And if a 4.6 knot ebb is running, you can add two hours or more. Pass under the Richmond-San Rafael Bridge just before maximum flood to ride the flood to Benicia.

Boaters looking for a calm passage should cross San Pablo Bay before early afternoon, while the winds are light and the seas flat. Sailors looking for more action can enjoy a boisterous broad reach by crossing later in the day. Occasionally, though, the winds blow directly out of the south, providing a beam reach in nearly flat seas. The Benicia harbormaster's office closes at 5:30, so plan to arrive before that time, or call ahead to make arrangements.

After passing the Carquinez Bridge, continue eastward along Carquinez Strait. At 3.0 miles on the port side, a square green daymark, #23, marks the remains of the old Benicia wharf. The entrance to the marina is 0.5 mile beyond Marker 23. Though harbor policy is to keep the entrance and marina dredged to a depth of 7 feet at low water, personnel often cannot keep up with the shoaling. While you're not likely to go aground at high water, don't count on more than 3-4 feet at low.

If you are approaching from the east, pass under the Benicia-Martinez Bridge and go 2.0 miles west to the Benicia Marina.

Recognize the marina entrance by identifying the breakwaters that extend 500 feet into Carquinez Strait. Enter the marina through the 60-foot-wide entrance between the two breakwaters. Traditional navigation lights are at the end of each breakwater.

Anchorage and Marina

Benicia Marina has no anchorage area, but a few options exist outside the marina. Some boaters anchor west of Marker 23 on the north side of Carquinez Strait. Depths close to shore are shallow, and the shelf drops off abruptly from about 6 to 50 feet in many places. Find an area with a depth of 6-10 feet at low water, and anchor in mud bottom with good holding. Expect heavy winds from the west in the afternoon to produce an uncomfortable anchorage.

Another anchorage is 0.22 mile east of the marina entrance, just past Sander's tow boat dock. This anchorage will give you protection from west and northwest winds, but avoid this anchorage when south winds blow. The area between the Benicia Marina entrance and Sander's dock is shallow close to shore.

A third anchorage, protected from southerly and westerly winds, is directly across Carquinez Strait from the marina. Anchor 500-1,000 yards east of the Ozol pier in 10 feet of water. **Do not anchor here when north winds blow.**

With 350 slips, Benicia Marina can normally provide guest slips for most visitors. Since this is a popular destination, you should call ahead. Tie up at the fuel dock, taking care not to block the pumps, while you sign in with the harbormaster.

Entrance to Benicia Marina

Benicia Marina   707-745-2628 and VHF 16

Note! Begin the trip back to San Francisco Bay early, and take advantage of an ebb. Winds normally blow at 20 knots or more on the nose across San Pablo Bay in the afternoon. By mid-afternoon the waves are steep and choppy. If you depart after midday on a flood, you will find yourself weathering quite a thrash to windward.

Facilities

One of the attractions of the Benicia Marina is its location. It is only a block east of First Street, the heart of town, where restaurants, shops, and other businesses abound.

At the Marina:
> Fuel Dock (gasoline and diesel)
> Grocery Store (with a modest deli)
> Launch Ramp
> Laundromat
> Pump Out

Attractions

The pleasures of a small town are easy to experience in Benicia. Many sites of historic interest are centrally located and near the marina. The historic California State Capitol, the Fischer-Hanlon House and Gardens, and the Tannery are but three sites meriting a visit. Walk out to the waterfront and marvel at the skill of the windsurfers in the Strait. Or, better still, get out and join them. The Strait here is one of the best windsurfing spots on the West Coast.

MARTINEZ
Chart #18652 and #18657

The only skyline of the modest town of Martinez, strategically located at the upper reaches of Carquinez Strait, is the monolith petroleum storage tanks erected for Shell Oil's Martinez Manufacturing Complex. Don't let the dominance of this skyline mislead you, however. Martinez really is much more than a company town, though the petroleum industry contributes significantly to its economic well-being. As a cruising destination, Martinez has much to entice you, even if you're not interested in admiring tanks on hillsides.

Martinez arose on this spot because California's only state-owned ferry began its run from this spot to Benicia in 1847—with the use of true horse power. This ferry was the primary access to the gold country for gold seekers coming through San Francisco. The sandy beaches, now long since silted over, the mild climate, and the cooling breezes blowing off the Strait were apparently beguiling. Some of the visitors to this stopover on the Argonaut Trail stayed on and founded a town. The last passenger ferry, the *Carquinez*, carrying cars to Benicia, made its final run on September 14, 1962, ending 115 years of ferry service between Martinez and Benicia.

The Central Pacific Railroad completed its connection to Martinez in 1879. Ocean-going vessels docked in Martinez to load grain brought by rail, scow schooners, and barges. At this time Central California was the largest grain-producing area in the nation. By 1884, grain wharves were continuous along 4 or 5 miles of the strait, but by the early 20th

Martinez Marina entrance

century these wharves were no longer profitable and fell into disuse and disrepair.

Sicilian fishermen stayed on when they docked their feluccas after tending their salmon, shad, and bass nets. One might assume some member of this Italian community was responsible for inventing the "martini," reportedly originating in Martinez. However, the local version is that the name is a shortened version of "Martinez," too much to pronounce after two or three martinis, and that the drink was first poured by Julio Richelieu to a thirsty returning miner in 1874.

Don Ygnacio Martinez, commander of the San Francisco Presidio between 1822 and 1831, held a Spanish grant to this area of rolling hills, Rancho El Pinole. The town named after him arose on the shores of what was then a much wider and deeper strait. The site of the present Martinez harbor was under 50 feet of water before this century. The silt from rivers flowing into Suisun Bay—the Sacramento and the San Joaquin—continues to create a perpetual challenge to all the marinas in the North Bay-Delta waters.

Approach

Boaters from San Francisco will go under the Richmond-San Rafael Bridge, across San Pablo Bay, under the Carquinez Bridge, and then 4.7 miles through Carquinez Strait. The Martinez Marina is on the south shore of the strait 1.0 mile west of the Benicia-Martinez Bridge and 0.2 mile southwest of the Shell Oil pier where ocean-going tankers

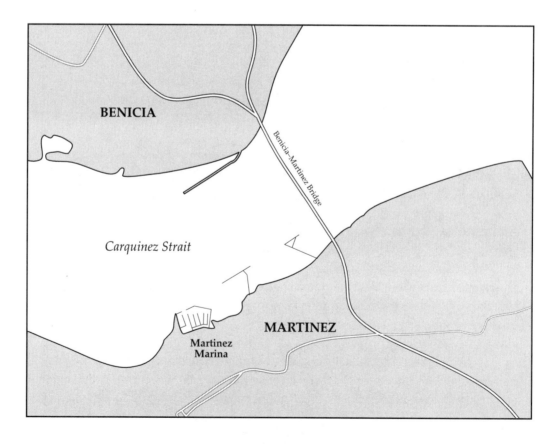

tie up. A large neon sign advertising the fuel dock is at the marina entrance, which is immediately east of an inactive ferry landing and a recently rebuilt fishing pier.

Anchorage and Berthing

There is no safe anchorage inside Martinez Marina. Some boaters swing to a lunch hook 0.6 mile west of the marina entrance during the day. However, this anchorage is shallow unless you're uncomfortably close to the ship channel. (The Benicia section of this book covers three other anchorages from which boaters can visit Martinez by dinghy or sportboat.)

Enter Martinez Marina only at high water unless you check with the harbormaster. Like most Carquinez and Delta marinas, Martinez has serious difficulties keeping up with the shoaling. Marina personnel attempt to keep the entrance dredged to a depth of 8 feet at low water, but constant shoaling frequently reduces actual depth to 4 feet or less.

Martinez Marina offers guest berthing at reasonable rates. Tie up at the long fuel dock and go to the harbormaster's office to check in.

Martinez Marina   925-313-0942 and VHF 16

Facilities

At the marina
> Amtrak
> Bait and Tackle Shop
> Boat Maintenance and Repair
> Fuel Dock (gasoline and diesel)
> Haul Out
> Launch Ramp
> Laundry
> Pump Out
> Showers

The marina is only a few blocks from Martinez, where you can find all the facilities of a small town.

Attractions

Excellent walking and biking trails are close by, many along the shoreline. The East Bay Regional Shoreline Park schedules bird walks regularly. If you miss one, take some bird seed to the small lake southeast of the marina, and surround yourself with as many geese and ducks as can fit on the grassy knoll.

In keeping with the Italian influence in Martinez, Waterfront Park has bocce ball courts. If bocce is not your sport of choice, one of the fourteen parks, several within walking distance of the marina, will surely have facilities to interest you.

The marina also has one of the better fishing piers around, made even more attractive because you don't need a license. A fisherwoman here reports catching bass, sturgeon, and flounder off the pier.

A short walk into town and you'll find the largest collection of antique shops in Contra Costa County. You'll also find one of the cleanest, prettiest towns around. Wide brick sidewalks take you past well-preserved stores and houses from the 1800s and classic structures from the first half of this century. On Thursdays, between May and October, a popular farmers' market occupies much of Main Street. Martinez has the sort of downtown for a leisure afternoon of strolling and browsing before returning to the quiet marina to watch sea and shore birds feeding at sunset.

SUISUN CITY
Chart #18656 or #18652

Part of the city's redevelopment project, Suisun City Marina, built in 1994, sits in the heart of Old Suisun City, a place with plenty of history and a world of charm. In 1990 the city began dredging and widening the badly silted Suisun Slough, a 12-mile water-way emptying into Suisun Bay where the Sacramento River meets San Francisco Bay.

City hall on Suisun City's waterfront

The native Patwins who inhabited these shores before the arrival of the Europeans harvested the many species of fish, fowl and game abundant in and around the slough.

The Gold Rush was instrumental in the birth of the settlement; beginning in 1851, miners came up the slough by boat as far as this site and then made their way by land to the gold fields. Beginning in 1851, steamers transported commercial goods to and from San Francisco. By 1854 the town had streets and a name: "Suisun," meaning "west wind," which does indeed blow through these hills. Suisun City continued to prosper as a port and, later, as the agricultural hub of Solano County. In 1869 Suisun City became a link to the East Coast via the transcontinental railroad. The town's prosperity waned when trucks replaced rail as the primary mode for the transport of commercial goods.

The redevelopment project begun in 1990 has restored vitality to Old Town and its adjacent waterfront. Main Street, one block from the marina, bustles with small-town activity and atmosphere. Ideal for visiting boaters, Main Street invites walking. You'll feel right at home as you stroll along the side streets of turn-of-the century houses and churches and wander into the shops and restaurants along Main.

Approach

The trip to Suisun City offers challenge, adventure, and diversity. Plan carefully to make certain you use the weather and tide to advantage. To begin with, consider the distance. Once at Vallejo, you are still about 23 miles from Suisun City, so plan accordingly.

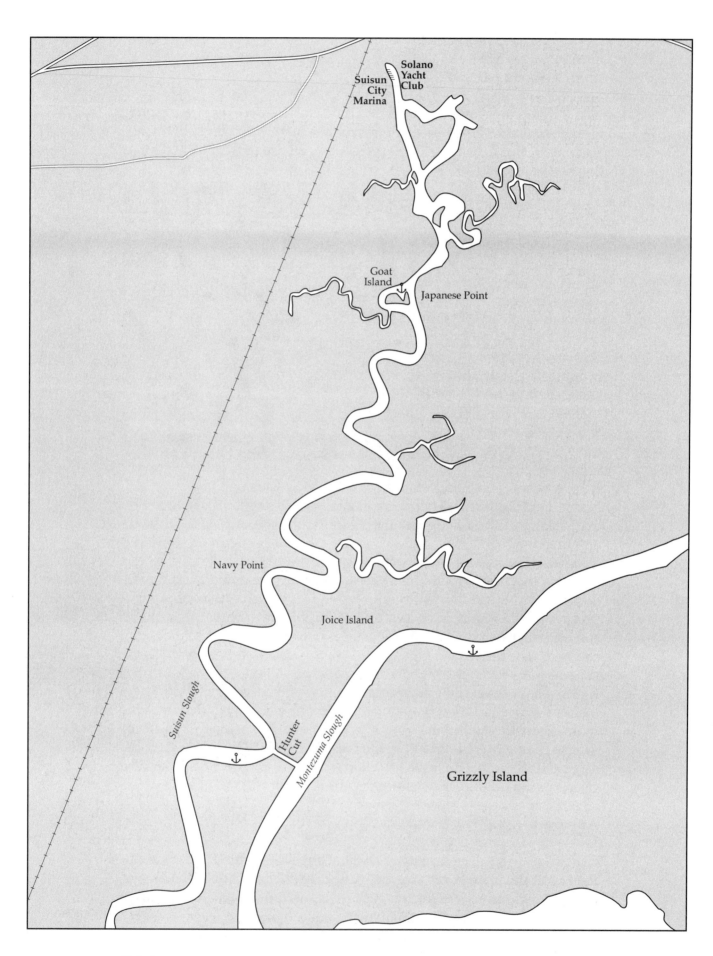

Attempt this trip only at or just before high water unless you are sailing a boat with a particularly shallow draft.

The challenge begins after you depart from the Benicia-Martinez Bridge. The channel to Suisun City is on the port side of Buoy 2; do not stray outside the channel to starboard, or you will be aground in short order. The Mothball Fleet (decommissioned Navy ships) will be on your port side as you proceed up the channel, passing markers 2, 4 and 6 on your starboard.

After passing Marker 6, continue on to Marker 9, the beginning of the channel into Suisun Slough. Do not turn into Suisun Slough at this entrance; shallow water between the entrance and Hunter Cut makes this portion of the Slough almost impassable. Charts show 10-20 feet of water in this portion of the Slough, but don't believe it. We recently made the passage at high water and found only 5-6 feet of water in many places.

Local boaters go from Marker 9 to Montezuma Slough to Hunter Cut . When you leave Marker 9, you might have trouble identifying the entrance into Montezuma Slough because the tule grass blends together and makes the slough hard to see. Follow a course of about 337 degrees mag. or use your radar, and you will soon see the entrance.

The trip from Hunter Cut up to Suisun City is picturesque, of course, since you travel through almost totally uninhabited marshlands. Powerboats have the advantage on this trip because those on the bridge can see over the levees and because they generally have shallower draft.

Local boaters warn visitors to be aware of the shoaling on the inside of the turn at

Winding along Suisun Slough

Navy Point. Swing this turn wide or you'll be hard aground, even at high tide.

Watch the chart closely as you pass Goat Island because the channel shoals markedly at Japanese Point. You'll need to remain alert to avoid going aground in these two areas, but otherwise you will need only to stay in the center of the channel to have ample water.

The trip to Suisun City is challenging, but no more so than the trip to Napa or Petaluma, and it certainly isn't as challenging as the trip to Alviso. Local boaters advise making the trip at high tide since shallow spots exist. Sailboats drawing 6 feet regularly make the trip, so plan the trip with confidence.

Winds are another factor to consider. In the spring and summer, the prevailing westerlies normally blow across Suisun Bay at 20-30 knots during the afternoon. Once inside the sloughs, however, the winds are not a problem.

Anchorage and Berthing

As you might expect, you can find endless spots to anchor in both Montezuma and Suisun Sloughs if you just want to get away from civilization and enjoy a quiet evening or weekend. Don't succumb to the temptation to pull off into one of the many small sloughs that branch off Suisun Slough, or you'll almost certainly find yourself aground. In fact, even if you decide to anchor in Suisun Slough, make sure you have enough water to remain afloat when the tide goes out. As with all slough anchoring, do not anchor in the middle of the slough because of boat traffic. And, because boaters transit the sloughs after dark, be sure to set your anchor light.

Guest berthing is available at the *Suisun City Marina* (150 berths). The *Solano Yacht Club* can provide guest berthing for members of visiting yacht clubs.

Suisun City Marina 707-429-2628

Solano Yacht Club   707-428-9701

Facilities

At Suisun City Marina
> Fuel (gasoline and diesel)
> Groceries
> Launch Ramp
> Laundromat
> Pump Out
> Restaurants
> Showers

At Solano Yacht Club
  Showers
  Other facilities above: 1 mile

Attractions

  Here you can discover, as did the native Patwins, the bounty of wildlife in these prime wetlands. Fishing is excellent, either from shore or from your tender. Catfish, striped bass, sturgeon, and salmon are among the tasty catches. If viewing is more to your taste, walk along the slough, where you'll see abundant waterfowl. Visit the modest but interesting Wildlife Center of the Suisun Marsh Natural History Association on Kellogg Street. From there, stroll over to Main Street past the attractive Town Plaza, a grass semicircle adorned with a granite and bronze stage and a segmented glass-domed gazebo. At the north end of Main and one block west is Rail Station Plaza, Amtrak's only Solano County stop between San Francisco and Sacramento.

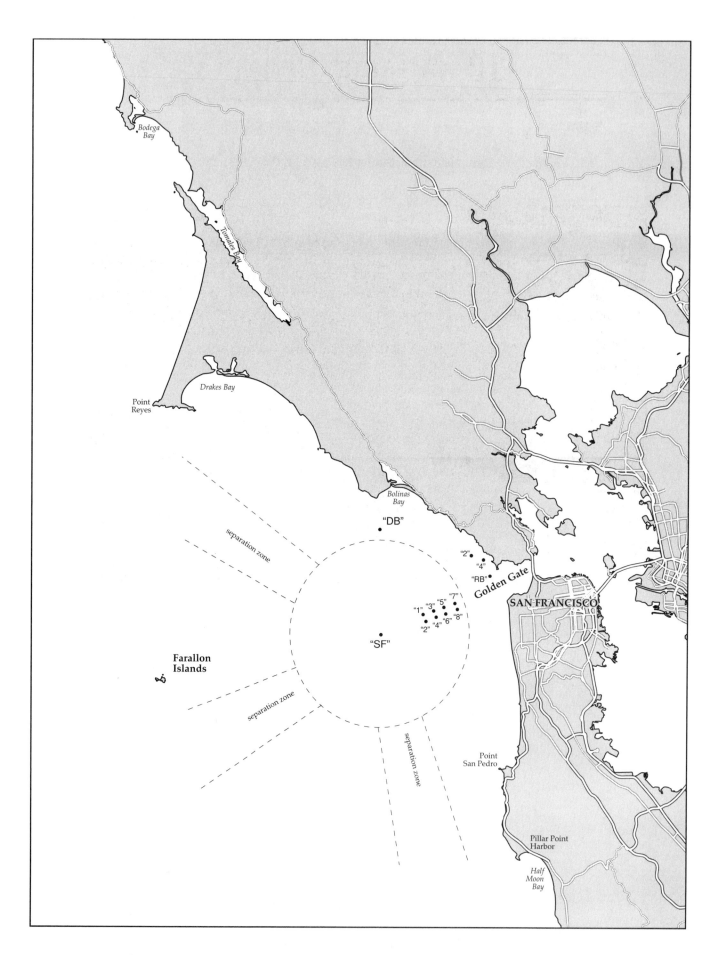

10 OUTSIDE THE BAY

*Not farre without this harborough [Drakes Bay] did lye certain islands. . .
having on them plentifull & great stores of Seals & birds.*
    —Sir Francis Drake

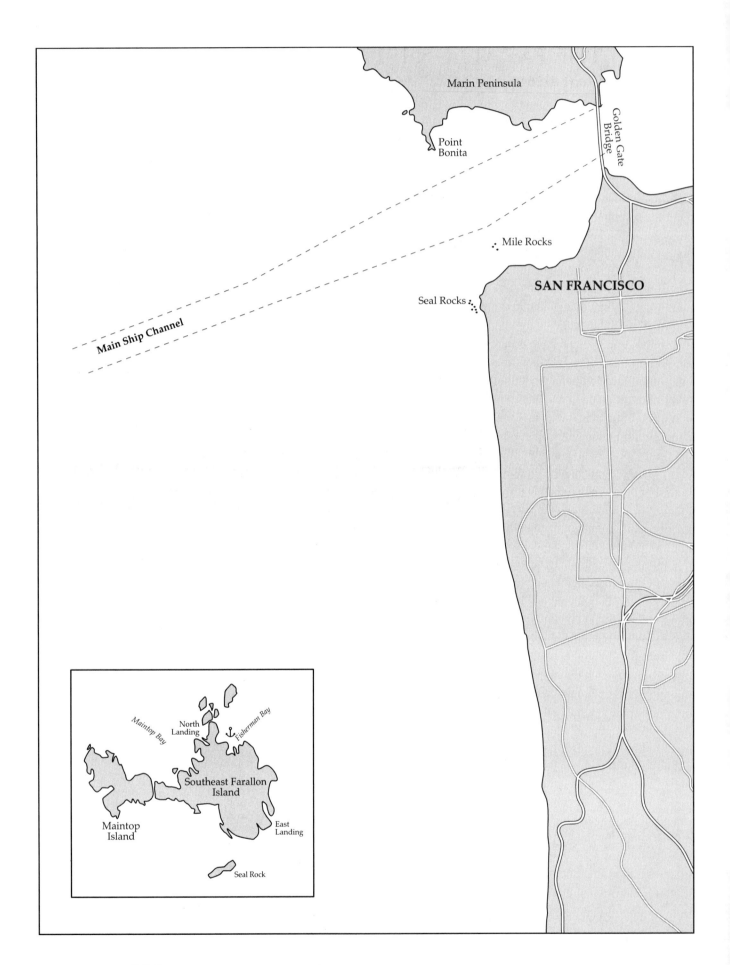

Marin Peninsula

Point
Bonita

Golden Gate
Bridge

Main Ship Channel

Mile Rocks

SAN FRANCISCO

Seal Rocks

Maintop Bay

North
Landing

Fisherman Bay

Southeast Farallon
Island

Maintop
Island

East
Landing

Seal Rock

THE FARALLON ISLANDS
Chart #18645

The Farallones (Spanish for "small rocky islands in the sea") lie 27 miles offshore from the Golden Gate Bridge. These rocky islands support only meager plant life, notably the Farallon weed, whose dark green color occasionally relieves the tans and grays of the rock-covered landscape. Sir Francis Drake landed on Southeast Farallon in 1579 to collect sea bird eggs and seal meat for provisions. He named the group of seven islands the Islands of St. James. In the

Southeast Farallon Island

early 19th-century, Boston fur sealers and Aleut otter hunters from Fort Ross used the Farallones as a base. The last Russian hunters left the Farallones, and California, in 1841. Fourteen years later, the Coast Guard built a lighthouse on the 365-foot peak of Southeast Farallon. From the late 1870s to 1972, when the light was automated, lighthouse keepers and their families lived in the two wooden houses still standing in the lee of this peak.

During the second half of the 19th-century, the Farallon Egg Company collected sea bird eggs on these islands to sell in the cities and mining camps of Northern California. The advent of chicken farming near Petaluma in the 1880s ended this enterprise but not before decimation of the common murre and cormorant populations. By 1900, the number of common murres nesting on the islands had dropped from 500,000 to a mere 15,000. Today these islands are a part of a National Wildlife Refuge and Marine Sanctuary, overseen by the staff and volunteers of the Point Reyes Bird Observatory. Once again the islands are alive with birds. Breeding here are 200,000 birds of 12 species, among them 80% of California's Cassin's auklets, the world's largest nesting population of ashy storm petrels, and a large population of western gulls. Another 350 species of migratory birds stop off to feed here in one of California's richest fisheries.

The Farallones are alive, as well, with California sea lions, elephant seals, and harbor seals sunbathing on the rocks or swimming in the coves. Great white sharks patrol these waters, preying on the pinnipeds. A school of porpoises may appear to gambol in your bow wave. Farther out you may spot migrating whales, most commonly grays but occasionally blues, humpbacks, and minkes.

The only anchorage, Fisherman Bay on Southeast Farallon, is at best marginal. Landing is forbidden by U. S. Fish and Wildlife Service regulations. Nevertheless, the Farallones make for a fascinating day sail when the days are long enough to permit a comfortable round-trip passage in daylight. The outward passage hard on the wind can be uncomfortable, but the abundant wildlife and the prospect of a fast broad reach home in the afternoon more than compensate for the discomfort. We have made the trip to the Farallones on our boat at least a dozen times and have found each trip different and exciting.

PASSAGE-MAKING STRATEGIES

General Comments

The winter weather is often poor off the Northern California coast. Late spring and early summer with their longer days are ideal seasons for a passage to the Farallon Islands, when the 20-knot winds will give you a thrilling reach home. Late summer and fall offer lighter winds and calmer seas, but you can encounter boisterous weather here year-round. Swells and wind waves regularly reach 7 feet or more, so be prepared for rough seas.

Whatever the season, plan your departure for early in the day, when the prevailing northwesterlies are lighter and the seas are calmer. If tidal conditions permit, pass under the Golden Gate Bridge just before sunrise so that you can be at or near the islands before the wind fills in strongly at midday.

Tide State

Exit the Golden Gate at slack water or during a moderate tidal flow. The Potato Patch becomes dangerously turbulent during both heavy ebb and flood tides. *Tides and Currents* shows, however, that heavy currents are running only a few days a month. Simply by moving your departure time an hour earlier or later, you can exit the Gate with a current of less than 4 knots on 20 days of a typical month.

Courses

Once outside the Golden Gate and well clear of off-lying rocks at Point Bonita, with the lighthouse approximately 100 yards off your starboard beam, set a course of 238° mag. for Southeast Farallon if no wind is blowing to push your boat south of the desired course. More ordinarily, though, you'll need to set your course 5-10 degrees more windward to assure landfall north of the island. Don't allow the wind to set you south of Southeast Farallon Island, or you will have a miserable time trying to lay the island against the large ocean swells and heavy winds that are normal in the area. If you depart at dawn, you'll probably motor sail most of the way, the passage taking the average small yacht about 6-7 hours.

The direct course to and from the Farallones passes through heavily traveled shipping lanes and congested fishing grounds. Maintain a sharp look out, and do not attempt this passage in thick, low fog. Most of the time the high fog will allow 1 to 2 miles visibility. For comfort on the outward passage, reschedule your trip if anticipated winds are over 20 knots.

Description

The low-lying Farallon Islands are rarely visible for more than 5 miles. Maintain an accurate DR plot, allow for current and tidal flow, and use radar or GPS if you have it. In typical hazy conditions, your first sight of the islands will be a shadowy protrusion on the horizon, but the main features will not stand out until you are about a mile off. Then you will see the gray and tan rocks of the 365-foot peak on Southeast Farallon with the white lighthouse atop it. Visible, too, will be the splashes of white water breaking on the sheer cliffs to the northwest of Fisherman Bay. Then the crane used by the PRBO personnel to hoist themselves and their equipment and supplies up the 70 feet from the water onto the island will come into view. Only then, you may begin to see the few green splotches of the Farallon weed. The two weathered white houses are not visible from this approach.

FISHERMAN BAY

The Farallon Islands are a National Marine Sanctuary, with a 300-foot restricted area around them except for Fisherman Bay, where you may anchor. Consider this bay a temporary stopping place; the surge and refracting waves from nearby rocks make for an uncomfortable stay, even in calm weather.

Once you have visually spotted the lighthouse, you can locate the anchorage at Fisherman Bay because it is only 400 yards north of it, on the north shore of the island. The anchorage is protected to the northwest by several rocky islets upon which the waves crash. An old crane and a small brown building are on the southwest shore of the anchorage. This crane, unlike the modern steel crane on the southeast corner of the island, is made of timber and is no longer used.

Anchorage

Anchor about 750 feet from shore in 50 feet or deeper water, or pick up the Coast Guard buoy if it's not in use. The latter, about 1,000 feet from the shore, offers even less protection from the surge and waves than an anchor spot closer in. If you anchor, lay plenty of scope, even on calm days.

Landing and Facilities

Landing on the islands is forbidden: they are protected as a wildlife refuge and marine sanctuary. If you want to anchor out overnight, plan to end your passage with the 18-mile run north to Drake's Bay. The course is to weather, but the anchorage is far more comfortable than that at Southeast Farallon.

Crane hoisting biologists onto island

DRAKES BAY
Chart #18645, #18647, or #18680

In their journal entries for the year 1579, Sir Francis Drake and members of his crew described a well-protected bay along the Northern California coast, where they careened the *Golden Hind* for five weeks while they made repairs on the ship's keel. In recent years some historians have questioned whether that bay was indeed the bay we now call "Drakes" or whether it lay farther north, perhaps in Campbell Cove, at the entrance of Bodega Harbor.

Later explorers clearly found this bay. In 1595 the sailing ship *San Agustin* went aground here in a storm, stranding the captain, Sebastian Rodriguez Cermeño, and his crew. Another Spanish captain exploring the California coast in 1603, Don Sebastian Vizcaino anchored

Fish buyers' pier at Drakes Bay.

in Drakes Bay on January 6, the day of the Feast of the Three Kings and thus named the rocky headlands "La Punta de Los Tres Reyes," which subsequently became simply "Point Reyes."

Whether or not Drake found shelter in the bay now bearing his name, many a modern day sailor has discovered its abundant rewards, one of which is indeed the fine protection the Point Reyes Headlands provides in the prevailing northwesterlies.

Another attraction for many San Francisco Bay boaters is the remoteness of Drakes. The shore and hills surrounding Drakes Bay are part of the extensive Point Reyes National Seashore. The nearest town is almost 20 miles away, and at night you'll see few lights except for those on the boats that moor or anchor here regularly. The sounds of city life will not intrude on the evening symphony of the rhythmic calls of the gulls and the black oystercatchers, accompanied by the splash of the brown pelicans diving for fish.

Approach

Drakes Bay is some 25 miles northwest of the Golden Gate. After clearing Point Bonita buoy and the Potato Patch, set a course for the buoy at Duxbury Reef, about 8 miles northwest of Bonita Light. When you pass the buoy at Duxbury, you can change course slightly for G"1" buoy off Drakes Bay and travel another 15 miles. Approaching Drakes from the north, go approximately 3 miles east after rounding Point Reyes before arriving at the buoy off Drakes Bay.

We recommend you make a trip to Drakes Bay only when the weather forecast calls for prevailing north or northwest winds of no more than 15 knots. (Never anchor in Drakes Bay in either south or east winds.) If possible, depart for Drakes early in the day, before the winds and seas have built up, and on slack water to avoid unpleasant conditions in the waters around Point Bonita and in the Potato Patch.

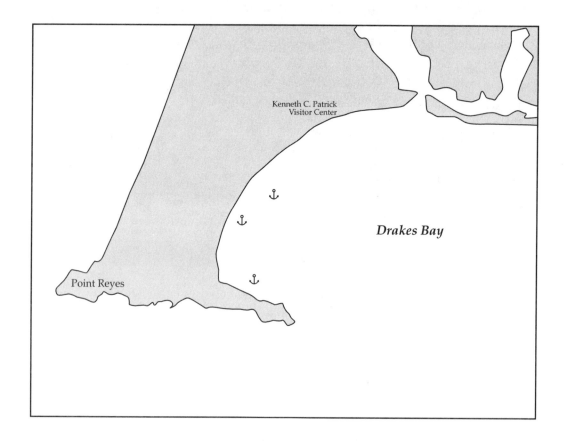

Anchorage

The best anchorage in Drakes Bay is off the westernmost of the two piers in the southwest corner of the bay. You'll recognize this anchorage area by the other boats—primarily commercial fishing boats—anchored or moored here. In fact, in some seasons you must choose an anchoring spot carefully because of the number of other boats in Drakes. On occasion, we've seen as many as 40 boats anchored in this bay on summer nights.

As you enter the bay, you'll see the Coast Guard buoy northeast of the pier. The water near the CG buoy is about 20 feet deep, but the depth near the old pier, where private and fishing boaters like to anchor, is closer to 15 feet. When the anchorage area is particularly crowded, both private and commercial boaters also anchor off the cliffs to the north of the pier in about 30 feet of water.

At Drakes Bay, dig your anchor in carefully. The bottom near the old pier has some grass and kelp that your anchor will have to penetrate. Farther away from the pier, the bottom is sand, especially near the cliffs to the north. For this reason, some boaters anchor near the cliffs even when the more popular area is not overcrowded.

Not only will the conditions on the bottom require you to anchor carefully, but the wind strength can also challenge your anchor. We have spent many nights anchored here when the wind blew in excess of 30 knots, and, yes, we learned about the grassy bottom the hard way, resetting our anchor numerous times until we were finally confident that it would hold. But the good news is that the water in Drakes Bay is calm even in heavy winds.

Facilities

At the trailhead parking lot:
    Restrooms
At the Kenneth C. Patrick Visitor Center (on the beach, approx. 3 mi. NE of the pier)
    Restrooms
    Showers
    Snack bar (open seasonally)
    Telephone

Attractions

Drakes Bay as a getaway site has more to offer than escape. For the nature lover, few spots in or around San Francisco Bay rival it.

For beach strolling, the golden sands of Drakes Beach curve for 4 miles, from the Historic Point Reyes Lifeboat Station to Drakes Estero.

For hiking rather than strolling, a trail leads up into the Headlands to Sea Lion Overlook and Point Reyes Lighthouse, the lighthouse in operation since 1870. From the Headlands you can watch thousands of common murres on the ledges below and harbor seals and sea lions drying out on the rocky shores or gliding and diving in the near-shore ocean. Between November and April, the migrating gray whales pass near to shore on their annual roundtrip from the Gulf of Alaska to the warm bays of Baja California, where they calve and mate before returning to Alaska in the spring to feed.

Birders from around the country come to the Point Reyes National Seashore that surrounds Drakes Bay to observe the hundreds of thousands of birds that frequent this flyway in their annual migrations, roughly between June and December. From the north, come ospreys, Arctic terns, Sabine's gulls, phalaropes, fulmars, jaegers, and fifteen species of hawks, as well as many species of songbirds. Depending on the month, you may see storm-petrels, shearwaters, albatrosses, Xantus' murrelets, skuas, loons, grebes, and diving ducks. It's a birders' feast for the eyes and the ears!

From the anchorage, take a sport boat ride along the beach to the Kenneth C. Patrick Visitor Center to see the exhibits of the wildlife in the Point Reyes National Seashore as well as of the Coast Miwoks who inhabited these lands before the Europeans arrived. (Be cautious about where you land your dinghy; the opportunities for a wet landing increase at this end of the beach.)

TOMALES BAY
Chart #18640 or #18643

The slender, pencil-like bay that opens up through a narrow gap in the southern reach of Bodega Bay is an anomaly of geology. The San Andreas Fault Zone, well-known for the destruction it periodically causes all along this portion of the Northern California coastline, separates the Bolinas Ridge to the east from the Inverness Ridge on the Point Reyes Peninsula. This fault zone runs along the length of Tomales Bay, from its mouth in Bodega Bay to its head, and continues in a more or less straight line to Bolinas Bay. The Peninsula is on the Pacific Ocean Plate, and the continual northwest shifting of this plate, a generally gradual shift estimated to have begun about 30 million years ago, has created Tomales Bay. The Peninsula took a giant leap northwestward of approximately 20 feet during the 1906 quake.

Spanish explorer Lt. Juan Francisco de Bodega y Cuadra, on the ship *Sonora*, was the first European of certain record to find the well-disguised entrance into Tomales Bay. He called this body of water, described as "a considerable river" by his sailing master, "de la Bodega." After the *Sonora* anchored at the mouth of the bay in 1775, the sailing master, Antonio Mourelle, noted in his journal the hazards of this entrance:

> *. . . in de la Bodega* [Tomales Bay] *on the first flow of the tide, in a contrary direction to that of the currents, the sea ran so high that our whole ship was engulfed while the boat along side was shattered to pieces.*
>
> *There is not sufficient depth of anchorage at the mouth of this port for a vessel to resist this violent surge. . . .*

In 1852, a group claiming title to a Mexican land grant called the five square leagues on the northeast side of the bay "Rancho Bolsa de Tamallos," the "Bolsa" perhaps signifying a pocket, and "Tamallos" being the name of the group of Coast Miwoks that had historically occupied the tract. "Tomales Bay" is the name that has survived.

While the name may have changed a bit over the years, one characteristic of this bay has remained constant: the hazards at the entrance.

In the first half of the 19th century, the Aleuts that the Russians at Fort Ross had brought down to hunt fur-bearing animals almost decimated the seal and otter populations of Tomales and other Northern California bays.

The next thriving industry of the Tomales region that remains in evidence today is the dairy industry. While the farming of some crops, notably potatoes and grain, has taken place alongside the bay, these hillsides have proven most nurturing for dairy cattle. With the coming of the Swiss immigrants in the 1870s, dairy farming became the mainstay of the region. Several dairies remain, though many have closed down, and much of the former dairy land has become part of the national park system.

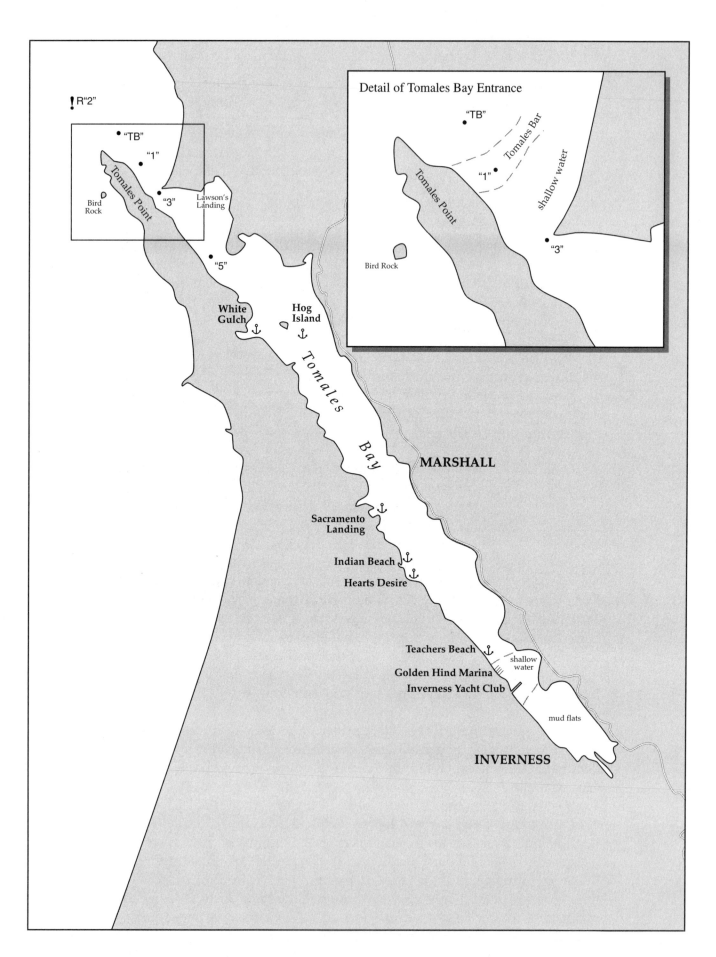

Detail of Tomales Bay Entrance

"TB"

Tomales Bar

shallow water

Tomales Point

"1"

"3"

Bird Rock

R"2"

"TB"

"1"

Tomales Point

"3"

Lawson's Landing

Bird Rock

"5"

White Gulch

Hog Island

Tomales Bay

MARSHALL

Sacramento Landing

Indian Beach

Hearts Desire

Teachers Beach

shallow water

Golden Hind Marina

Inverness Yacht Club

mud flats

INVERNESS

Approach

We can think of no other destination where the timing of your approach is as critical as at Tomales Bay. Traveling to Tomales from San Francisco Bay, we like to anchor overnight at Drakes Bay so we can round Point Reyes early the next morning before the winds and large swells make conditions uncomfortable. By leaving at or shortly after dawn and setting a course to round Reyes about a mile off the point, we may still encounter slightly uncomfortable swells, but they are not likely to be dangerous.

One local boater who has spent his entire 80-plus years in and around Tomales Bay told us he crosses the bar only between 0800 and 1000 because the seas are most predictable during those hours. Although we've crossed the bar far fewer times than he, we too have noticed how much lighter the winds and how much calmer the waters off Tomales Point and Sand Point are before 1000 hours.

The entrance into Tomales Bay lies approximately 16 miles northward from Point Reyes. Since the desired time to cross the bar into Tomales is early morning on high slack water on a day when no large seas are running, you may have to spend a day or two at either Drakes or Bodega Harbor to

Coast Guard sign at Inverness warns boaters about the entrance bar.

wait for the optimum conditions. We once departed Drakes Bay just before dawn and arrived at the Tomales Bay entrance at the perfect time, but the odds of repeating that feat are low. The last time we visited, we spent three days happily exploring Bodega Harbor while we waited for desirable conditions at the entrance to Tomales.

Approaching Tomales from the north, you'll probably be approaching from Bodega Harbor. From the entrance into Bodega Harbor, the run to the "BW" buoy, known as "TB," some 600 yards from the bar, is a short 5 miles.

Although as much as 7 or 8 feet of water covers the bar at the entrance to Tomales Bay at low tide, you must nevertheless cross this bar at high tide. Waves coming directly from the open ocean and into the northwest-facing entrance of Tomales can often be 6 feet or higher, with force enough to drive a boat onto the bar.

However, if you carefully time your arrival and departure at the

Tomales bar, you can cross it safely. First, do not try to enter Tomales Bay when swells of more than 5 feet are running. Second, enter only at high slack water or just before slack when the flood tide is still running to avoid the dangerous waves that build when ebbing water meets the waves coming in from the open ocean.

Whether approaching from the north or south, you'll be able to assess the conditions at the bar from the "BW" buoy. When you've confirmed that conditions are right, identify the C"1" buoy and set a course midway between the buoy and the shore. The C"1" buoy is positioned over the bar in 8 feet of water (at low water, of course). After you're beyond C"1," lay a course for Marker 3, located off Sand Point, watching your chart carefully as you go (Chart #18643 should be close at hand as you enter).

Local boaters warn that the bar at Sand Point often extends out into the channel, especially after a winter of heavy rains and shoaling, so favor the shore of Tomales Point as you pass by the marker. Observe the shallow water some 1,000 yards beyond Marker 3 and proceed cautiously. Providing you're indeed entering on high slack water, you should have no trouble.

Past Marker 3, pay strict attention to the channel markers, for water depths outside the channel are shallow for the first 4 miles. Beyond Marker 10, you need not worry about staying in a channel until you are almost as far south as Inverness.

One member of the Coast Guard who is stationed at Bodega Bay has crossed the bar more than 100 times without incident, and he recommends that visiting boaters faithfully follow these guidelines:

1.   Never enter at night; the buoys are not lighted.
2.   Never enter on an ebb unless in flat calm conditions.
3.   Hug the Tomales Point side of the entrance as you pass Sand Point.
4.   Call the Coast Guard on VHF 16 or Lawson's Landing (707-878-2443) if doubtful about conditions at the bar.

The foregoing comments underline how treacherous the entrance into Tomales Bay can be. But, with careful planning and attention to the sea conditions, you can safely navigate past Sand Point and revel in the placid waters, generally warm weather (particularly on the eastern side), and slow-paced life of the several excellent anchorages along the shores of this treasure of a destination.

Anchorages

The only marina in Tomales Bay is at the Golden Hind Inn in Inverness, at the extreme south end of the navigable portion of the bay. Not only is the marina small and usually full, but it is as shallow as is the water just outside the harbor (the chart shows only 2 feet outside the harbor). Given this situation, you'll likely anchor out when you visit this beautiful bay. Anchorage sites are plentiful along the shores of Tomales Bay. We'll simply point out a few favorites.

White Gulch, slightly more than 3 miles into the bay past the bar, on the starboard side of the channel west of Marker 7, is the first recommended anchorage. Drop your anchor in about 15 feet of water. The mud bottom provides excellent holding (and a messy anchor when you hoist).

Anchorage at White Gulch, with Hog Island in the background.

On the hillsides above the anchorage, tule elks that have been re-introduced to this peninsula graze as they did for centuries before they were hunted to near extinction after 1860. In addition to elk-watching, hiking ashore here is excellent, although you can expect to get your shoes muddy as you get from your tender to the land. Occasionally, winds race down the canyon at White Gulch, but for the most part the days and nights in this anchorage are calm and quiet.

A second good anchorage on the west shore is the cove just north of *Sacramento Landing,* about 3 miles south of White Gulch. The shoreline here provides excellent protection from both north and west winds. Anchor in some 12 feet of water in a mud bottom with good holding.

A mile farther into the Bay are the adjacent anchorages *Indian Beach* and *Hearts Desire.* In the summer months, swimmers, kayakers, and hikers often crowd the beach and water at Hearts Desire; park personnel put out perimeter buoys in the summer to keep boats out of the swimming area. We prefer the quieter anchorage off Indian Beach, where we anchor in about 10 feet on a sand and mud bottom.

You can take your tender ashore on either beach.

Between Hearts Desire and Inverness (about 6 miles away) are other small beaches that will entice you to stop. We usually go on to the Inverness anchorage about 500 yards north of the marina at the Golden Hind Inn, near where a few boats are on moorings. We anchor in an area shown on the chart as having 6 feet of water at low water, recognizing that we might be sitting in the mud in an extremely low tide. Beyond this anchorage, the bay hasn't enough water for boats other than those with unusually shallow drafts.

Be sure to put out adequate scope and set your anchor well when you anchor north of the Golden Hind. Afternoon winds regularly pick up to 20 knots or so, generating 3-4 foot wind waves that will almost certainly pull out a carelessly set anchor.

From this anchorage, you can take your sport boat ashore and tie up at the dock

Quiet anchorage at Marshall.

in the marina behind the Golden Hind, being careful not to block access for other boaters. After tying up you can go to dinner at Bartleby's restaurant or walk to the restaurants and shops in the town of Inverness, about 1 mile farther south.

Along the eastern shore, approximately across from Sacramento Landing, an anchorage off the small town of *Marshall* is easy to recognize because of the boat yard on the shore, the boats docked and moored here, and the small community of houses and businesses. Anchor in 15 feet of water, with a mud bottom, just outside the moored boats. Or you may have the option of renting a vacant buoy from the boat yard. When space is available at the docks, the owner of the boat yard will also give you permission to tie up to go ashore and have a meal at the deli or the restaurant.

Although we haven't anchored at *Hog Island,* other boaters have told us they like to anchor in 15 feet of water about 100 yards south of the island. This anchorage, protected by the island and within easy sport boat range of many spots worthy of exploration, offers you another option for consideration.

Facilities

> *At Hearts Desire:*
> > Showers (outdoor)
> > Restrooms
> *At Inverness:*
> > Gas (at service station, 1 mi.)
> > Grocery Store, with ATM (1 mi.)
> > Launch Ramp
> > Post Office (1 mi.)
> > Propane (1 mi.)
> > Restaurants (one at the anchorage; several 1 mi.)
> > Yacht Club Dock (0.5 mi.)
> *At Marshall (on Bolinas Ridge):*
> > Boat Maintenance and Repair
> > Grocery Store and Deli
> > Haul Out
> > Restaurant
> *At Lawson's Landing:*
> > Launch Ramp

Attractions

Once you've entered the wonderfully protected waters of Tomales Bay, you'll know all the careful planning to get here has been amply rewarded. This bay, a part of the Gulf of the Farallones National Marine Sanctuary, is a haven for not only boaters but for wilder life of many varieties. Migratory sea and song birds using the flyway along this coast between June and December feed in or around the waters of the bay. Harbor seals haul out and even calve on the mud flats. You may free dive for abalone here, dig clams, go crabbing, or fish for monkey face, wolf eels, sea trout, cabazone, blue cod, perch, striped bass, and halibut. Or you may simply go to one of the five oyster farms on the east shore and purchase your dinner.

Tomales Bay is replete with hiking possibilities accessible from any of the anchorages. The "Point Reyes" pamphlet available from the National Park Service shows the many trails from the beaches in Tomales.

From White Gulch, a trail heads up the hill, past a herd of tule elk, to the Pierce Point Ranch, a former dairy now a National Park Service display. You can wander through the ranch, learning about the dairy industry that continues to be of economic importance to the Tomales Bay area. After this tour, you can walk down the ocean side of the peninsula for .5 mile to McClures Beach or hike the 3+ miles along the Tomales Point Trail and look at all the sea birds on Bird Rock.

Of particular interest, the 0.5-mile Indian Nature Trail, heading northwest from the beach at Hearts Desire, has numerous markers identifying native plants, such as the California huckleberry, toyon, poison oak, bay, California hazelnut, and Coast live oak, and explaining how the Tamallos used these plants for foods, medicines, and ornamentation. The trail continues on another mile beyond the markers.

For a more urban experience, explore the two diminutive towns accessible from the anchorages on foot or by sport boat. Inverness, originally a resort town and then the site of a fish hatchery, is by far the larger of the two. The several restaurants and shops lining its main street attest to its appeal to tourists. Marshall, on the eastern shore of Tomales Bay, was a busy railroad stop in the early years of the 20th century. It was also the site of the West Coast's first wireless communications system, run by Guglielmo Marconi, the inventor of the wireless telegraph. Marshall is today in the heart of a thriving oyster farming industry. In each town, you'll have a short but thoroughly delightful walk, especially if you stop to visit with the friendly local people!

Besides Indian and Hearts Desire beaches, other good swimming beaches clustered along the southwest shore include Pebble, Shallow, and Shell. On the other side of the bay is Tomales Bay State Park, for swimming, hiking, and picnicking.

BODEGA HARBOR
Chart #18640 or #18643

Historians and archeologists are still debating the location of the one event that may eventually be the greatest claim Bodega Bay can make to lasting fame. In 1579, Sir Francis Drake, frustrated in his attempt to find the fabled Northwest Passage linking the Pacific and Atlantic oceans, turned southward. He found a secure bay lying beneath a headland, where he and his crew sheltered themselves on the beach for five weeks while they repaired the keel of the *Golden Hind.* Although Drakes Bay, 20 miles to the south of Bodega Harbor, has traditionally gotten the nod as the site of this first landing of a European in Northern California, the discovery in 1963 of a stone wall at Campbell Cove, tucked in behind Bodega Head, has convinced some that this and not Drakes Bay was the site of that momentous landing.

However, none can dispute that some 200 years later Russians used this harbor they called "Port Rumiantsev" for their fur trade out of Fort Ross. The stone wall may prove to have been erected not by the English in 1579 but by the Russians in the early 1800s.

Whether the Russians or the English were the builders of this historic wall, both groups were latecomers in the human history of Bodega Bay. The Coast Miwoks harvested food from this bay for an estimated 4,000 years before any Europeans landed here.

In 1841 General Vallejo and the Spanish crown contested the Russians' claim to this port, and in 1843 a Mexican land grant ceded the 35,000-acre Rancho Bodego to an American, Captain Stephen Smith, who three years later became the first private citizen in California to raise the Bear Flag.

With the encouragement of Smith and others, farmers begin to migrate here, with potatoes a particularly successful crop. Two prosperous potato farmers, John Keys and Warren Dutton, started a shipping company at Bodega Harbor to transport to market the much prized Bodega Red potatoes, as well as dairy products, grain, fish, and other produce of the region. The busy harbor was also the anchorage for pioneer ships of many nations. Unfortunately, the creeks and bay began to silt badly, and a narrow gauge railway transiting this coastline between 1875 and 1933 became the primary mode of transporting both goods and passengers in and out of Bodega Bay.

Today, fishing is once again the primary export from this bay. At Spud Point Marina, completed in 1985, 80 per cent of the 244 berths are allocated to commercial fishing vessels, and the slips in the adjacent Mason's Marina are almost exclusively taken up by the commercial fishing fleet.

Approach

Approaching from the south, go approximately 20 miles northward from Point Reyes to get to Bodega Bay. Identify the three buoys located in Bodega Bay—R"2" off Tomales Bluff, "BA" ("Jingle Bells" to local boaters) off the south end of Seal Rocks, and R"12" southwest of Bodega Head. These three buoys can be difficult to sight if heavy seas are running or low fog has settled in. You may want to use a GPS or radar if you have one aboard your boat.

Regardless of conditions, do not enter Bodega Harbor until you have a visual sighting of "BA." Bodega Rock will be easily visible from "BA" in all except the foggiest weather, but other rocks northwest of the buoy are below the water. Set a course for the entrance from "BA" that will take you east of Bodega Rock.

When the prevailing northwest wind is blowing, the surf may break southwest of the rocks off Bodega Head as well as to the east of the entrance channel. Although this breaking water appears dangerous, you can readily see the clear water of the channel.

You might be tempted to use the shortcut between Seal Island and Bodega Head if you see local boaters doing so, but we can't recommend it unless you can follow someone with local knowledge through the pass. Coast Guard personnel are adamant that this is not a viable channel except in the calmest of weather.

The entrance channel into Bodega Harbor runs from east to west for the first 0.5 mile before

Entrance to Bodega Harbor.

making a northward run into the harbor between Bodega Head and the peninsula that extends westward from the mainland. On this peninsula, called Doran Beach, you'll see many parked RV units as you enter the channel. In the channel, you'll be in protected water, a blessed relief after the rough water typical outside the channel.

The channel changes course three times, but it is well marked. Stay in the channel, which has 12 feet of water, for the water just outside the markers is shallow enough to guarantee going aground. On gusty days, winds blow down the channel briskly.

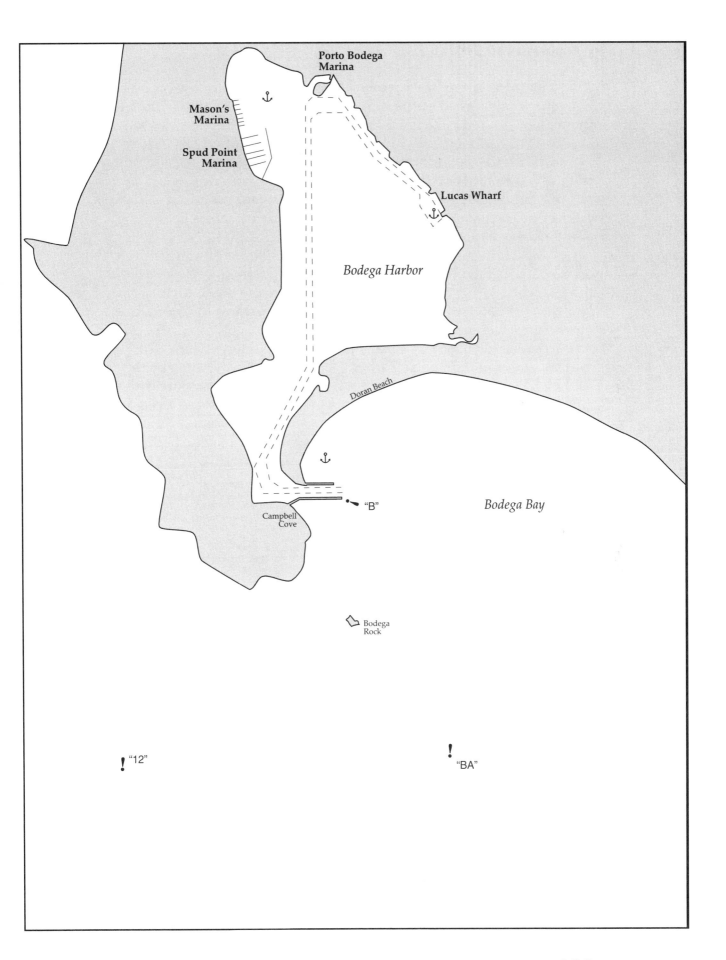

Porto Bodega
Marina

Mason's
Marina

Spud Point
Marina

Lucas Wharf

Bodega Harbor

Doran Beach

"B"

Campbell
Cove

Bodega Bay

Bodega
Rock

"12"

"BA"

Anchorage and Berthing

Bodega Harbor has three anchorage areas. The first, an excellent anchorage in calm conditions or in prevailing northwest winds, is immediately outside the entrance, north of the north jetty. This jetty, almost 1,000 feet long, provides protection from southerly swells, and Doran Beach to the north provides protection from northwest winds. In fact, you're likely to find a few fishing boats or a cruising sailboat already anchored here when you arrive at the entrance to Bodega Harbor. Anchor in 10-20 feet of water. If a south or a west swell is running, you'll not want to anchor here.

Most cruising boaters anchored here take their dinghies ashore on the beach behind the north jetty, but another possibility is to go inside the channel and tie your dinghy to the side of the small dock at the launch ramp south of the Coast Guard station, making sure you don't block access to the ramp.

A second anchorage area is just outside Mason's Marina in the northwest corner of Bodega Harbor. You will often see fishing boats at anchor or on moorings in this area, but we can't recommend this anchorage for three reasons. First, the bottom is soft mud that does not provide good holding; in fact, boats anchored here regularly drag. Second, the water is so shallow that boats typically sit on the bottom at low water. And, finally, the waters here are in protected tidelands.

The third anchorage area at Bodega is at the end of the channel that branches east off the main channel at the north end of the harbor. This channel begins in front of Porto Bodega Marina and ends behind

Stay in the well-marked channel at Bodega.

the Bodega Bay Boat Club. Though small, accommodating only two or three boats, this anchorage is secure and provides easy access to the restaurant on Lucas Wharf, the post office, and other businesses in the town.

The mud bottom in this anchorage provides good holding in water about 12 feet deep. However, a local boater who has anchored here numerous times says he anchors both bow and stern in this anchorage to prevent the tide from turning his boat beam-on to the west wind that frequently blows through the anchorage during the summer months.

The first marina along the channel, approximately 1.5 miles from the entrance into Bodega Harbor, is *Spud Point Marina,* a modern facility designed and run to serve pleasure and commercial fishing boats, both resident and transient. To enter this marina, turn to port after passing buoy G"33", and follow the pairs of buoys past a breakwater on the port side. Depths in the channel and inside the marina are about 12 feet. In this 244-berth marina, "A" dock accommodates boats from 50-80 feet; "B" and "C" docks handle shorter boats. The harbormaster monitors VHF 16 and 68, but, if you don't have a radio, you may leave your boat in any of the empty transient slips, identified by a 5-inch red anchor on the dock box, while you check in at the harbor office.

The second marina, *Mason's Marina,* is immediately north of Spud Point Marina. The staff at Mason's also welcomes visiting boaters; however, working fishing boats generally fill all the slips here. Mason's can accommodate boats up to 40 feet, and depths inside the harbor are at least 7 feet at low water. If you'd like to experience the ambiance of a small working marina, you might be able to get a slip assignment by calling ahead.

The third marina, *Porto Bodega,* is at the north end of the main channel in Bodega Harbor. Marina staff welcomes visiting boaters here, too. Like Mason's, this marina can handle boats to a maximum of 40 feet, and depths here are also about 7 feet at low water. If you arrive looking for a slip, you can call on VHF 16 or 71 or on CB 35; however, the marina staff recommends you call before you depart from your home harbor to check for slip availability. Of the three marinas at Bodega, this is the closest to the restaurants, market, and other businesses of the town, but the docks and facilities are not quite as modern as those at Spud Point.

Bodega Coast Guard	707-875-3596 and VHF 16
Lucas Wharf Restaurant	707-875-3571
Mason's Marina	707-875-3811
Porto Bodega Marina	707-875-2354, VHF 16 and 71 and CB 35

Facilities

At Spud Point Marina:
> Boat Maintenance and Repair
> Bait and Tackle Shop
> Chandlery
> Deli/Mini-market
> Fuel (gasoline and diesel)
> Haul Out
> Laundry
> NOAA Weather Display Station
> Public Transportation
> Pump Out
> Showers

At Mason's Marina:
> Deli/Mini-market
> Fuel (gasoline and diesel)
> Propane
> Showers

At or near Porto Bodega:
> Bait and Tackle
> Grocery Store
> Launch Ramp
> Post Office (0.5 mi.)
> Propane
> Restaurants
> Showers

At Doran Beach and Westside Park:
> Launch Ramps

Attractions

Besides the opportunity to experience a coastal cruise and good facilities at their destination, visiting boaters can find plenty of other reasons to stop off at Bodega Harbor for a few days, or even weeks. As you would expect, many of the attractions are in and around the water.

You might start your day with a hike along Westshore Road and up to Bodega Head. Along the way you'll pass a "pond" where ducks

The dramatic coastline at Bodega Head

splash down. This pond is, in fact, Hole in the Head, a 12-storey-deep excavation planned to house a nuclear reactor, a project abandoned in 1964. Atop Bodega Head, you'll take in a coastal scene of rugged brown cliffs and boulders assaulted by crescendos of foaming white water. Between November and April the spouting of the migrating gray whales gives away their locations. Orca, humpback, and blue whales, though in much smaller numbers than the grays, also appear along this coast.

Instead of returning the way you came, you can continue north along trails to Bodega Dunes State Park, its varied habitats offering up a multitude of treasures for birders.

After this vigorous walk, you may be ready to relax on one of the beaches of Bodega. When the sun breaks through the fog (more common in the fall than in the summer), inspiring you to take to the water, Campbell Cove Beach, at the mouth of the harbor on the port side, has a well-protected sandy beach, where even young children can play at the water's edge safely. Much more impressive is Doran Beach, the long peninsula of sand separating the south end of the harbor from the bay. On the bay side are the beach, hiking trails, clam flats, and a salt marsh. Across the road, on the harbor side, are the mud flats of the southern portion of the harbor, where thousands of marbled godwits, great egrets, great blue herons, snowy plovers, and killdeer may be feeding at low tide.

You may have guessed that you're sure to see more birds than people around this harbor. In fact, the town of Bodega Bay is well known for its birds, as depicted by the director Alfred Hitchcock in his suspense masterpiece *The Birds*. The only building left in town that is recognizable in Hitchcock's film is the old school house; fire has destroyed the others.

PILLAR POINT HARBOR (HALF MOON BAY)
Chart #18645, or #18682

San Francisco Bay sailors planning a trip to Pillar Point Harbor generally call this destination "Half Moon Bay" for good reason: it is tucked into the northern corner of Half Moon Bay. However, the town of Half Moon Bay is some 5 miles farther south on Highway 1, and Pillar Point Harbor is, in fact, in the tiny town of Princeton-by-the-Sea.

By any name, though, this destination calls sweetly to San Francisco Bay sailors. It is clearly the favored destination for many sailors who want to venture outside San Francisco for a few days.

Despite its proximity to the city, this harbor—protected by outer and inner breakwaters and thus one of the safest harbors in the United States—promises Bay Area sailors a dramatic change of atmosphere. You couldn't call it "sleepy," for Pillar Point Harbor has one of the largest and busiest fishing fleets in Northern California, with an annual haul of 10 million pounds of fish. (And, by the way, you, too, can easily get in on the act: you may fish off the pier without a license.) The dozens of fishing vessels leaving to go out to sea and returning with their catches of salmon and rockfish keep the waters and

Pillar Point fishing boats crowd the harbor.

docks at Pillar Point alive with the hum of an old-fashioned commercial fishing harbor.

Costanoans lived and fished along these shores for centuries before the Spanish explorer Gaspar de Portolá founded Mission Dolores in 1776. Soon after, the coastside became the grazing land for the horses, cattle, and oxen from the mission. In the 1840s Spanish dons with land grants established large ranches here. Grazing livestock dot much of the land beyond the neighborhoods and towns around Half Moon Bay yet today.

In the late 1800s Half Moon Bay, the oldest town in San Mateo County, dating back to 1840, grew more and more prosperous. The two wharves north of town, Amesport Landing at Miramar and Pillar Point, handled the large volume of shipping for this otherwise isolated region. Portuguese sailors from the Azores ran a whaling station at Pillar Point between 1860 and the 1890s. In 1908, the Ocean Shore Railway established a coastal route between San Francisco and Tunitas Glen to carry passengers from the city to the wide sandy beaches of Half Moon Bay. That same year, the railway laid out the resort towns of Princeton-by-the-Sea and El Granada (across Highway 1 from Pillar Point Harbor). The Ocean Shore Railway line lasted only until 1920, after which date these beaches and hills regained their former isolation.

This isolation led to the next spurt of activity, during Prohibition, when the rumrunners from Canada hid in this quiet harbor, where they could anchor undetected in the hidden coves and thick fog.

Now, Highway 1 has made the area accessible so that houses cluster on the hillsides above Half Moon Bay, and tourists come from north and south to sample both the natural and man-made wares. But either anchored or docked at Pillar Point Harbor, you'll find yourself much more a part of the natural than of the civilized world.

Approach

San Francisco boaters undertaking a cruise to Pillar Point Harbor experience the joys and challenges of coastal passage making. To begin with, this cruise requires careful timing of the departure from San Francisco Bay. We strongly recommend exiting the bay on slack water or on a *slight* ebb or flood. Although some boaters choose to depart when a strong ebb is flowing to make the trip from the Golden Gate to the open ocean more quickly, by doing so they increase the risk of encountering dangerous seas as they cross the Potato Patch. As the strong ebb meets the winds and currents of the ocean, huge seas often form, seas large enough to capsize a boat transiting the area.

Another consideration for boaters making the trip to Pillar Point is the time of day. The winds are generally stronger during the afternoon hours, and, when strong winds blow out of the northwest, as they commonly do, these prevailing winds can create a boisterous ocean. To avoid these seas, and the resulting uncomfortable boat motion, time your exit from the Bay early enough to pass under the Golden Gate Bridge well before noon. Then you can have the anchor down inside Pillar Point Harbor by mid afternoon.

After passing under the Golden Gate Bridge, set a course along the south side of the ship channel. Stay at least 100 yards off Mile Rocks and Seal Rocks as you make your way seaward; large seas build up in these areas, rendering a closer route uncomfortable or even dangerous. Resist the temptation to turn to port for a run down the coastline immediately after clearing Seal Rocks; shallow water and huge waves make this shortcut dangerous. Continue along the south side of the ship channel for at least a mile before turning. If large seas are running, wait until you are close to the R"8" buoy of the ship channel, some 3.5 miles seaward of Seal Rocks, before turning. If you turn earlier,

The large anchorage at Pillar Point.

the almost inevitable erratic seas will not be kind to you and your boat.

After the turn, the run to the G"1" buoy off Pillar Point is typically a 19-mile broad reach. The G"1" buoy, approximately 1.0 mile southwest of Pillar Point, is easily identified by the radar towers and white buildings on the bluffs above the water. Do not attempt to go directly from G"1" to the harbor entrance, however, for shallow water and rocks abound in the area. Rather, go 1.5 miles on a course of 090 mag. to the G"3" buoy before turning toward the entrance, which is slightly less than 1.0 mile from the G"3" buoy.

Approaching Pillar Point Harbor from the south, you must navigate around the reef 2.0 miles south of the entrance. A G"1" buoy marks the southern edge of the reef, and an R"2" buoy marks its northern edge. You can pass safely on either side of the reef once you've identified it, but be certain to pass to the east of the G"3" buoy after you've passed the reef.

If you're approaching Pillar Point Harbor in thick fog, be especially careful to identify each of the buoys. If you cannot find the buoys, do not attempt to enter the harbor.

Anchorage and Berthing

Immediately inside the breakwater is a large anchorage area with a few private mooring buoys positioned randomly throughout. The mud bottom provides good holding in approximately 15 feet of water. Leave enough space between your boat and the mooring buoys so you won't find a large fishing boat sitting a few feet off your gunnel when you awaken the next morning.

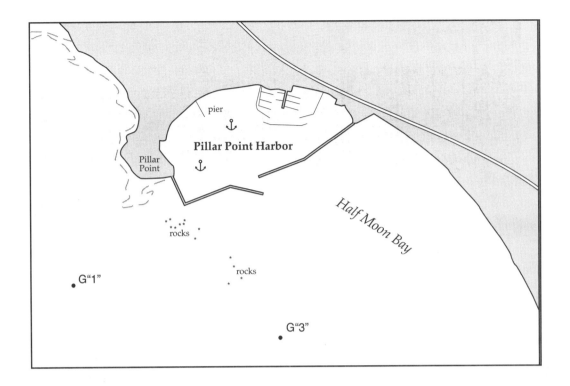

An inner harbor is located behind the inner breakwater to your starboard when you first enter the harbor. The harbor office attempts to provide guest slips to visiting boaters, but demand often outstrips availability in the summer months.

Many pleasure boaters prefer to anchor out, away from the bustle of this busy commercial harbor, and use their tenders to go ashore. A convenient dinghy dock is directly in front of the harbor office.

Pillar Point Harbormaster 650-726-4382 or 650-726-5727
and VHF 16

Facilities

ATM
Boat Maintenance and Repair
Chandlery
Fuel (gasoline and diesel)
Grocery Store
Haul Out
Launch Ramp
Laundry
Life-saving Vessel
Medical Services (2 miles)
Post Office (0.5 mile)
Propane
Public Transportation
Pump Out

Restaurants
Restrooms and Showers

Attractions

One of the primary attractions of Pillar Point Harbor for pleasure boaters is the vastness and security of its anchorage, making it ideal for rafting up a sizable number of boats for a weekend of merriment.

Whether you are in a raft-up or anchored alone, you'll find plenty of entertainment even if you never venture beyond Pillar Point Harbor. Gulls, cormorants, brown pelicans, and terns busily feed in the waters of the anchorage or rest on

Pelicans at Pillar Point.

the rocks. Sea lions add their distinctive barking to the commotion on the breakwaters. Great blue herons and snowy egrets wade in the marsh on the northwest side of the anchorage, and black-crowned night herons swoop in overhead for their evening meals.

If you prefer to purchase rather than catch your own fish, a fish market right at the harbor can accommodate your taste.

The Coastside Trail traversing the ocean bluffs between Pillar Point Harbor and the town of Half Moon Bay promises additional natural wonders. The ocean itself, and the life dependent on it, is, of course, ceaselessly fascinating, but along the 5-mile trail you'll also see the seasonal wonders of the land—California poppies, blue lupine, and beach primroses; song birds and raptors; brush rabbits and jack rabbits.

From this trail, paths lead down to the sandy beaches of Half Moon Bay: El Granada, Vallejo, Miramar, Naples, Dunes, Venice, or Francis.

A much shorter walk is the one through Pillar Point Marsh and Shoreline, on the west wide of the harbor. Both fresh water and salt water feed this unique marsh. If you walk on around the point, you can see tidepools and basking sea lions. Just west of the point is one of the world's most challenging surfing spots, Mavericks Wave.

INDEX